WHAT WOMEN REALLY WANT . . .
AND HOW THEY CAN GET IT

WHAT WOMEN REALLY WANT . . . AND HOW THEY CAN GET IT

L.A. JUSTICE

CARROLL & GRAF PUBLISHERS, INC.
NEW YORK

First Carroll & Graf edition 2000

Carroll & Graf Publishers, Inc.
A Division of Avalon Publishing Group
19 West 21st Street
New York, NY 10010-6805

Library of Congress Cataloging-in-Publication Data is available.
ISBN: 0-7867-0766-6

Manufactured in the United States of America

For my mother, Helen Herbstman,
who taught me the importance of eating right and exercising.

■

And for my father, Sidney Herbstman,
who taught me to follow my dreams and never give up.

ACKNOWLEDGMENTS

To all the amazing and courageous women whose stories have made this book possible.

Thanks to editor Donald McLachlan for suggesting the title, as well as Dori Miningham for giving me the names of Bob Diforio and Marilyn Allen, my agents, who turned this manuscript into a "done deal" in record time. Bob and Marilyn, thanks from the bottom of my heart.

A heartfelt thank you to Herman Graf and Kent Carroll for taking a chance on a new author. And to Martine Bellen, editor, Nancy Gillan, copyeditor, and Claiborne Hancock of the publicity department.

Thanks to Jerome R. Miller, Esq.; and Aimee M. Devereux, Esq.; for handling my legal matters; Flora Cousins for her wonderful poems and great enthusiasm; and Jane Greer, Ph. D., who took time from her hectic schedule to write a terrific preface.

To my paramour, Tim Roethele, thanks for the many life lessons you have taught me, thanks for taking those great photos of me, and a thank you from the bottom of my heart for creating the amazing Web site www.whatwomenreallywant.NET.

And most important, I owe a debt of gratitude to my daughters, Zena and Ananda, for their patience, support, and terrific ideas—many of which have been included in the text.

TABLE OF CONTENTS

PREFACE

Dr. Jane Greer

THE DECLARATION OF Independence promises life, liberty and the pursuit of happiness, but no one ever teaches you how to be happy. The assumption is that once you figure out "what you want to be when you grow up." happiness will be part of the package. Of course, that's not always the way it works.

Most women find out sooner or later that they are responsible for their own personal fulfillment. While that may not sound like a wonderful thing at first, upon reflection it becomes one of the most freeing realizations a woman can make. How wonderful it is to discover that you are writing your own script for life! The power to play a fulfilling leading role and have a "happy ending" is truly in your hands.

While everyone has different ideas about the elements that go into having a meaningful life, there are some common threads that unite the majority of women. Based on the high volume of letters that I receive through *Redbook* magazine's online column, "Ask the Relationship Doctor" (http://redbookmag.com/askdr-greer) and "Relationship Rx" (www.momsonline.com) on *Oxygen*, I can confidently say that L.A. Justice has ingeniously managed to cover the topics that women ask about the most. Her book is divided into chapters on happiness, love, financial security, peace of mind, power, success, health, respect and last, but definitely not least—aging gracefully.

What Women Really Want . . . And How They Can Get It is chock full of practical hands-on techniques and tips that get you thinking, help you to prioritize your values, and define what you really want. It also assists you in determining what's stopping you from going after your dreams and offers positive steps to take so you can create the life you yearn to have and live it with vitality. This enlightening book is complete with information that you may think you know, but don't. Once you pinpoint what you really want, you'll be ready and motivated to open the door to a more meaningful and satisfying quality of life.

In a very real sense, L.A. Justice has put together a course book that could be called Fulfillment 101: Lessons for Life. She helps you to find and actualize your own recipe for a meaningful life by getting you to zero in on the missing ingredients. Best of all, the process doesn't feel overwhelming because she breaks it down into doable, manageable, obtainable steps so it becomes a winning formula within reach; one which will guarantee your own personal triumph!

Peppered with humor, this book doesn't talk around the issues—it gives you straightforward practical advice, maps out specific steps to take and points out what to focus on along your way. You learn how to mentally train yourself to create your vision. You also get in touch with your vulnerabilities and discover what you're missing by answering the questionnaires provided. This discovery process can be an incredible breakthrough in itself. Once you can clearly see where you are, it's much easier to plan your path for the future.

An important part of actualizing any goal or dream is believing that it's possible. The affirmations L.A. provides can help you to shape and firm up your belief in yourself, and fuel your desire and commitment to yourself for improvement and self-growth.

By taking the time to read this book, you are taking a fundamental step toward empowering yourself and moving on in the metaphorical footsteps of many women who we've all come to know, love and admire. You'll find out how women as diverse as Madonna, Barbara Walters, Tina Turner, Goldie Hawn and Oprah Winfrey have risen above incredible obstacles and made their dreams come true. You'll also hear how L.A. learned to toughen her own emotional skin so she could keep her eyes and her heart on what was most important to her. The natural outgrowth of reading these success stories is the firm feeling, "If they can do it, I can do it too!"

Believing that you can do it is of paramount importance because self-esteem is a prerequisite for most of your other goals in life. Believing in yourself is one of the most fundamental elements that everyone strives to attain. Yet, this essential ingredient can elude you if you have unrealistic expectations of yourself and set goals that truly cannot be accomplished. Taking a solid assessment of your abilities and strengthening your weak spots increases your self-esteem. Taking action-steps toward actualizing your dreams gets self-confidence flowing and bolsters your feeling of self-worth.

This book will not only give you a "can do" attitude, it will also provide you with some new role models. While you are striving to be your best, finding out how other women have made it can help to expand and shape your vision. It can also spur you on toward your own picture of fulfillment. By walking in their footsteps, and learning from their triumphs and mistakes, you take advantage of the road they have already paved.

By following these inspiring women's leads and putting the tools that L.A. gives you to use, you will soon discover that other women are following your lead and walking in your footsteps!

INTRODUCTION

*I*T'S HUMAN NATURE not to be satisfied. Whether it's a bigger home, a new car, a husband, a baby, a lover, a successful career, or simply less stress, we all want something that we don't have. Women, in particular, have an aching desire to attain their secret dreams. Even if a woman's life appears perfect to others, something nags inside her. Timid ladies want to be empowered, heavy ones want to be slimmer, and most single women want a loving relationship.

Although many women are dissatisfied with some aspect of their lives, they don't take the actions needed to effect a change—to make their dreams come true. The problem is that although they are frustrated with "their lot in life," too many women accept what they have, even if it is not enough. "This is all I deserve," they complain to anyone who will listen. "I'm not entitled to more."

This is nonsense. If you yearn to be a high-powered executive, to shop on Rodeo Drive, to have a kind-hearted man kissing your feet, you can achieve your dreams. If you want power, peace of mind, or to age gracefully and in good health, then aim for those goals.

Among the women that I interviewed for this book, happiness, success, financial security, peace of mind, and good health were found at the top of the list. Other aspirations include:

Respect	Acceptance
Love/romance	Companionship
Freedom to be oneself	Mental well-being
Spirituality	To be admired
Power	Friends
Wisdom	A family

Traditionally women don't want to compete with men; they feel inadequate; they are reluctant to earn more than their spouses; they don't have the energy, drive or ambition—or they are afraid to be seen as "mannish" if they assert themselves.

Remember the song from *My Fair Lady*, "Why Can't a Woman Be More Like a Man?" Well here's the rub. We don't want to be more like men. We want to remain feminine while at the same time being entitled to the things that many men have: respect, happiness, success, wealth, and mental well-being, without sacrificing our families or our womanliness, and without feeling guilty.

Women now account for forty-six percent of the work force, making them an integral part of the business world. Some women are learning to become more assertive and to take responsibility for making their wildest dreams come true. Amazingly, female-owned businesses employ one of every five U.S. workers. More than one-third of all companies are owned by women.

Even with these impressive and encouraging figures, women still have to battle to earn as much as men for comparable skills.

Gillian Anderson of the television show *The X-Files* was paid $500,000 for each episode while her co-star David Duchovney made twice that much. When she wanted her salary raised to an equitable amount, the producers threatened to kill her character. Fair? You bet not. Although women are making great strides toward equality in the workplace, they must continue to battle, and battle positively, by clearly stating what they want and by hanging in there until they get what they want.

"Women trailblazers of the next decade must learn to use positive power behaviors," says Priscilla V. Marotta, Ph.D., director of the South Florida group Women of Wisdom. "Their feminine wisdom will positively affect their lives, businesses, and society."

The purpose of this book is to help you pinpoint what you want, determine what is holding you back from achieving your goals and give you positive and practical steps for getting there. Each chapter contains the stories of famous women and how they accomplished their objectives. The questionnaires will show how you defeat yourself. Advice from experts will help you take charge of your life. And daily affirmations will empower you.

Thirty years ago if a woman had said she wanted to be president of the United States, she would have been laughed right out of politics. While there hasn't even been a female vice-president yet, the day may come in our lifetime. Meanwhile, women are now CEOs of major corporations and run their own businesses successfully. Oprah Winfrey is the richest woman in the field of entertainment and she didn't have an inheritance or a husband to boost her. She started from the bottom and took her talent to the top with grit, determination, and a positive "can-do" attitude.

If you have the inner drive, nothing will dissuade you.
Whatever it is you want to accomplish in your life,
if you are truly ready and trust in your divine powers to manifest it,
the teachers will be there. You will be guided.
Money will not make a difference. You will find a way.

—WAYNE DYER

∎

Life isn't always fair. When you wallow in despair or complain about what is wrong with your life, you undermine yourself by languishing in negativity and self-pity.

"The fact that life isn't fair doesn't mean that we shouldn't do everything in our power to improve our own lives or the world as a whole," says author Richard Carlson. "Pity is a self-defeating emotion that does nothing for anyone, except to make everyone feel worse than they already do."

When I was married, we rented an apartment. All my friends lived in small houses. In time they moved into more spacious homes while we stayed put. I cried myself to sleep wanting a house, even a tiny one that I could call my own. Alas, it was not meant to be. We divorced and I moved to Florida. With nobody to fall back on, all my energy was directed toward owning a piece of real estate. Nothing was going to stop me—not lack of money, not moving to a strange area where I didn't know a soul. I was unemployed when I bought my condominium. Since that day thirteen years ago I have upgraded to a larger, more spacious condo and I did it by myself.

Once I stopped whining about how life wasn't fair, I sprang into action. With hard work, determination, and sheer willpower, I have put both my daughters through college, bought and sold half a dozen cars for the three of us—and still have a few dollars left over.

I've been called opinionated and aggressive. I have learned not to care. Some men don't like me because I am self-sufficient. Some women resent that I am happy. That's their problem. One man loves me and I think that's truly marvelous. I wake up each morning itching to see what the day will bring. And it never disappoints. It is truly amazing how much can happen in 24 hours.

What do YOU want? Whatever it is, you have the power to get it. You can make your dreams come true if you put enough time, energy, and thought into achieving it. We each have within ourselves our own private Department of Human Resources, which we should not forget in times of need. I found mine and you can find yours, too.

If you think that to become happy, you must make greater efforts
than others, or that you are not worthy of happiness because of
your past mistakes, you will never be happy—just as you thought.
—MASAMI SAIONJI

■

The habit of happiness guides you to stay in touch with any
negative feelings as they arise ... and not hide them
for days to weeks to years.
—BARNET MELTZER, M.D.

■

One

IF YOU WANT TO BE HAPPY

Happiness is not guaranteed as anybody's inalienable right.
Only the pursuit of happiness is.
—WILLIAM COUGHLIN

■

WHAT WILL MAKE you happy? A new car? A bigger house? A higher-paying job? Someone to love? A baby? Getting married? Getting divorced?

Here's the lowdown on happiness: You have the power to be happy right now—even if you are dirt poor and living alone, with no job and no car. For happiness means being satisfied with what you have—even if it's nothing.

"Happiness is not acquired through drugs, alcohol, or a temporary perk, like a new job or a new boyfriend," says Dr. Brian Greer, a psychiatrist in Boca Raton, Florida. "It's about bringing a positive purpose into your life."

Yet, sadly, many of us postpone our happiness thinking things will be better . . . someday.

We tell ourselves that we'll be happy when our bills are paid, when we get out of school, get our first job, a promotion, says author Richard Carlson. "We convince ourselves that life will be better after we get married, have a baby, then another. Then we are frustrated that the kids aren't old enough—we'll be more content when they are. After that, we're frustrated that we have teenagers to deal with. We will certainly be happy when they are out of that stage. We tell ourselves that our life will be complete when our spouse gets his act together, when we get a nice car, are able to go on a nice vacation, when we retire. And on and on and on!"

The truth is, life keeps moving forward. And there's no better time to be happy than right now. If not now, when?

> My philosophy is that I can be unhappy for a little period of time,
> but I don't like to feel unhappiness for long periods of time.
> —GOLDIE HAWN

■

After her enormous triumph in the blockbuster hit, *The First Wives Club,* which netted more than $100 million at the box office, Goldie Hawn suddenly found movie scripts and offers rolling in faster than a tidal wave.

While the preceding years had been a roller coaster ride of good times and not-so-good times, "Giggling Goldie" always had a huge smile on her face, radiating cheer, charm and bliss.

Amazingly, for the past thirty years, Goldie has remained afloat in the shark-infested waters of Hollywood and has kept not only her sanity but also her positive outlook.

"As a kid people would ask what I wanted to be when I grew up," she says. "I didn't say I wanted to be a big star. I wanted to be happy—and that's still the only thing I want."

Growing up in Tacoma Park, Maryland, Goldie began taking dance lessons at the tender age of three. By sixteen she was playing Juliet in a stage production of *Romeo and Juliet.* After dropping out of college at age eighteen, she worked as a professional dancer in New York City and clawed her way up from the very bottom. Before she became Hollywood's favorite ditzy blonde, she was a go-go girl, gyrating in a cage at discotheques in

Manhattan and New Jersey. So when friends offered to drive her to California, she didn't think twice about hopping into the car.

While doing a one-time stint as a dancer on an Andy Griffith TV special, she was spotted by an eagle-eyed agent who negotiated a deal for her on *Rowan & Martin's Laugh-In*. The show, an overnight sensation, became one of the most popular TV shows of the 1960s, and it swung Goldie Hawn right up to stardom.

With peace symbols, stripes, and slogans painted all over her briefly clad body, she mugged wide-eyed at the cameras, giggling nonstop. When she was given the opportunity to introduce guests, she muffed her lines and cracked up. The producer, George Schlatter, loved it.

"Goldie has an innate charm that completely bowls you over," he says.

To get a rise out of her, the crew tossed cold water on her from the sidelines. Instead of complaining as some actors would have done, she blossomed like a flower.

"I totally connected with the character," says Hawn. "She was looked upon as dizzy, dumb, vacant, giggly. What I was really feeling was pure joy. It didn't matter whether I made a goof or whether someone else made a goof—it just tickled me."

She was twenty-three. The year was 1968. And Goldie Hawn was an instant hit. Not only did she keep audiences chuckling, she received two Emmy nominations.

But things are not always as they appear. Although she was laughing on camera, Goldie was in a downward spiral that made her a virtual recluse. When not rehearsing or filming the show, she would hide in her home watching TV and sipping tea. Her weight dropped to a dangerous 96 pounds. The stress of fame was more than she could handle. Therapy was the answer.

"The real reason that I got professional help was that I felt I was beginning to lose my joy," she says. "What I got out of therapy was clarity of the situation."

A string of movies—some memorable, some forgettable—followed her departure from the show. Her first one, *Cactus Flower*, made in 1969 with Walter Matthau and Ingrid Bergman, won her an Oscar for Best Supporting Actress. Since then the vivacious star has had her share of problems. Yet she remains level-headed and upbeat.

While watching a compilation show of *Laugh-In* sketches a number of years ago, she had tears streaming down her face. They were not all tears of joy. "I've grown up," she admits. "I've gone through the trials and tribulations of life. I've lost my parents since then. I've had two failed marriages. I've had career ups and downs. Yet the essence of that person I was has remained the same."

The essence of that person is an innate charmer who awes everyone she meets. She is diplomatic under duress. Says a Hollywood insider, "No one, but no one, hates Hawn—an amazing feat for someone who has been in showbiz for as long as she has. She simply refuses to make enemies."

Hawn is the first to admit she sees no point in taking an adversarial position.

"Everybody who's ever done me wrong is back in my life," she says. "It's deeply important in a business like this to forgive people."

That forgiveness means she harbors no resentment, hate or hostility, which leaves plenty of room in her emotional stockpile for good feelings of love, respect and happiness.

"Until you can forgive people, you can't really move on with your life," says Goldie, who continues to be one of Hollywood's A-list favorites.

In fact Goldie, a longtime believer in transcendental meditation and the mind/body connection, is producing a documentary—a "feel-good flick" called *In Search of Joy*, which will chronicle how people around the world have found inner happiness. And who is better qualified to make it?

The act of forgiving allows you to eliminate the negative and accentuate the positive. It is impossible to be happy and glowing when you are miserable and irritable.

"I really do feel joy inside," she adds. "I wake up happy. I guess all of us like to be around people who make us happy. And that's part of my thing. When I was born, God went, 'Bing! Okay, you're going to be happy. You've got that little button of joy in there, and now you're going to pass it around.'"

That button of joy helped her survive two divorces.

She wed actor/director Gus Trikonis in 1969; they split up in 1976 and she had to ante up a reported $75,000 as a divorce settlement. It was love at first sight when she met comedian/singer Bill Hudson on a transcontinental flight. They married in 1976 and had two children, Oliver and Kate. But in 1980 that marriage also ended in divorce.

She says that her success probably contributed to the breakup of both marriages—but she didn't sit around bashing men. Instead, she had a few well-publicized affairs, then hooked up with handsome Kurt Russell when they made the movie *Swing Shift* in 1982. And they've been together ever since, without any legal and binding contract. Their love and respect, their son, Wyatt, and the family they have created, is the glue that keeps this handsome couple together.

Kurt Russell believes Hawn has a natural desire and ability to seek out joy. "Goldie's wonderfully naïve at times, but she's also very much aware of what's going on around her," he says.

Goldie Hawn does not depend on others for her good feelings. Her happiness springs from a well of cheer deep inside. She has vowed to be true to herself and to never settle for anything that doesn't make her happy.

"Wanna know my secret?" she asks. "I love life. I wake up every day excited to wake up. You want to know what I think? I think you have to stop feeling sorry for yourself and thank the day instead of scowling at it."

Remember the compliments you receive. Forget the insults.

—MARY SCHMICH

■

WHAT'S HOLDING YOU BACK?

> What hampers your happiness is not your husband, nor your wife,
> nor your children, nor your parents-in-law. What hampers you is
> yourself. No one else. Your wrong thoughts, emotions, and knowl-
> edge stand in your way. Happiness is not something that others
> give you. You must create it with your own hands.
> —MASAMI SAIONJI

∎

For years psychologists have been charting misery, trying to get a fix on why people are so miserable. In fact, way back in 1776, Samuel Johnson wrote that we are "not born for happiness." Fast-forward to 1930, when philosopher Bertrand Russell declared that most people are unhappy.

"Depressed adults are in one sense like children in a bad mood: They typically recall their parents as rejecting, punitive, and guilt-promoting," says David G. Myers, Ph.D., therapist, author and professor of psychology at Hope College in Holland, Michigan. "It's like viewing life through dark-colored glasses."

As one of his patients put it: "As I look into the past, I become convinced that everything I've ever done is worthless. Any happy period seems like an illusion. My accomplishments appear as genuine as the false facade of a Western movie."

Who is happy?

New studies based on the premise of "positive psychology" indicate that most people are at least moderately happy, regardless of age or gender. Recent polls indicate that three in ten Americans are "very happy" and six in ten say they are "pretty happy." Only one in ten says they are "not too happy."

"When you go out and randomly sample the world at large, people present a happier picture of life than you might expect," says David G. Myers. "By and large, most people live with positive emotion from day to day."

Our essential nature is happiness. However, most people rely on things like money, love or appreciation from others to make them happy.

Wayne Dyer, author of *Pulling Your Own Strings*, says: "If you are perpetually in a state of seeking your pleasures from external sources, you are convinced that your happiness comes from those sources. As you pursue this external-oriented pleasure, you are kept from the experience of knowing the bliss of a pure heart. Consequently, you destroy yourself little by little."

Studies have found that while scads of money can buy freedom and empower those with huge bank accounts, it cannot guarantee happiness. Eventually, the stress of daily life, the constant struggle to make more or keep what you have, takes its toll.

"Realizing that well-being is something other than being well-off is liberating," adds Myers. "It liberates us from spending on eighteen-hundred-dollar dresses, on luxury cars, on yachts and huge homes—all purchased in a vain quest for an elusive joy. It liberates us from envying the lifestyles of the rich and famous. It liberates us to invest ourselves in developing traits, attitudes, relationships, activities, environments, and spiritual resources that will promote the well-being of ourselves and others."

Money cannot buy happiness, but neither can poverty.

—ANONYMOUS

■

To illustrate this old adage, here is a short scene from the life of actor Will Smith.

With his celebrity status firmly established with the hit series *The Fresh Prince of Bel Air*, Smith and his friend Jazzy Jeff set up a 900 phone line to advertise their 1989 album entitled "And In This Corner." The money poured in.

"One year I spent $800,000," says Smith. "I went through it so fast it made my head spin. Being able to buy anything you want makes you a little crazy."

He started with the "boys' toys"—cars, seven of them, including a Corvette, truck, motorbike, Camaro, and Suburban wagon. There was a solid-gold necklace spelling out "Fresh Prince" in diamonds. And, of course, a mansion. He flew to London and Tokyo to buy clothes.

"I spent a long time trying to figure out how things could be going so well, and I could be so unhappy," he confesses.

And then the IRS came rapping. It was not the kind of rap Will Smith had in mind. Suddenly, everything fell apart. "One day I had a mansion, the next, I couldn't pay the gas bill," says the *Independence Day* star.

> Some days you're the pigeon, some days you're the statue.
> —KATHY LEVINE

■

Smith's story is an excellent example of a person expecting *things*, including money, to make him happy. He eventually resolved his dealings with the IRS, but it was a costly lesson.

In a nutshell: No person and no external circumstances can make you happy. YOU, and you alone, are responsible for your happiness!

Sadly, we let others influence the way we feel. Some examples:

Children can be the light of your life. But while you can derive much happiness from them, babies fuss, they cry, they teethe. They have endless complaints and problems, they get sick, they make a mess. You'll be up late at night and running on little steam during the day. In their teenage years they can bring sorrow as well as joy. Do you let it get you down?

If you have a husband or boyfriend or significant other, is your relationship constant? Or are there problems? If you're like most people, you'll have ups and downs—just like Goldie Hawn and the rest of us.

If you work, your boss or coworkers may give you grief on a daily basis. People are often unmindful of others' feelings when they talk—like the editor who dismissed a reporter friend of mine with the flip comment, "I don't have time for you."

Of course it hurt her feelings! Coworkers gossip behind your back and make rude comments to your face. You might hate your job or fear being downsized or fired. A zillion things—both large and small—can happen during the day to make it go wrong . . . like the time I had a flat tire on the way to stress-reduction class. I was uptight and unhappy at the thought of being late. Then I looked around and realized it was a beautiful day and I had a chance to enjoy the scenery while waiting for a tow truck. It's about making lemonade out of lemons.

When I finally made it to class, an interesting thing happened. During a discussion about toxic people—those negative, irritating people who can turn a nice day upside down—the instructor said this: "Just remember, nobody can rob you of your happiness."

That struck home with me, and it might also for you. During any given day, 99 percent of the things that happen to you will be uplifting. It's that tiny one percent that sours the whole day. Instead of recalling the positive things, we say the day has been just downright awful.

Interestingly, researchers at the University of Chicago found that teenagers typically bounce back from a gloomy experience in less than an hour. A tiff with a friend may seem the end of the world, but once the phone rings the feud is forgotten.

How long does it take for *you* to let go of the bad feelings and let the happy ones return ?

The good news is that as we mature, adult mood swings become less extreme. We tend to look beyond the moment. That means that even when things go wrong, you should be able to get over it fairly quickly. Perhaps it will take more than an hour or two, but it's important to let go of negativity as soon as possible and focus on the positive, uplifting aspects of your life. The longer you drag around those pessimistic feelings, the less happy you will be

The next time your children, your partner or a coworker, boss, friend or relative says or does something to upset you, remember, *nobody can rob you of your happiness without your permission!*

Researchers have also found that contentment does not come from being slim or rich. It starts with your genes and ends with your attitude. David Lykken and Auke Tellegren, at the University of Minnesota in Minneapolis, suggest that we each have an inherited "happiness setpoint"—a level of well-being that we naturally return to—no matter what is happening in our lives.

"You inherit a predisposition for a certain level of happiness," says Lykken in his book *Happiness*, "but you can influence the waves on your lake of happiness and learn to ride above your set point."

Even if you come from a family with a penchant for depression, you can override it if you choose to. Lykken cites the case of Eve, a thirty-four-year-old marketing consultant, whose mother's gloom-and-doom approach to life had stunted Eve's efforts to be happy.

"My grandmother was a manic depressive," explains Eve. "And long after her own mother's death, my mother was still wallowing in self-pity over her love-deprived childhood. I finally decided I wasn't going to let biology determine my destiny. I can't say I'm perfectly baggage-free today, but I have tried to figure out what makes me happy, and it's really made a difference in my day-to-day contentment."

The power of the mind can get us through any tough situation as long as we are not waiting for others to provide the answers or the solutions to our problems.

> So many people look at me and say, "She should be happy," but
> what they don't realize is that I'm still a person inside just like
> everybody else ... people expect you to always be happy just
> because you have what they think is physical beauty or you have
> money and you're an actress.
> —HALLE BERRY

■

Happiness is far more within your control that you think. In 1952 Norman Vincent Peale wrote *The Power of Positive*

Thinking. It became an instant best-seller and has sold millions of copies over the years.

"You can think your way to failure or unhappiness," he wrote. "But you can also think your way to success and happiness. The world in which you live is not primarily determined by outward conditions and circumstances but by thoughts that habitually occupy your mind."

Success does not create happiness, nor does a portfolio of mutual funds, or having the perfect spouse or ideal offspring, or a high-paying job and a boss who thinks you're wonderful. They help, sure, but if you are counting on these fleeting moments to give you everlasting bliss, you might as well be searching for the pot of gold at the end of the rainbow.

If you want to be happy (and who doesn't?), know that *you* are holding yourself back. Nobody else. You are the rainbow. And you are also the pot of gold. You are everything you need to be.

When you say, "Basically, I'm not a happy person," or, "Basically I'm happy, but right now I'm not because things aren't going very well," you are probably sitting on the "pity pot" waiting for some payoff—a new guy, a raise or a promotion, a better car, a windfall—to put a smile on your face.

Those are all temporary fixes. Let's get down to brass tacks and see what's making you unhappy. Take a look at this questionnaire and see how many things in it apply to you.

Always keep happiness on your agenda,
along with your other tasks and goals.

— A N O N Y M O U S

■

PEANUTS reprinted by permission of United Feature Syndicate, Inc.

HAPPINESS QUESTIONNAIRE

Read each question carefully, then mark Yes or No. Be honest with your answers. These are key items in your quest for happiness.

1. Do your feelings of happiness stem from the way people talk to you?
   Yes_____No_____

2. Do your feelings of happiness stem from the way people treat you?
   Yes_____No_____

3. Can one negative thing (a cross word, a situation that doesn't go right) ruin your day?
   Yes_____No_____

4. Do you see the "down" side of things?
   Yes_____No_____

5. Do you see the negative side of people?
   Yes_____No_____

6. Are you judgmental?
   Yes_____No_____

7. Do you find it difficult to forgive others?
   Yes_____No_____

8. Do you get your good feelings from your spouse, children, parents or friends?
   Yes_____No_____

9. Do you let a bad mood linger for days?
   Yes_____No_____

10. Do you always need to be right?
    Yes_____No_____

11. Does it make you unhappy if you are not right?
    Yes_____No_____

12. Do you cling to those feelings?
    Yes_____No_____

13. Are you waiting for someone or something to make you happy?
Yes_____No_____

14. Are you jealous of other people's happiness?
Yes _____No_____

15. Are you waiting for luck or chance to bring you happiness?
Yes_____No_____

16. Are you working toward a positive goal?
Yes_____No_____

17. Can you accept being wrong?
Yes_____No_____

18. Can you snap out of bad mood within a few hours?
Yes_____No_____

19. Is there something you can do that will give you joy?
Yes_____No_____

20. Can you let go of negative things and move on?
Yes_____No_____

KEY TO ANSWERS:

If you marked Yes on more than half of questions 1 to 15, you are holding yourself back from attaining happiness.

If you marked No on more than half of questions 16 to 20, you are keeping yourself from experiencing joy.

FINAL QUESTION:

What can you find within yourself to bring you joy?

POSITIVE STEPS YOU CAN TAKE

You grow up the day you have your first real laugh—at yourself.
—ETHEL BARRYMORE

■

In her book *Girl Talk*, Sharon Wegscheider-Cruse says there was a time in her life when she thought she'd die of "terminal seriousness."

"There was plenty to be somber about," she writes. "Yet I couldn't help but notice that there were many people around me, with even worse problems, who still had a sense of humor and a lightness of heart. I wondered how they did it. Since that time I've learned that facing the realities of life is easier with a sense of humor."

David G. Myers likens happiness to cholesterol levels. He says: "Both are genetically influenced and yet both are, to some extent, under our control. By diet and exercise, we have some influence on our cholesterol levels; likewise, there are certain things we can do that will have a bearing on our happiness."

If you're one of the 40 million viewers who watch QVC, one of television's home-shopping channels, you will know Kathy Levine. She laughs, she bubbles with excitement, she is gung-ho about everything. And it's not just an act. She is one of the most optimistic ladies I've ever met.

Kathy has been married and divorced, and has had her share of rotten dates. Now approaching the big 5-0, she's making the most of every minute of every day.

"I'm not about to sit around and cry in my beer until Mr. Right comes along," she says firmly. "I've taken up flying and sailing. Coupled with my job, the joy of a loving dog, my family and good friends, that should keep me busy for awhile."

Kathy, however, is like the rest of us. Bad things happen to this upbeat lady. But she does not let them color her world. She had a nasty bout with a plastic surgery procedure; she was taken for a financial ride by a smooth-talking swindler; she cared for her sick father in a nursing home until his death; and she's had plenty of bad-hair days and my-clothes-don't-fit days.

"I don't believe life is a dress rehearsal," she says. "This is the real show and I seize every day with optimism and joy. Sure, there are those bummer days when nothing seems to go right. So I pout, stamp my feet, eat a piece cheesecake, go shopping. I feel better and I get over it."

Kathy says the key to her happiness is personal satisfaction from a good day's work or reaching out to help someone else.

"It sounds very Pollyanna but when I'm inner-focused, thinking only of myself, wallowing in a personal dilemma, I get slow and dull. Who wants to be around that? When I'm focused on others or goal-oriented, I'm in high gear—bright, clear-minded and charged with energy. It feels better that way. There's something to that karma business. Everything we put out to the universe, positive or negative, comes back to us."

Kathy is right.

Studies have shown that the primary trait of happy people is positive self-esteem. Folks who believe themselves smart, healthy and sociable, who can maintain an optimistic outlook and keep bad things in perspective, have a better chance of remaining happy when dark clouds gather overhead.

> Go forth into the busy world and love it. Interest yourself in its life,
> mingle kindly with its joys and sorrows.
> —RALPH WALDO EMERSON

■

We all experience highs and lows. When things don't go right, you must not let it undermine your innate happiness. "Being unhappy is a habit," says Wayne Dyer. "Being depressed is a habit. There are many, many people who have spent a large portion of their lives with very little in the way of material possessions, yet their habit was not to be depressed about it."

This means you can choose to be unhappy or happy. Or, as Abraham Lincoln once said, "People are just about as happy as they want to be."

The key to happiness, or anything else you really want, is to realize that *you* can become your own worst enemy. It's called "self-defeating" behavior. However, you can just as easily turn that negative attitude into a positive one.

You have the power to change those troublesome habits or customs. Dyer says: "Know within yourself that you will find your physical self automatically following a new course. You can rid yourself of habits that come from allowing others to manipulate you. Instead, shift your inner world and create a purposeful, spiritually fulfilled human being."

Overcoming self-defeating behavior, including unhappiness, is a challenge. But it can be done. In fact, happiness is less often found around the corner than right in front of us!

There are a number of ways that you can stop worrying and get happy. These six points can get you started down the yellow-brick road to bliss.

1. *Be determined to get happy*. If your plan is to be happy and stay happy, no matter what happens during the day, you stand a much better chance of going to bed in a good mood instead of a funk. Rick Foster and Greg Hicks, who interviewed hundreds of happy people for their book *How We Choose to Be Happy*, found that striving for happiness is the first and most basic step toward finding it.

2. *Take charge of your life*. True satisfaction also means taking responsibility for your choices and your well-being. Louise, a twenty-eight-year-old reporter from Atlanta, sums it up best: "Sometimes I look back and wish I'd made different choices. But then I take a deep breath and say, I'm going to be content with those decisions because they were mine and I made them the best I could. And I'm very happy with the sum of my choices—the way my life is today."

3. *Don't expect to feel great all the time.* Happiness is like the ocean. It ebbs and flows; it has peaks and troughs. And you need to know when to go with the flow. "Sometimes you have to go after what you want and try to push things to go your way," says Jerry Ruhl, Ph.D., co-author of *Contentment: A Way to True Happiness.* "But sometimes you'll be happier if you step back and just let go and accept what comes to you."

4. *Learn from your lows.* After a trauma, some people regain their equilibrium faster than others. Television personality Katie Couric seemed to bounce back after the devastating death of her husband. Remember what Lykken and Tellegren said about the happiness setpoint: You *can* influence it. Experts suggest that the best way to regain your sense of joy is to experience the pain fully, then find something positive to focus on.

5. *Be grateful.* Cherishing all the positive aspects of your life will boost your mood. "When you're focusing on and appreciating what's good about right now, anxieties about the past and the future fade away," says Rick Foster. In other words, count your blessings. It will make you feel more satisfied and it will promote contentment.

6. *Give to others.* "When you give, you feel connected to other people," advises Jerry Ruhl. That does not necessarily mean money, although that works also. It can also be time and energy, or a compliment on a coworker's outfit, a friendly conversation, sharing a recipe, letting someone get in line in front of you, giving a helpful hint—anything that improves someone else's day will brighten yours, too.

If you can consciously shift your outlook to compare yourself with people who have less than you, rather than envying those with more, you'll feel much less dissatisfied with your life.

—HOWARD CUTLER

■

A study conducted at the University of Michigan found that there is a connection between high self-esteem and general satisfaction with life. Even more than family, friends, income or work, satisfaction with self leads to a feeling of well-being. The study found that people who like and accept themselves feel good about life in general.

"This should come as no surprise," says David G. Myers. "Self-help books exhort us to respect ourselves, to dwell on our good points, to be positive about ourselves: Cut the self-pity. Stop the negative talk. To discover love, first love yourself."

We all feel inferior now and then. It's natural to compare ourselves to others—whether it's looks, grades, income, marital status, parenting prowess, earning ability, smarts, clothes, or the cars we drive and the houses we live in. But healthy, happy people are not defensive about their position. They strive toward achievement of realistic goals and they feel accepted for what and who they are.

"Happy, too, are those who gain the sense of control that comes with effective management of one's time," adds Myers. "Unoccupied time, especially for out-of-work people who aren't able to plan and fill their time, is unsatisfying. For happy people, time is filled and planned. They are punctual and efficient. For unhappy people, time is unfilled, open, and uncommitted; they postpone things and are inefficient."

One way to manage your time is to set large, long-term goals, then break them down into smaller daily tasks. Increasing your control through goals achieved will improve your health, mental outlook, and emotional foundation.

Can you find happiness at work? You definitely can.

Researchers have discovered that when you are in "the flow" of a project, you reach a state of mind that engages and challenges your skills without overwhelming them. I have found that when I'm writing an article or book that is absorbing, time means nothing. Every time I sat down to write *What Women Really Want*, I was filled with a sense of enjoyment.

Sure, it was hard work and yet I was in the flow, savoring every minute.

The same can happen when you are exercising and reach that place called "the zone." Chemicals produced by the brain cause a release of certain proteins, called an "endorphin rush," which improves health and energy levels. And it provides a natural antidote to depression and anxiety.

Religion is another avenue to happiness. Since happy people are less self-directed and more concerned with the well-being of others, if you belong to a community of faith it will allow you to focus your energy on a larger mission than just yourself.

> I wake each morning with the thrill of expectation and the joy of being truly alive. And I'm thankful for this day.
> —ANGELA L. WOZNIAK

∎

Most of us have more ability, creativity, energy, and desire than we use. So why aren't more of us positive and productive?

Sharon Wegscheider-Cruse says it's self-denial.

"In my office I kept a bowl of graham-cracker crumbs. Why? To remind my clients that it's too easy to settle for the crumbs when we deserve the whole cookie!"

Negative and limiting behavior makes you settle for less than the whole. That leads to depression and misery. It's important to dream your dream. Visualize it and take whatever action is necessary to make it come true.

"It may require an attitude adjustment," adds Wegscheider-Cruse, "but it's worth the struggle. Self-acceptance, self-confidence, and a loving, caring sense of self are all connected."

If you truly want to be happy, you will first need to drum up some good feelings about yourself. Confidence promotes energy and a willingness to try new things, take chances, explore untried options.

You might have to work at it, so here are few ways to lift those spirits and enjoy life:

- *Walk tall with shoulders back.* Unhappy people slouch. Happy people not only stand taller, they take bigger steps when they walk.
- *Look people in the eye.* Holding a steady gaze shows you have nothing to hide, that you are up-front and sincere.
- *Smile.* You can actually fool your brain into believing you are happy if you grin, and your radiance will be reflected back to you in the faces of others.
- *Dress in clothes you like.* Anything that makes you feel good about yourself will lift your mood. Find your power color and wear it often.
- *Set goals for yourself.* Once they are set, make a plan to reach them. Achieving your objective is a surefire way to make you glow with worthy feelings.
- *Find things you like doing.* A steady diet of simple delights is the key to true happiness. And when you are in the midst of a project there is no time to mope.
- *Take an interest in others.* Focusing on the needs of those around you lets you stop worrying about your own problems.
- *Learn from others.* Find someone whose confidence you admire and tap into his or her spirit.
- *Pretend to be happy.* Positive thoughts and behavior raise serotonin levels in the brain, which stimulate your body into feelings of pleasure instead of pain.
- *Remain resolved.* Pessimists use the word "try," optimists assume they will succeed.
- *Avoid toxic people.* Whiners, complainers and critical people drag you down. Steer clear of these negative influences.
- *Take time for you.* Whether it's a nap, a bath by candlelight, a massage, facial, manicure or a walk on the beach, do something just for YOU every day—and do it without guilt.
- *Touch your spiritual side.* Whether or not you attend church, you can tap into your higher self to find a sense of contentment.
- *Exercise.* Any kind of workout that raises your heart rate will release mood-altering endorphins to lift depression and stave off anxiety.

- *Reduce stress*. Relaxation techniques, such as yoga or medi-tation, will help get rid of pressure, which promotes a sense of well-being.
- *Nurture close friendships*. A strong connection with other people can support you during times of illness, job loss, death of a loved one or accident.
- *Laugh*. Giggling, chuckling, and chortling not only oxygenate the body, they produce a relaxation response that lowers blood pressure and heart rate and stimulates endorphins.

Happiness comes of the capacity to feel deeply, to enjoy simply, to think freely, to risk life, to be needed.
—STORM JAMESON

■

A messy divorce can be grounds for unhappiness. Actually, any breakup or loss can be demoralizing and debilitating: My separation included three years of my sleeping on the living-room couch. Yet I managed to find moments of happiness at the disco roller-skating rinks that were popular at the time. Three nights a week I grabbed my skates and went out for an evening of exercise and camaraderie with other people who enjoyed the sport. Despite difficult times at home, I can now recall those days as some of the most enjoyable in my life.

Stephen R. Rue, a prominent divorce attorney in New Orleans, says, "There is no question that getting divorced is a very stressful event in one's life. The commencement of a divorce proceeding brings concerns about children, money, property, and being single again.

"You may experience anxiety, doubt, denial, depression, lone-liness, guilt, anger, sadness, feelings that overwhelm, forgetful-ness, and frustration. You also may feel a sense of relief. Moving past the familiar to the realm of the unknown is never easy."

He adds: "We must learn to laugh at ourselves and not take ourselves too seriously. We might as well smile, laugh, and celebrate a new beginning. After all, what other choice do we have? Certainly not to return to unhappiness."

Anger and bitterness will eat you up. The person most hurt by the rage is yourself. Forgive your spouse for your own sake, and for the sake of your children. This is not to say that you should forgive and reconcile, but rather, forgive for the sake of being happy. Forgive for the sake of being healthy. Forgive for the sake of moving on, he advises.

So remember: You will survive. You will be happy again— unless you allow guilt to steal your happiness.

"Do not wallow in your guilt and certainly do not let guilt motivate your decisions," says Rue, who has helped thousands of men and women through their divorces. "If you feel guilty about events that led to your breakup, forgive yourself. Forgive and live."

The grass looks greener on the opposite side of the fence.
—TRADITIONAL PROVERB

■

In his book *Count Your Blessings*, author John F. Demartini says we can feel sorry for ourselves over what we think is missing in our lives.

He relates the story of Theresa, who said to him, "When I was single, I thought I needed love to be happy. Now I'm in love and I'm still not happy." She added that her top priority had been to find her soul mate, convinced that when she met him, the void in her life would be filled. Then she met Matt. But even with Matt, Theresa felt unsettled. She thought a new job would be the answer—or a baby. "Maybe that would make me happy," she said.

Theresa's search for happiness was leading her on a wild-goose chase. So Demartini encouraged her to look inside her heart for the mission or purpose that she would love to pursue and let that be her true beacon and guide in life. "You'll always experience happiness and sadness," he says. "But if you work toward your inspired mission or purpose in life, you'll have a more steady focus and you can embrace both sides of life more powerfully."

Happiness is the joy and comfort that permeates your being when you're completely at peace, advises Sharon Wegscheider-Cruse. "It bubbles up as an all-is-well feeling. People who are chronically happy tend to be sick less often, and live longer. Likewise, to be angry or to harbor hostility weakens the immune system."

Since it's never too late to change the way you think, keep these ideas in mind as you strive for a happier you:

- Identify why you feel unhappy.
- Take action to eliminate those circumstances.
- Identify what will make you happy.
- Start taking action toward that goal.
- Let go of the things or people who feed into your unhappiness.
- Surround yourself with positive, upbeat people.
- Let go of grudges and other negative behavior.
- Do not cling to feelings of guilt.
- Forgive yourself.
- Try not to take insults personally.
- Count your blessings.
- Try to see the positive instead of the negative.
- Don't sweat the small stuff.
- Don't worry. Be happy!

It *is* possible to become a happier person. Always remember, however, that money, fame, fortune, and love have nothing to do with it. You can be starving, alone, and the most obscure person on the planet, and still be happy!

If you are in a "bad" place—an abusive relationship, a terrible job, a crime-ridden neighborhood—attaining happiness may seem an overwhelming task. If this is the case, the first thing you must do is remove yourself from the situation.

That may sound easier than it is. However, by setting small goals for yourself you will be focused and motivated to make that change. You will be surprised at how much you can accomplish when you try.

Feeling victimized or out of control is distressing. Working with a specific purpose in mind is motivating. Your attitude allows you to experience the joy that is rightfully yours. One of the keys to happiness is to calm the mind. Stop worrying, stop feeling guilty, stop obsessing over things you cannot change. Instead, take positive action. Connect with another person. Make a difference.

All permanent and lasting change must come from the inner you. And daunting though that may seem, there is good news: That change *can* come from you. Nothing is missing. You have everything you need right now. Feelings of joy or sorrow are not the result of what has happened to you but, rather, are what you *decide* to keep inside you.

Happiness is the result of personal attitudes, the way you relate to others, and a positive sense of self-worth. We can all be that way!

> I'm happy all the time. I can't help it.
>
> —GOLDIE HAWN

■

THE FAMILY CIRCUS®   By Bil Keane

THINGS THAT MAKE ME HAPPY (Dolly)

Watching the sun settle down into its nest.

Being kept warm with affection.

Letting the swing tickle my tummy.

My good ol' friendly bed.

Reprinted with special permission of King Features Syndicate

AFFIRMATIONS

Affirmations are reminders, or sayings, that you can repeat as a daily mantra or prayer to help you achieve the state of mind you want. Write each one (or the ones you select) on a separate Post-it and stick them where you'll see them every day: on the bathroom mirror, on the kitchen coffeemaker, on the refrigerator door. Don't become fixated on them, but each time you see one, read it out loud to yourself. It may not seem like much—you may even feel silly at first—but do it. The results may surprise you.

Here are a few to help you achieve a happier frame of mind.

- I cannot make others happy.
- Only I can make myself happy.
- Nobody can rob me of my happiness.
- I choose to be upbeat instead of in the dumps.
- I breathe in and I smile, I breathe out and I'm at peace.
- I will set goals for myself and work toward them.
- I will stop my self-defeating behavior.
- I will create my own good feelings.
- I will reach out to others in a spirit of giving, and will not wallow in self-pity.
- I will not depend on anyone or anything except myself for my happiness.

When people are content, they experience happiness and peace, and never find life unbearable no matter how poor their living conditions or health may be. Contentment comes from demonstrating your given power to the fullest by putting your whole heart and soul into everything you do.

—MASAMI SAIONJI

∎

RECOMMENDED READING
ON HAPPINESS

Anthony, Robert, Ph.D. *How to Make the Impossible Possible.* Berkley Books.

Burns, David D., M.D. *Feeling Good.* Avon Books.

Carlson, Richard, Ph.D. *Don't Sweat the Small Stuff...and It's All Small Stuff.* Hyperion Books.

His Holiness the Dalai Lama and Howard Cutler. *The Art of Happiness.* Riverhead.

Demartini, John F., Ph.D. *Count Your Blessings.* Element Books.

Dyer, Wayne, Ph.D. *Your Sacred Self.* HarperCollins.

Levine, Kathy. *We Should Be So Lucky.* Pocket Books.

Lykken, David. *Happiness.* Golden Books.

Myers, David G., Ph.D. *The Pursuit of Happiness.* William Morrow & Co.

Rue, Stephen R., Esq., *Voodoo Divorce.* Forbes/FCP.

Ruhl, Jerry, Ph.D. *Contentment: A Way to True Happiness.* HarperSanFrancisco.

Saionji, Masami. *The Golden Key to Happiness.* Element Books.

Wegscheider-Cruse, Sharon. *Girl Talk.* Health Communications, Inc.

Also try happiness online: The Secret Society of Happy People (www.sohp.com).

Two

IF YOU WANT
FINANCIAL SECURITY

Can anyone remember when the times were not hard,
and money not scarce?
—RALPH WALDO EMERSON

■

*H*OW MUCH MONEY would you consider enough? One hundred thousand dollars in the bank? Five hundred thousand? A million? Two?

Most of us wish we had more money to take the pressure off and allow us to make choices—perhaps to travel, or leave a job or a spouse, or start a business, or just to feel good. Yet, somehow, what we have is never enough. That is why the credit-card industry is thriving and the bankruptcy courts are overloaded. This country is sinking in debt. Winning the lottery is a dream shared by tens of millions, but only a lucky few take home the jackpot. And, amazingly, many of these winners end up filing Chapter 11!

You can have financial security. But first you must be comfortable with the idea of managing your money. Many women have built a wall of resistance when it comes to taking responsibility for their own finances. It's easier to let someone else do it: a husband, a boyfriend, a CPA, a stock broker. Too often we hang back from getting to know how to manage our money and make it work for us.

That sort of shyness breeds ignorance, and ignorance breeds fear, says Neale S. Godfrey, author of *Making Change: A Woman's Guide to Designing Her Financial Future.* "But a woman cannot afford to be ignorant about money or afraid of dealing with her finances."

The fantasies of the old TV sitcoms have lulled us into a sense of complacency that someone else will make everything all right and we need not worry our pretty little heads about money matters.

Wrong. The days of Ozzie and Harriet are over.

Very few women have a clear idea of how to relate to money, however this much is clear: You must take responsibility for your own financial future with hard work and sound financial investments. You cannot spend more than you earn, which means you must live within a budget. Always!

The idea of being empowered when it comes to finances can be frightening and even overwhelming. To enable you to identify where and how your finances fall short, think about these questions:

1. How can you increase your wealth?
2. What money habits do you want to change?
3. How can you stop spending too much money?
4. What are your feelings about money?
5. What do you want to learn about your managing money?

Think about the value you place on acquiring money, the motivation you have to earn it, the discipline you have to keep it and how you like to spend it—on yourself and others. Says Sharon Wegscheider-Cruse, a Nevada-based therapist: "Money is a wonderful way of making our lives fuller, richer and more varied. Money can make life easier and more comfortable. Best of all, you'll have choices. When there is no money, the choices are few.

Your time and energy are directed to making it. But when you have even slightly more than you need to take care of your bills, you can relax a bit and enjoy life without the constant worry."

Where are you in the scheme of things?

> Think early about investing for your retirement. Old age isn't for sissies and certainly it's not for poor people!
> —LIZ SMITH

■

Barbra Streisand was so poor growing up that her only doll was fashioned out of a hot-water bottle! She started her career singing in Greenwich Village gay bars, lived in a cold-water flat and begged her friends for food—or went without. Now she commands a cool $10 million for a single Las Vegas show. She's come a long way, baby. Her net worth is an estimated $100 million. With or without a husband, she'll never worry about money again.

And at age twenty-four, the lovely songbird known as Jewel is also set for life. But it wasn't always that way. Raised on a homestead outside Homer, Alaska, Jewel Kilcher's family was so poor they had no running water or electricity. Her threadbare childhood made her an unlikely candidate for fame and fortune.

Her dad's folks, Grandpa Yule and Grandma Ruth Kilcher, moved from Switzerland to Alaska for free land under the Homestead Act. Grandma Ruth, who had studied opera in Europe, became one of the first female journalists in Alaska. Grandpa Yule was a scholar who spoke twelve languages and invented his own musical instruments. Along with his seven siblings, Jewel's father, Atz, was home-schooled.

On Jewel's mother's side, Grandpa Jay and Grandma Arva Carroll settled in the interior of Alaska during the 1930s, then moved to an island and lived in a one-room cabin with a dirt floor. Grandpa Jay was a trapper and Grandma Arva was a pioneer wife. They had four children, including Jewel's mother, Nedra. In time they moved to Seward, where Grandpa Jay designed power stations and built an airplane from scratch. He later developed a business around his love for airplanes.

Eventually the Carrolls moved to Homer where Atz, a social worker and musician, met Nedra, a poet, painter, and artist. They made two albums and had three children: Jewel, Atz, Jr., and Shane. The kids were raised in a log cabin without electricity, running water, or a telephone.

Jewel's parents divorced when she was eight; she stayed with her dad, singing in saloons for a few dollars. At age eighteen, she moved to San Diego to be with her mom and got a job as a waitress. Hungry and broke, she nibbled the uneaten food left on customers' plates. She and Nedra were so strapped for cash that she stole toilet paper from fast-food restaurants. They begged and borrowed enough money to buy two old vans and they each moved into one.

Jewel took showers at the homes of friends or washed up in a lavatory at the local department store. Homeless, confused, and in despair, she turned to music as her salvation—writing more than 100 songs and poems during those poor and lonely times.

She was "discovered" in a San Diego coffeehouse in 1994. Her first CD sold 10 million copies. Since then she's signed a $2 million book deal and written a best-seller—*A Night Without Armor*. Her albums skyrocket to the chart-top at the speed of light. She tours America and Europe, singing, and she has a starring role in the film *Ride With the Devil*. The old VW van has been replaced with a rambling country home filled with huge pillows, wood paneling, flowers, and a sumptuous pool and Jacuzzi. But deep down inside, Jewel Kilcher is still that little girl from the farm.

"I grew up with dirt under my nails . . . you never get over that," she says.

For a barefoot babe, she's made out just swell.

WHAT'S HOLDING YOU BACK?

The biggest temptation is to settle for too little.

—THOMAS MERTON

■

If you grew up during the 1950s and '60s, chances are you were told that women were expected to marry, have children, and live happily ever after. That was the myth back then. And what a myth it was! Nobody talked about what happens if you could not find a spouse, or if he was not a provider, or if you got divorced.

I fell victim to that legend and was KO'd when my marriage fell apart. Not only did I have nothing, I was out in the cold with two children and a former spouse who refused to pay support. I could have gone to court and we could have battled for years. It would have cost a fortune, which neither of us had. Instead, I picked myself up, dusted myself off and started all over again. Now I own a condo and two cars. When my daughters need help financially, I am there for them. I have never let them down. And I have two IRAs, mutual funds, and a bank account. I'm not rich, not by a long shot. But I'm comfortable and I have done it on my own.

"No matter where you are, even if you're at the beginning, if you manage your finances successfully you can create security for yourself," says author and financial expert Tina B. Tessina, Ph.D. "No matter how small your income, you can begin saving and planning to invest. Every woman today needs to know how to manage her own finances."

Unless you had a clear-cut picture of what you wanted to be when you grew up, chances are you fell into a job. Perhaps you lucked out and you are making a decent salary. Perhaps you found yourself in a dead-end job and you are too frightened to quit and start something new. Or maybe you feel you are not smart or clever or talented enough to do anything else. Or maybe you became exactly what you wanted to be, then found it was not what you wanted after all.

You can make excuses or you can make money.
But you can't do both.
—RICHARD CARLSON

∎

Excuses are nothing more than an expression of fear. You might be fearful of stepping out of your comfort zone, of making more than your partner or of taking time away from your family.

"Successful people face the same frustrations, hurdles and fears as everyone else," says Richard Carlson, Ph.D., author of *Don't Worry, Make Money.* "The difference is, rather than feeling defeated or immobilized by their fears and worries, successful people conquer them. Courage is best described as 'doing it anyway.'"

When you make excuses—no matter what they are—you keep yourself locked in a negative cycle. You think the excuse is valid, which prevents you from moving forward with your life. It's another self-defeating habit. But it can be broken. Successful people—including women who are set financially—do not let their fears and excuses dominate their lives. What was Jewel thinking as she lived in her van with no running water and no electricity? She was thinking, "I'm going to break out of here somehow!"

And she did.

Instead of feeling overwhelmed by negative internal dialogue, financially successful people are able to stay focused on what they are doing and what they want to accomplish.

Lydia, a single parent with two young girls, worked as a legal secretary for a cheapskate who wouldn't give her a five-dollar-a-week raise. When her boss gave everyone else in the office a raise, the writing was on the wall. Lydia scanned the want ads, updated her resume, went on interviews and landed another job—one that paid $50 more a week. She gave notice and never looked back.

No matter what you do for a living, there are better-paying jobs. If you have no skills, there are trade and technical schools. Community colleges offer night courses. Where there's a will, there's a way.

When I was laid off from my last full-time job, I went into business for myself. I had business cards printed and contacted every editor I knew. Within two years I had doubled my salary. Best of all, I am now my own boss!

Do you say, "I can't," or "I'm not smart enough," or "I have no talent"? Take those negative phrases out of your vocabulary starting right this minute. Why say "I can't" when you can say "I will"?

We all grew up with a lot of baggage about money. The generation before us did not talk about finances. Our mothers cooked and cleaned and bought groceries. Dad paid the bills. You may still feel that there will be conflict, danger, and hurt in your marital situation if you start taking too much of an interest in the details of household finances.

Now know this:

- Women live an average of seven years longer than men.
- There are five times as many widows as widowers.
- Divorce ends nearly half of all marriages.
- Only one out of every seven divorced women receives spousal support.
- At some point in their lives, nearly 90 percent of all women will have to take charge of their own finances.

As the *Chicago Tribune* columnist Mary Schmich said in her mock 1997 graduation speech that became the hit pop song "Wear Sunscreen": "Don't expect anyone else to support you. Maybe you have a trust fund. Maybe you'll have a wealthy spouse. But you never know when either one might run out."

Essentially, women have two possibilities: be independent, or be dependent. The latter generally means being dependent on a man, although it can just as easily be on another woman or on Mom and Dad. Dependence is dependence.

If you want financial security, you must learn a new set of life skills to shore up your cash reserves. It may mean breaking old habits, like overspending or buying on credit. It will mean sorting through options and selecting priorities.

Recently my friend Tim and I took a long scenic bike ride through a fabulously wealthy neighborhood. When I pointed to the luxurious homes and expensive automobiles and asked, "Isn't this mind-boggling?" he stared at me and said, "Why?"

"How do people get to live in houses like this and drive cars like that?" I asked, pointing to a Rolls-Royce.

"They set their minds to it," he answered simply. "They know exactly what they want and they spend nearly every waking minute maneuvering toward it. They only associate with wealthy people, they only date people with money and they don't let anything come between them and their bank accounts."

There are plenty of women who want to marry rich. But nobody can predict when that rug may be yanked right out from under you. And if you are starting from scratch, know this: You can do it. You can design the financial life you want.

As a first step, take a look at the following questionnaire for an overview of all the ways in which you defeat yourself. The section that follows the questionnaire offers practical tips for getting a jump-start on becoming financially secure.

> In overcoming overspending, you may be trying to give up a compulsion that's as powerful as cigarettes are to a smoker.
>
> —OLIVIA MELLAN

■

FINANCIAL QUESTIONNAIRE

Women traditionally hold themselves back financially. Answer these questions truthfully to get a handle on where you stand with regard to money.

1. Do you know how much you make per year, month, week, and/or hour?
Yes_____No_____

2. Do you know how much your husband or partner makes?
Yes_____No_____

3. Can you live within a budget?
Yes_____No_____

4. Do you put away a certain amount of every paycheck?
Yes_____No_____

5. Do you have an IRA?
Yes_____No_____

6. Do you have a savings account?
Yes_____No_____

7. Can you balance your checkbook?
Yes_____No_____

8. Do you handle the finances in the family?
Yes_____No_____

9. If not, do you understand how the finances are handled?
Yes_____No_____

10. Do you have a cash reserve equal to at least six months of your salary?
Yes_____No_____

11. Are you satisfied with what you make?
Yes_____No_____

12. Are you kept in the dark about money by your partner?
Yes_____No_____

13. If yes, does it bother you?
Yes_____No_____

14. Do you spend money when you cannot afford to?
Yes_____No_____

15. Do you buy things to cheer you up?
Yes_____No_____

16. Do you buy most things on credit?
Yes_____No_____

17. Would you like to have better control of your financial future?
Yes_____No_____

18. Do you buy things you don't need?
Yes_____No_____

19. Do you go to sales just for the bargains?
Yes_____No_____

20. Do you buy cars, clothes, jewelry, and designer labels as status symbols?
Yes_____No_____

KEY TO ANSWERS:

If you marked No on more than half of questions 1 to 10, you are not taking control of your finances.

If you marked Yes on more than half of questions 11 to 20, you have a problem with budgeting your money.

FINAL QUESTION:

Write down three ways you can improve your financial status.

_____

_____

_____

POSITIVE STEPS FOR
FINANCIAL HEALTH

Do not value money for any more or any less than it's worth; it is a
good servant, but a bad master.
—ALEXANDER DUMAS

■

Financially speaking, where do you want to be a year from
today? Five years? Ten years? What are you doing about making
that dream come true?

In 1984 Michele Hoskins of Calumet City, Illinois, was in the
middle of a divorce. The thirty-six-year-old parochial school
teacher had three young daughters and a rocky road ahead of
her. "I knew it would be impossible to live well on my teacher's
salary once I was a single parent," she says.

Michele's dream was to live well. And she knew it could be
done, but she had to risk everything to get what she wanted.

Her great-great-grandmother, America Washington, a slave in
Arkansas, had invented a recipe for a special syrup. It had been
passed down from generation to generation, but only the third
daughter of each family was given the recipe.

"My mother was the third daughter among her siblings so she
got it," Michele explained to me. "But I was the only girl in the
family. Rightfully, it should have gone to my youngest daughter,
but I pleaded with Mama to give it to me."

Michele got the recipe but she could not get conventional
bank loans. So she begged a $25,000 loan from one of her broth-
ers and set to work brewing up huge batches of Butter Creme,
Honey Creme, and Maple Creme syrups in the attic.

"It was clear that I'd have to risk everything to get what I
wanted," she admits.

And risk it she did. She sold her condominium and its
furnishings, gave up her teaching job, and went on welfare. She

and her daughters moved back into her parents' house. But her brother and parents, who could not see her vision, made her life a sticky mess by suing her for trying to take the recipe public. A court decided in Michele's favor and within five years the syrup was being sold in 48 stores in the metropolitan Chicago area.

Just when she thought her future was set, Michele began having blinding headaches. Doctors found a tumor on her pituitary gland. Michele prayed for a miracle—and she got it. Surgery, followed by an herbal regimen, cured her. Now her company, aptly named Michele Foods, Inc., boasts contracts with national retail chains. They supply Denny's restaurants, among others, and Michele is very comfortable as president and CEO of a company that does upwards of $10 million in sales each year. A few years ago she was courted by General Mills, which does not have a syrup product line. They felt teaming up with Michele Foods made good sense.

Michele, who has been a guest on Oprah Winfrey's TV show, says: "Everyone has the power to enjoy life. But you have to work hard to reach your dreams."

Getting ahead financially is a complicated procedure, and not everyone has a secret family recipe that will generate millions of dollars in revenue. But we can all dream. First you must decide what you want to do. Then visualize yourself doing it. Now determine what you must do to get there.

"When I started at Chase Manhattan Bank, I imagined myself in an office on the seventeenth floor," says author and motivational speaker Neale S. Godfrey. "I furnished the room—rugs, desk, paintings on the walls. I imagined myself in the boardroom, in meetings, even in the executive ladies' room. It was a good daydream, but ultimately I couldn't see myself there. Then I started visualizing myself working out of my home—traveling and teaching, giving lectures and seminars, but based in an office right in my home—and it started to feel right. Amazingly, way back then, I imagined an office in a suburban home very much like the one I have now."

Though difficult, it is important not to compare yourself to others to your own detriment. Instead, strive for a higher position, better salary, and more money in the bank. Admire and emulate those who have more, rather than those who have less than you.

When I was married and living in a small apartment with my two daughters, four of us sharing one bathroom, I looked at my friends who were moving from starter homes to larger, more spacious quarters, and I felt deprived. I could, of course, have compared myself to those who had less—families of six or eight living in one or two cramped rooms with no running water. Instead of striving to better our circumstances, I wallowed in self-pity. Now I know better.

But while we may have no control over the conditions into which we are born, we *do* have the power as we mature to make the most of our opportunities.

With affirmations, you can influence your subconscious to believe that everything is possible. Once you have faced the issue of money and addressed it, you need to put your words into action. Use your mind to formulate a plan to create realistic goals that will bring the money to you.

By imagining abundance and a bountiful lifestyle, you will let go of the negative "poor me" attitude that holds you to the past. Then you can move forward to your goal of a better, richer life.

> Don't be influenced by what others do or say. Don't be put off when some of your friends are buying high-priced and high-powered cars and moving into larger homes. Let them have those goals. Only you know what you want to do with your own money.
>
> —ELIZABETH LEWIN

■

It will take time to put your dreams in motion. That does *not* mean you should wait around for that raise and promotion, or for you to get a better job or complete your education or technical training.

As of right now, you must start living within your means so you can start saving. Set reachable goals. If you are married, those goals might involve your spouse. Whether you are with someone or alone, write down your objectives, giving them a dollar amount and a time frame. Committing your plan to paper makes it real—something you can watch as you get closer to your dream. You may have a short-term goal (new furniture), a medium-term goal (a new car) or a long-term goal (a European vacation or early retirement).

No matter what your specific goals are, be aware that setting aside money will be difficult until you get into the habit. Planning for tomorrow means beginning today! Right now— even though it's murder living from one paycheck to another. For years I would bring home my check, pay my bills and cry. There was never enough. Looking back I cannot imagine how I managed. However, I put away $25 from every check. Hard? You'd better believe it. Now I have a cushion which allows me to fly by the seat of my pants as a freelance writer.

An even more impressive financial success story is recounted by Cynthia Kersey in her book *Unstoppable*.

Sheri Poe, an aerobics enthusiast, wondered why her back and feet ached after each workout. Her research revealed that women's athletic shoes were scaled-down versions of men's shoes, although the female foot is shaped differently. Sheri and her husband, Martin Birrittella, decided to start a company to manufacture athletic shoes made specifically for women. The problem was that they had no experience and no capital. Neither of them had a college degree. And their competitors were Nike and Reebok, two monster companies that dominated the industry.

But Sheri asked, "Why not?"

First she polled hundreds of athletic women to determine the need for specially formed shoes. Then she and Martin took a third mortgage on their house and borrowed from friends, family and anyone else who was interested in their project. "They thought it was insane to think we could break into this market with no experience and create a new brand in such a competitive field," admits Sheri.

Instead of being dissuaded, Sheri and Martin started a company called Ryka and found an investment banker who loaned them $250,000. He also gave them a letter of intent to go public with their company in the spring of 1988. But in the fall of 1987, the market crashed. Sheri and Martin were in shock. They thought they were going belly-up before they even began. However, the banker assured them there was still interest in Ryka, and the public offering five months later raised $4 million. They were in business.

When the first pair of shoes was shipped, Sheri realized the manufacturer had not followed her specifications and foot form, but had simply made a smaller version of a man's shoe. Instead of giving up, she contacted retailers and had them ship back the footwear. Then she had new shoes made and shipped. To make up for the season that was lost, she offered her athletic footgear to aerobics instructors at a discount. She sent samples of the shoes to Oprah Winfrey and was ultimately invited to appear on *Oprah*. She wrote to England's Princess Diana, enclosing a pair of shoes—all of which boosted sales into the millions.

Only six years after going public with their stock, Ryka was raking in $15 million. They have since merged with Global Sports, Inc., and now Sheri is developing children's products.

> I believe the reason that we were able to do this was because we saw a need in the market, had incredible passion, and were committed to making it happen.
> —SHERI POE

Whatever your goal is, you must first know how much you make and how much you spend. Then you must make MORE than you spend and if you can't make more, you must start spending less. That will allow you to start saving. You must take charge of your money. Unless your goal is to be financially independent, enlist the aid of your spouse or significant other if you have two incomes.

"You cannot make sound financial decisions for the future without gathering and maintaining personal financial information that is factual, detailed, and fully accurate," says author Elizabeth Lewin. "Erroneous financial information can lead to disastrous financial decisions. Yet the human tendency is to guesstimate."

Here are some of the sources you will need in order to find out how much you are worth. Assemble statements, invoices or receipts from:

- Checking and savings accounts.
- Certificates of deposit.
- Money-market funds and treasury bills.
- Stocks and bonds (your most recent statements).
- Pensions, including IRAs, Keogh plans, 401(k)plans, tax-deferred annuities, and/or corporate pension plans.
- Real estate that you own.
- Life-insurance policies (face value or current cash value).
- Other assets, including automobile (if you own it), collections of gold, silver, coin, crystal, stamps, antiques, jewelry, furs, etc.

You will also need to know your liabilities—how much you owe. So consider these possibilities:

- Mortgages.
- Credit-card debt, including department stores and gas cards.
- Loans for automobile, education, personal IOUs.
- Automobile insurance.
- Taxes (unpaid to IRS or quarterly, if you are self-employed).

It takes time and effort to gather correct figures. And once you have them, it takes an even greater effort to set priorities on your spending habits.

Spending money is fun. If you are like me, $50 can fly out of your wallet in less than 10 minutes. And unless you sit down and account for every penny, you may not even know exactly where it went. If you work, eating lunch out every day can gobble up a huge amount of cash. So can a spur-of-the-moment trip to the mall or an impulsive purchase. While I do not consider myself a spendthrift, I was poor for such a long time that there are occasions when I splurge just to make myself feel good. And I'm willing to bet most women do the same thing.

"There are specific attitudes toward money that characterize overspenders," says Olivia Mellan, a reformed overspender. "The basic definition is this: If your spending habits create a problem for you or others around you, you're probably an overspender. It's as simple (and as complex) as that."

So what can you do? First you must get a handle on why you spend more than you can afford. Like an alcoholic, you need to admit that you have a money-spending problem. It's hard to say no, to deprive yourself when everyone around you is buying. But how much of what you buy do you really need, and how much of it is frivolous spending?

Temptation surrounds us. We are bombarded nonstop with advertisements—on TV, on the radio, in magazines and in newspapers. Cash has been replaced by credit cards. And now at-home TV shows and Internet shopping slurp up billions of our dollars without our ever having to leave the house!

"Deep inside, most overspenders believe money can buy, or substitute for, love or happiness," says Mellan. "It's like feeding yourself empty calories. This emotional malnutrition can lead to low self-esteem and other psychological problems."

Overspending usually falls into these specific categories:

1. To show affection for others by buying presents for them.
2. To alleviate stress or a bad day.
3. To reward oneself.
4. To seek status by buying only brand-name merchandise.
5. To "save money" by buying items on sale, even if you don't need them.
6. As an uncontrollable urge.
7. To "get revenge," show power or feel superior.
8. For the thrill of it—intentionally putting yourself at risk.

The bad news is that it's hard to quit cold turkey. Even worse, overspending can wreck a marriage or a relationship. Not surprisingly, arguments about money are the number one cause of divorce in America. Overspending can blow your budget to pieces and it can land you in bankruptcy court—or worse, in jail.

The scope of this book doesn't allow a psychological analysis of why people overspend or how to stop. However, if you perceive yourself as being in this category, you might want to seek out a competent therapist or financial counselor who can offer advice on consolidating your debts and help you understand the psychological reasons behind your spending habits. Once you have broken the vicious cycle, you can start saving. And remember, cliché it may be, but it's true: A penny saved is a penny earned.

The basic rule for shopping is: Get the best buy for the best price.
—NEALE S. GODFREY

■

For too many of us, "The American Way" is to buy now, pay later. With our paychecks stretched beyond their limits, and with millions of workers being downsized, we are relying on plastic even for such necessities as groceries and gas. On the other hand, many people like the convenience of charging everything and writing a single check at the end of the month.

However, too many women juggle the plastic, not always expertly. They "max out" one card, then start on another, paying the minimum each month, or maybe a little more. It's a terrible cycle of debt-plus-more-debt. If you want financial security, beware the credit card!

Of course we all know the benefits of credit cards. We live in a society where they are absolutely necessary for renting cars, reserving hotel rooms and airline tickets, ordering from catalogs, even getting Internet service. And when there is an emergency, they provide instant cash. The idea is not to get rid of your cards, but to use them wisely. Enjoy the convenience they provide and never accumulate more debt than you can pay in full when the monthly statement arrives.

Since your goal is to free up as much money as possible for your retirement, take a good hard look at how you handle credit and debt, warns Elizabeth Lewin. "Are you charging on credit card the ordinary items that have life spans shorter than the time it will take to pay for them? Taking cash advances so you can buy the things you used to pay cash for?"

Here are some tips for using your credit cards wisely.

- Only use cards with no annual fee.
- Watch for offers with low introductory percentage rates. Before taking one, find out how high the rate will rise at the end of the introductory period.
- If necessary, maintain two cards: one for large purchases, to

be paid off over time; and one for small items, which you pay in full every month.

- Always pay more than the required minimum amount. If you have a debt of $1,100 at 18 percent, it will take 12.5 years to pay off if you pay the minimum due—and you will have paid $2,480 in interest! By adding $10 per month, you cut the debt to six years and will have spent only $676 in interest.
- To avoid hefty late charges, always pay your bill (whether in whole or in part) on time.

Says Lewin: "If you can't afford to pay cash, you can't afford to buy it on credit. A finance charge is money spent for nothing more than convenience."

> I had plastic surgery last week. I cut up my credit card.
> —HENNY YOUNGMAN

■

What is your dream? To own a home or a horse farm? To travel to exotic lands or have enough for your retirement? All that's holding you back is money. Right? Wrong.

"To make your assets grow, keep them in motion," advises psychologist John F. Demartini. "Money is a form of energy, and energy in motion is more productive than energy at rest."

He adds:

- Money must circulate to grow.
- You must *spend* money *and save* money to *make* money.
- It makes no difference how much you make. The secret lies in how well you manage what you have.
- The law of fair exchange means you will not get something for nothing.

"One of the most successful paths to wealth is the path of an inspired dream," says Demartini. "When we have a mission or a purpose bigger than we are, and our vision stretches beyond our own lifetime, we become like magnets attracting the resources we require to fulfill our inspirations."

All financial management experts will tell you these truths right up front: (1) pay yourself first, (2) save at least 10 percent of what you earn, (3) invest in your dreams, and (4) time is money—don't procrastinate.

And know this: *Every day you don't save is a day you add more to your work.*

> Nobody is safe from the ax of unemployment or from the upheaval of an unhappy marriage, from the death of a loved one or an unexpected illness or accident.
>
> —BENJAMIN F. DOVER

■

If saving money is a mystery, now is the time to learn. Check your local community college for courses, read the newspaper for seminars, contact your bank for free investment classes, ask your friends to recommend a good CPA (certified public accountant). Take notes and ask questions. A financial advisor can provide you with timely information to build your financial security. On the Internet you will find financial websites such as www.financialengines.com. In concept, these retirement calculators take into consideration your age, salary, pension (if you have one) and current investments, and the future income you'd like to have. They do not account for the millions of possibilities that could occur between now and then, such as emergencies at home, job loss, or the stock market crashing. However, the search engine may give you a ballpark idea of how much you need to sock away now so you can live comfortably later.

No matter how you approach your long-term saving plan, begin by budgeting.

"Budgeting, like dieting, is one of those actions many women have good intentions about, but don't seem to accomplish," says author Tina B. Tessina. "The good news is that budgeting is much easier than dieting."

Here are some of her tips for getting started.

1. *Know your income.* In a notebook, keep track of everything you earn.
2. *Write down your fixed bills* (rent or mortgage payment, utilities, groceries, insurance, car payments, credit-card payments, taxes, etc.).
3. *Make entries as you spend.* Keep the ledger or notebook handy. If you have to dig it out you won't make the necessary notations. Write down other expenses such as medical bills, stamps, clothing, gas, lunches out, dinners, etc.
4. *Analyze your expenses.* Record what you spend. Account for every dollar. Without this system in place, it's amazingly easy to lose track or to spend hundreds of dollars on nothing of value.
5. *Tally the money going out against the money coming in.* Often it's a negative balance. That means you're sliding further into debt each month.
6. *Using that list as a guide, see where you can cut expenses.* If you're really behind the eight-ball, perhaps it's time for a second job or one that pays better—or, even if temporarily, think of *all* your money as "non-spend" cash.

Saving money is the single most important thing you can do for yourself—even if it seems impossible with pressing bills and those emergencies that pop up with maddening regularity. If you take home $400 a week, first put $40 in a savings account. That's only ten percent. Once you have a small nest egg, take it out of the bank (which pays a piddling three percent interest) and invest the money into either a certificate of deposit (CD), a mutual fund, a money-market account or real estate. That's a good start, and there are other ways to increase your savings.

Owning your own home or condominium is an ideal investment since mortgages can be less expensive than rent. The first thing I did when my marriage ended was to borrow the money for a down payment on a condo. My mortgage, including maintenance, is less than $500 a month, but I could easily rent my place for almost $1,000. If I didn't own it, I couldn't afford to live here!

If you have a life partner or spouse and own property, make sure your name is on the deed. That way, half is yours no matter what happens in the future.

Many employers do not offer a 401(k) pension plan. If you are counting on Social Security to help you through your old age, think again and plan ahead. Individual Retirement Accounts come in many forms: regular rollover, SEP-IRAs, Keoghs, and Roth IRAs. Ask a financial planner which of these makes the most sense for you. You might also think about making your money grow with mutual funds.

"Mutual funds are a group of stocks put together by financial companies who hire experts to watch the market," advises Tessina. "And they are less risky than individual stocks."

And while you're asking, find out about annuities, a type of insurance policy: you pay a premium now for a guaranteed income at retirement age. Inquire, too, about earnings that compound themselves. Because compounding can produce dramatic results the longer these accounts are held, it's important to start as early as possible.

When shopping for securities, be aware of brokerage fees and operating expenses. Many mutual funds charge a sales commission, called a "load" to cover marketing costs. Most of these charges are in the three-percent range. So if you invest $1,000, you lose $30 up front for administrative fees. Ask about "no-load" funds (mutual funds with no fees) and aggressive funds with proven track records.

This kind of information was Greek to me just a few years ago. My money sat in a bank savings account earning virtually nothing. Now my cash is growing by leaps and bounds in mutual funds and money-market accounts. Make your money work for *you* so that you can have financial peace of mind.

Financial experts advise thinking long-term, not for next month or next year. Look toward leaving your money invested for three to five years—or longer. You must build in the time needed to recover from inevitable slumps in the stock market. In Chapter Six, If Success Is Your Goal, you will read about a remarkable woman who made millions in the stock market.

To have a better picture of what you are getting into, here is a list of terms you should have an investment counselor explain— or look them up yourself: money-market accounts, mutual funds, stocks, bonds, bond funds, certificates of deposit, treasury bonds, treasury notes, government savings bonds, municipal bonds, tax-exempt bonds, and corporate bonds.

Also ask about safety of principal, income return, long-term capital growth, tax minimization, market risk, inflation, interest rate risk, liquidity risk, and emotional risk.

Once your money is invested, there are a few things to remember. It takes time for money to grow. It's not like fruit, which ripens quickly, or a plant that flowers overnight. Price swings are common. The market fluctuates up and down. Don't get scared and sell when it's down. In fact, a "down market" is a good time to buy because prices are cheaper (if your reasons for buying in the first place haven't changed). It will swing up again. Be wary of tips from well-meaning friends and neighbors, and listen instead to those in the business. And remember, any get-rich-quick scheme that sounds too good to be true is probably a rip-off. Don't be suckered into throwing away your money by being greedy. Patience is a virtue in the investing trade.

Do your homework, and don't check the price quotes every day or you'll drive yourself bonkers. Keep a diversified portfolio. By putting all your eggs in one stock, you could be wiped out. That's why mutual or bond funds are a wise choice; your investment counselor will help you choose the best one for you.

Never invest your money in anything that eats or needs repairing.
—BILLY ROSE

■

The exception to Billy Rose's advice, of course, is kids. If you have children, the financial demands can be endless. They can deplete your resources faster than a gas-guzzling car. As parents, we hate to say no. So say yes to a weekly allowance. It is the best way to teach your youngsters the value of a dollar. It will also help you budget *your* income and expenses. Tell them what the cash covers (movies, clothes, snacks when they're out with their friends—and whatever else you think should be included). When they ask for a raise, negotiate. And don't fork over the bucks if they run short before payday. It's a good lesson on how to live within their means, and it will help when they get to the real world and have to make one paycheck last until the next. That's what's called "stretching the dollar." By setting your children up on a fixed income you are doing them a great service for the future. If they are old enough, have them open a free checking account in their own names.

Today is the day to take that first step toward ensuring your own financial security, and here is a list of additional positive ideas to keep in mind as you begin to amass your wealth.

- If you earn a salary, you should be entitled to spend or save a portion of that money any way you want—even if you are in a committed relationship with a joint account. By having your own savings, you are creating a form of independence for yourself, should the need ever arise.
- If you want to move up to a better job, consider going back to school for a specialty course (paralegal, computer training) or getting a license (real estate, brokerage) or earning that next degree.
- If you want to start your own business, invest in yourself. The payment will be well worth it.
- Even if you are afraid to take that first step, do it anyway. Not only will you survive, but you'll also make progress toward your goals.
- Save, save, save. Then invest, invest, invest.
- When you are goal-oriented, you will pick up the skills and tools that are necessary to get to the finish line. By focusing on the positive you can accomplish anything.

Suze Orman, a former Wall Street broker turned motivational speaker and author, says it takes grit to face the issue of money. That's because money is charged with passion. "Your emotional state ultimately determines your financial state," she says.

Her message is that until you find out why you have trouble saving money, keeping track of it or taking risks investing it, you'll find yourself having trouble in other areas of life, too. Frustrations about money will spill over into a lack of confidence everywhere else.

Money is something we shy away from—even (perhaps especially) in intimate relationships.

Orman says: "Financial intimacy is such an important part of our lives. You have to know as much about your mate's financial hygiene habits as you do about his other personal habits. It takes courage to open yourself to money, to ask others to do the same and to make true wealth one of the goals of true love."

Tough times don't last. Tough people do.

—OLD TEXAS PROVERB

■

AFFIRMATIONS

No matter what your financial situation is now, it can be improved. Use these daily affirmations for setting yourself in motion.

- I will invest in my inspirations.
- I will start saving for tomorrow today.
- I will pay myself first.
- I will make an effort to learn more about my finances.
- If things are bad now, they will get better.
- I appreciate the wealth I have.
- I can make my money work for me.
- I can earn more than I am earning now.
- I will live within my budget and not treat money irresponsibly.
- One year from now, I will have twice as much as I have today.

**There's nothing in life we are more afraid to face bravely
and honestly than our money.**

—S uze O rman

■

RECOMMENDED READING ON
FINANCIAL SECURITY

Carlson, Richard. *Don't Worry, Make Money.* Hyperion Press.

Covey, Stephen. Living the 7 Habits: Stories of Courage and Inspiration. Simon & Schuster.

—. The 7 Habits of Highly Effective People. Simon & Schuster.

Demartini, John F. *Count Your Blessings.* Element Books.

Dover, Benjamin. *Life After Debt.* Equitable Media Services.

Fox, Arnold, M.D., and Barry Fox, Ph.D. *Beyond Positive Thinking.* Hay House.

Lewin, Elizabeth. *Kiss the Rat Race Good-Bye.* Pharos Books.

—. *Your Personal Financial Fitness Program.* Pharos Books.

Malaspina, Margaret A. *Don't Die Broke, How To Turn Your Investment Savings Into Lasting Income.* Bloomberg Press.

Mellan, Olivia. *Overcoming Overspending.* Walker and Co.

Godfrey, Neale S. *A Penny Saved.* Simon & Schuster.

—. *Making Change: A Woman's Guide to Designing her Financial Future.* Simon & Schuster.

Orman, Suze. *The Courage to Be Rich: Creating a Life of Material and Spiritual Abundance.* Riverhead Books.

—. *Nine Steps to Financial Freedom.* Crown.

Quinn, Hope Stanley, and Lyn Miller-Lachmann. *Downsized But Not Defeated.* Andrews McMeel Publishing.

Tessina, Tina B., Ph.D. *The 10 Smartest Decisions a Woman Can Make Before 40.* Health Communications, Inc.

Wegscheider-Cruse, Sharon. *Girl Talk.* Health Communications, Inc.

Never Fear

Never fear anything because
If you do, whatever you fear
May come upon you.

Reach out in faith
When fear comes your way
Take the amount of faith you need
To make it through the day

—FLORA COUSINS

∎

Three

IF YOU WANT PEACE OF MIND

When the mind is stirred up, all things are stirred up.
The mind is not stirred up, there is nothing stirring.
—ZEN PROVERB BY DAIJU

■

*T*HE SAYING "SILENCE is golden" is particularly true if your world is bustling with activity. For many working women with families, time alone is a precious commodity. Women who are being verbally or physically abused need harmony in their shattered lives. And single women with busy careers crave serenity to relieve stress. In other words, there are myriad reasons that women yearn for peace of mind.

If you are like most women, your thoughts are filled with constant "mind chatter"—endless lists of things to do, dialogues that may never take place, rehashing the past and worrying about the future.

Whatever the nature of your mental prattling, one thing is for certain: It offers no peace and quiet—even if you are sitting in a meadow with nothing pressing to do.

"We all know what a struggle it is to release obsessive thoughts that insist on swirling around in our heads almost as though they have a life of their own," says Lama Surya Das, a spiritual teacher. "When we try to relinquish old behavior patterns and habits, we can almost feel the physical pain or wrench. We get so foolishly stuck—in how we think and how we act. We keep repeating the same mistakes, day in and day out. Why can't we simply switch gears?"

Switching gears is difficult, even under the best circumstances, and under difficult or painful conditions it can seem downright impossible. Battered wives can attest to this, but it may take years of abuse before the lesson sinks in and the victim learns that nothing will change the abuser. She must let go and move on.

Singer and legend Tina Turner was one of those women. Ultimately, she gave up everything she had worked so long and hard to achieve in order to attain peace of mind, body and spirit. However, she had to be pushed beyond the edge to leave her husband Ike and start anew—an incredible journey from the bottomless pit of chaos to the bliss that peace of mind can bring. Remarkably, today, at sixty years of age, she is more celebrated, more prosperous and more respected than ever before.

Anna Mae Bullock—a poor but free-spirited youngster—was born in 1939 in Nut Bush, Tennessee. Although she sang in the local church, the rural community in which she grew up could not prepare her for the untamed world of high rollers, cocaine users, and atrocious beatings that would become her life.

When she was seventeen, she met musician Ike Turner, who was touring with his band. During intermission Anna Mae bravely stepped onto the stage, gingerly picked up the microphone and belted out the lyrics to one of Ike's songs. He was amazed that this skinny country girl could sing with such raw and unaffected power. Intrigued, he began the makeover that would turn Anna Mae into the incredible, soulful, charismatic Tina Turner.

As her manager, mentor, and lover, Ike sent Tina to a dentist, bought clothes that would show off her fabulous legs, and moved her into his home. Over the next decade they released a string of hit records. Not only did Tina become the main attraction of the show, but Ike also renamed the band the Ike and Tina Turner Review. After having a son by one of the other band members, she became pregnant with Ike's son. To legitimize their relationship, he insisted they marry. In her autobiography, *I, Tina*, she says that love had nothing to do with it. He simply wanted to bind her to him legally. In spite of his violent temper and constant womanizing—and against her better judgment— she agreed to the marriage. In 1962, they found a hole-in-the- wall office with a justice of the peace in Tijuana, Mexico. That's where they got hitched.

"All I remember is this guy pushing this paper over to me across a table and me signing it," recalls Tina. "And I thought, this is my wedding."

In time their family grew to six—Ike and Tina, their two sons, her son from a previous affair, and Ike's son from his former marriage. Although their act was making them rich, Tina often had to perform battered, bruised and bleeding.

"Ike was beating me with phones, with shoes, with hangers . . . Choking me, punching me—it wasn't slapping anymore," she confesses. "One time, right before a show, he punched me in the face and broke my jaw—and I had to go on and sing anyway, with the blood just gushing in my mouth. I felt like I could not take it any more."

They toured nonstop, playing in smoky dives. Exhausted and physically abused, Tina swallowed 50 Valium tablets just before a show in Los Angeles. She wanted to die.

Peace was not a word in Tina's vocabulary at that time. Her commitment was to her boys, the band's hectic tour schedule, and her adoring fans. She was married to a man with a cocaine habit and a short fuse. Then one day he brought home a woman named Valerie Bishop. Ordinarily this would have been Tina's cue to make herself scarce. But Valerie was different. She was a "chanter."

And she saved Tina's life.

"I listened as Valerie told me about Buddhism," recalls Tina.

"And something inside me went bling!"

Valerie gave Tina a chant, which she immediately began testing.

"Now this sounds kind of silly, but the chant was helping me to rearrange my place in the universe," she confesses. "I could feel the power deep inside me, stirring up after all these years."

As she continued chanting, Tina realized her dream of breaking free from Ike was a possibility. But it would take a few more years and tens of thousands of chants until she summoned the courage to make her move.

That night came while they were on tour. The date was July 1, 1976, and Ike, irked over something trivial, pulverized his rocksteady wife in the back of a limousine in Dallas, Texas. Suddenly Tina was fighting back with every shred of dignity she still possessed. Her days as a victim were over. The new Tina had emerged.

"I was really chanting a lot by then—chanting was the only tool I had," she says.

Bloody, battered, with 36 cents in her pocket, she begged the hotel manager to let her stay overnight. To his credit, he did. That was the beginning of Tina's new life.

The divorce was as ugly as their marriage. The bickering dragged on for months until Tina realized that walking away from it all was her only shot at peace.

"She just gave it all away," says her divorce lawyer, Arthur Leeds. "He kept the studio, his publishing companies, his four cars, all the property, but none of the debt. Tina walked out with what was on her back, essentially—and her name."

Says Tina: "My life is more important."

Slowly, painstakingly, this incredible lady pieced her life back together. And all the while she chanted.

"God gives us a connection, but you have to dig for it," she says. "Contacting that place within you helps you make the right decisions."

One of those decisions was to hook up with a new manager, who put her back on the charts with "What's Love Got to Do With It?" and the CD "Private Dancer." Tina was on top again—

this time without Ike and with nobody but herself controlling her body and mind.

Not only a pop icon and first-class diva, today Tina Turner is also an inspiration to all women who must start again from scratch.

Whether she is on tour or at her palatial home in the south of France, Tina finds peace, harmony and tranquility within herself. Twice daily she kneels in before a small shrine hidden away in a niche in the back stairwell.

"Chanting is about contacting the subconscious mind," she says. "And when you find the right words to connect with that, it's stronger than anything you can get from a man. But you must do it for yourself."

Today she lives with Erwin Bach, a German businessman sixteen years her junior. She is happy at last, and at peace with herself and the world.

"There's no place else I want to be," she says, watching the sunset over the Mediterranean. "Just listening to the music of the planet—the sounds of life."

Before you can get what you want, you have to know what you want.
The first step is to identify the hunger,
for only then can you determine how to feed it.
—NANCY O'HARA

■

WHAT'S HOLDING YOU BACK?

The more impatience we feel when trying, in fear and anxiety, to
escape difficulties and adversities, the farther we stray from the
true path. When we stop being impatient, stop trying frantically to
escape, and calm ourselves, we hear the inner voice of guidance.
That voice is always trying to reach us.

—MASAMI SAIONJI

∎

Into each life some rain may fall—although at times it might
seem like a deluge. "All these terrible things keep happening to
me," you might say. "It's just not possible for me not to worry."

Yes, that's true. Each of us will inevitably experience many
mind-numbing and soul-searching moments. They may be hurtful, frustrating, annoying, emotionally or physically devastating,
painful, or joyous. Bad things do happen. There are stressful
times. Or, as some philosophers would say: "That's life."

We cannot stop the universe, or change the things that happen
to us—or the people who make those things happen. We can
only change ourselves. And this turmoil provides us with a wonderful opportunity to learn a valuable lesson.

"There must be a conscious commitment to change an impossible situation to a possible opportunity," says psychologist Robert
Anthony. "Our goal in life should be to convert what we know
into positive results through awareness and self-correction."

Impossible situations are wake-up calls for creativity. "Every
problem or stumbling block that comes our way is a chance to
change for the better," he explains.

Problems can help you grow. Adverse experiences are tests.
But if your mind distorts and magnifies the situation, your
thoughts become dominated by it. The situation itself may be
real—like the beatings Tina Turner suffered—or it may be imagined—the "what-ifs" we constantly dwell on. Or you may create

your own turmoil by yearning for things you cannot have. And, of course, we all carry baggage from our childhood years.

Author Wayne Dyer says: "Peace is not the absence of conflict. There will always be conflict. But as you learn to shut down your inner dialogue and become more peaceful, you will begin to know the presence of God in your life. That presence will be felt in both your body and your inner world."

Roadblocks to inner peace are everywhere. They come in all shapes and sizes: an alcoholic parent or spouse, abusive family members, a difficult child, a crummy job, money problems, an unhappy marriage, toxic friends, or the lack of friends or someone to love. Some difficulties are external, stemming from situations inflicted upon us by other people. Some are dilemmas we create for ourselves. These roadblocks drain our energy and immobilize the human spirit.

Confusion from unexpected problems—an accident, a serious illness, a sudden layoff, or the abrupt end of a relationship—when added to the stress of the daily grind, can lead to self-destructive behavior. All too often alcohol, drugs, overeating or even suicide is the "solution." And yet, we have within ourselves all it takes to handle anything.

Stress, one of the leading causes of illness and mental turmoil, can result in these emotions:

Anger	Guilt
Anxiety	Jealousy
Hostility	Fear

Anger and fear are considered survival emotions, explains Brian Luke Seaward, author and motivational speaker. "In times of danger, one or both of these emotions serve as a motivation to move, run, hide. They are meant to last only long enough to get out of harm's way. However, we allow these feelings of anger and fear to linger for days, months and even years."

Harboring unresolved anger leads to frustration and general resentment. We feel as though we have lost control of our lives.

When things don't go as planned, it's natural to feel frustrated. But instead of cracking up or dropping out, or making yourself sick with worry and guilt, remember that *less is more*. This is true for people who demand perfection from themselves, from their coworkers and especially from their children and loved ones.

"I have yet to meet an absolute perfectionist whose life was filled with inner peace," says author Richard Carlson. "The need for perfection and the desire for inner tranquility conflict with each other. Rather than being content and grateful for what we have, we are focused on what's wrong with something and our need to fix it. When we are zeroed in on what's wrong, it implies that we are dissatisfied, discontent."

There are always better ways to do something—situations that can be improved upon, behavior that can be modified. But if you try to change those things that cannot be changed (someone else's accustomed way of doing things, for instance), you are bound to fail. Have you ever tried to get someone to stop smoking? Or lose weight? Or change a particular habit? It's a setup for anger and frustration and discordant feelings all around; certainly not fertile ground for peace of mind.

> Each of us needs to withdraw from the cares which will not withdraw from us. We need hours of aimless wandering, or spates of time sitting on park benches, observing the mysterious world of ants and the canopy of treetops.
> —MAYA ANGELOU

■

Some days can be overwhelming—so much so that even the usual methods of solace, such as a hot bath, a delicious dinner, a drink, a pill, are not enough to soothe frayed nerves. That's when you need something more. For Tina Turner that "something more" was chanting, which quieted her mind and purged her inner demons until she was strong enough to take action to change the situation. You can use any mantra, or saying, to give you strength to make a change in your life; or you can use meditation techniques to let all mind chatter fall away; or turn to God (or the higher power you believe in) and pray for help.

"If stress is totally eliminated from your mind, the illness and discord that you have had until now will disappear in an instant," suggests author Masami Saionji. "You can conquer stress with your own power. Recognize your own capacity as it is. Accept it without resistance. Don't overestimate or underestimate yourself—both can cause stress. Have absolute faith and confidence in the wonderful ability that is inherent in human beings. In short, faith in yourself is the best medicine."

Problems are transition points—stepping stones to higher awareness and, ultimately, inner peace. You never have a problem that you cannot solve, either by yourself or with the help of others. One answer is to rise above the problem—take step back and look at it from a broader perspective, or through the eyes of another person.

"What we must always keep in mind is that nothing is ever completely negative or hopeless, or ultimately to be despaired," says Lama Surya Das. "Every cloud has a silver lining. Things can be turned over. We can see the light. In this faith, we live and flourish."

Don't worry about the future.
Or worry, but know that worrying is as effective as
trying to solve an algebra equation by chewing bubble gum.
—Mary Schmich

■

PEACE OF MIND QUESTIONNAIRE

By answering Yes or No, you will get some idea of where your problems attaining peace of mind may lie.

1. When given a choice, do you choose to argue?
    Yes_____No_____
2. Do you seek confrontations?
    Yes_____No_____
3. Do you compare yourself to others?
    Yes_____No_____
4. Do you set yourself up for competition with others?
    Yes_____No_____
5. Do you worry about money?
    Yes_____No_____
6. Do you fret constantly?
    Yes_____No_____
7. Do you need constant approval and attention?
    Yes_____No_____
8. Do you set up unrealistic deadlines or box yourself into tight time schedules?
    Yes_____No_____
9. Is your head filled with constant mental chatter?
    Yes_____No_____
10. Are you in an abusive situation?
    Yes_____No_____
11. Are you always giving in to the needs of others?
    Yes_____No_____
12. Are you often stressed?
    Yes_____No_____
13. Do you let others run your life?
    Yes_____No_____
14. Do you say "Yes" when you mean "No"?
    Yes_____No_____

15. Are you putting off getting attention for a medical problem you have?
Yes_____No_____

16. Do you make time for yourself each day?
Yes_____No_____

17. Do you pray, chant, or meditate?
Yes_____No_____

18. Do you find time to care for yourself?
Yes_____No_____

19. Do you attend church regularly?
Yes_____No_____

20. Do you get enough exercise?
Yes_____No_____

KEY TO ANSWERS:

If you answered Yes to questions 1 to 15, you are holding yourself back from attaining peace of mind.

If you answered No to questions 16 to 20, you are doing yourself a disservice.

FINAL QUESTION:

Name one change that you feel would help you attain peace of mind.

_____

POSITIVE STEPS TO GIVE YOU PEACE

Stop talking, stop thinking, and there is nothing
you will not understand.
—CHINESE SAGE SENG T'SAN

■

At any given moment, you have the power within yourself to choose peace over turmoil. Tina Turner found it with Zen Buddhism; others find it with God; still others in nature, in yoga or in the art of meditation. While Tina changed her living situation, not everyone is able to make that adjustment. The care and attention children require—as well as their normal activities—can distract you when you seek peace and quiet. However, there are ways you can ensure your own inner tranquility.

Although Margaret Denio and her husband, Dom, were raising eighteen (yes, 18!) children, she did not let the chaos of their large household upset her peace of mind. And, more amazingly, she found the time and energy to further her education by taking night courses at the local community college.

Margaret and Dom, a high-school teacher and baseball coach from upstate New York, welcomed their first son, Tom, into the world in 1950. Dom Jr. was born eleven months later. In quick succession over the next twenty-two years came Bill, Theresa, John, Mary, Matt, Ann, Rosemary, Ellen, Paul, Martha, Margaret, Michael, Patty, Steven, Beth, and Robert. From the days of President Truman, through Elvis, JFK, the Beatles, the Vietnam War, Woodstock, and Nixon, Margaret was either pregnant or giving birth, except for the years 1969 and 1970.

"I was thrilled every time I got pregnant," says Margaret—a strict Catholic—now seventy-one, with an empty nest and a retirement condo in Florida. "We always managed financially. We weren't rich, but there was plenty of love to go around."

A typical day started with 20 people eating breakfast at the massive dining-room table. When the kids left for school, Margaret went shopping.

"I bought in bulk—often ten chickens at a time. Once, we bought a whole cow," she told me. "In the afternoon I'd cook dinner—huge pots of stew or spaghetti that everyone could dip into as they came home from sports practice, band and chorus rehearsals, or their jobs. On Sunday we sat down as a family."

The happy homemaker explains that she delegated chores to everyone, which helped relieve her burden. The older children helped the younger ones with schoolwork. And Margaret says she learned to escape by immersing herself in a good book.

"I just tuned out the noise and got into whatever book I was reading at the time," she says. "I was so filled with love and happiness for my huge family that I rarely got blue. But on those occasions when I needed a break, Dom would tell me to go out somewhere and take time for myself. I never turned down his offer."

Raising children is like being pecked by chickens.

—ANONYMOUS

■

Re-read the questionnaire for a moment and note how many Yes answers you checked off. These things are guaranteed to block peace of mind: confrontations, arguments, comparing yourself to others, competing to get ahead, striving for riches, worrying about the future, feeling guilty about the past, putting yourself under pressure to do it faster and better, constant mental chatter, seeking perfection in yourself and others, living in the past, being involved with people who will hurt and undermine you, holding onto anger, carrying a grudge, always having to be right.

The Zen master Dogen said: "If you don't let go of worldly worries about the future and making a living, you'll regret it. Follow the Way, or all your days and nights will have been lived for nothing."

When you are peaceful, you are fulfilled. Before you sit down
to meditate, keep the following points in mind. Allow them to
become part of the inner you.

- Being right is not important.
- Yelling or arguing only sets you up for more stress.
- Letting go of anger will help you find peace.
- Judging others adds to your lack of peace.
- Worrying about things you cannot change
  accomplishes nothing.
- When the mind is in turmoil, peace is impossible.
- Replace fear with forgiveness.
- Replace guilt with kindness.
- Replace anger with love.
- Peace is healing.

The best way to find inner peace is to visualize what you
want. One of the modern-day masters of stress reduction is Jon
Kabat-Zinn, Ph.D., founder of the Stress Reduction Clinic at the
University of Massachusetts Medical Center.

This is what he advises: "To achieve peace of mind, people
have to kindle a vision of what they really want for themselves
and keep that vision alive in the face of inner and outer hard-
ships, obstacles, and setbacks."

He says he once believed meditation alone was powerful
enough to effect a healing. Now he knows it takes more.

"Time has taught me that some kind of personal vision is
also necessary. For some that vision might be one of vibrancy
and health, for others it might be one of relaxation or kindness or peacefulness or harmony or wisdom. Your vision
should be what is most important to you, to be at peace with
yourself, to be whole."

You don't need to avoid or deny anything.
It is enough to just know about it. When you are busy trying to

avoid something, it's still affecting you. Simply cease to be affected
or impelled by anything and you'll find you are free.
—ZEN MASTER CAOSHAN

■

Effective visualization is like dreaming, but it is far more than
that. It's focused imagining, with the power of your will behind it.

"The mental images you form must absolutely support what
you want to create and should be visualized with as much detail
and clarity as possible," says Grandmaster Tae Yun Kim.
"Unfortunately, when we have idle time, many of us have a habit
of running all sorts of negative pictures through our minds. But
once you are aware that visualization is a powerful part of the
creative process, use this wonderful tool to achieve your goals."

Grandmaster Tae Yun Kim, a martial arts master and author of
Seven Steps to Inner Power, says you alone have power over the
good and bad events that shape your life. Her own struggles to
attain her goals are a living testament to that concept. She says:
"I have discovered that how I dealt with circumstances was
much more important than the circumstances themselves."

Her earliest memories were filled with horror as the Korean
War ravaged her country.

"I was five years old, and I couldn't understand why explosions were everywhere, why people were trying to hurt me," she
writes. "I remember running day and night as my family fled the
Communist invasion. I couldn't understand why the world was
suddenly crazy. Why would anyone want to kill me? My play-
mate was a year older than I. I was so tired, but she kept encouraging me to keep running. She was a short distance from me
when another explosion blew her apart."

Kim says she will never forget that sight. But it was too terrible to seem real.

"To call that a bad experience would be an understatement.
But even then, in the midst of the bad, was the formation in my
mind of something uniquely good. At that moment I made the
decision not to run anymore."

Two years later, on a misty blue-gray morning in the Kinchom Province, she was enthralled to see her uncles practicing an ancient form of martial arts known as Jung Su Won, which means "the way of uniting body, mind and spirit in total harmony."

"Nothing in my mind seemed so mystical and yet so natural . . . more worthwhile and exciting. It was important . . . perfect . . . and I had to learn this art," she admits.

But girls were expected to marry and have babies. Kim persisted until her uncles conceded, assuming she would give up when she realized how physically demanding the art would be. Instead, she wore slacks to hide her bruises. Her family said she brought shame upon them acting like a boy. None of this mattered.

"At the age of eight I discovered not everyone thought I was crazy," adds Grandmaster Kim. "A martial arts master recognized my desire and accepted me as a student."

People may say of a journey that it's long and they'll not bother to start. Take one step on the longest journey and you've shortened it.

—GRANDMASTER TAE YUN KIM

■

One effective way to achieve the state of mental awareness that allows effective visualization is through meditation. Meditation is a naturally occurring rest state—in other words, resting while remaining awake and alert. It's not a short nap, although beginners often doze off, especially if they are lying down.

Meditation helps you switch mental gears. When you awake in the morning, it calms the mind for the day's events. In the evening, it relaxes you for a good night's sleep. At your desk during the day, it helps you cope with stress at work. If you can snatch a minute here or five minutes there, it will help calm the spirit and make you feel more alert and relaxed. Consider meditation a mini-vacation for the mind.

When you sit quietly, you will experience the ebb and flow of many thoughts. To form a pattern or rhythm, repeat a mantra (or short saying) while you relax into your meditation. Or simply listen to the sound of your breath going in and out as you still your mind to reach that place of divine serenity. There are many postures and procedures for meditation. This one is typical.

1. Sit calmly on the floor or on a flat pillow which you use specifically for meditation.
2. Cross your legs so you are comfortable, or sit in a straight-back chair, feet flat on the floor.
3. Sit straight, palms facing up, resting gently on your lap.
4. Close your eyes gently. Close your mouth and let your tongue relax.
5. Breathe in deeply through your nose, hold your breath as long as you comfortably can, and then exhale slowly and softly. Your breathing should be quiet and gentle.
6. Let worries or concerns or clamorous thoughts and feelings flow away. Initially, your conscious mind wants to keep thinking and will try to do so. Just continue breathing and refuse to pay attention to intrusive thoughts and feelings. Let them go, let them pass. Eventually, you will feel your mind start to clear.
7. Relax your mind and determine to let all thoughts flow to you freely. Do not become attached to any of them. Notice them but do not force yourself to analyze or think about them. You can do that later. Experience the peace that follows as your shoulders relax and you enter into the state of meditation.

Patience is a quality of heart that can be greatly enhanced with deliberate practice. Think of life itself as the classroom, and the curriculum is patience.
—RICHARD CARLSON

∎

Young children, demanding bosses, testy spouses, irritated customers, long lines, traffic jams can all teach you the art of patience—if you are willing to learn. When the pressure starts building, aim for five minutes of calmness. This will take perseverance, but it can, with practice, be achieved.

"The simple act of gearing my mind toward patience allows me to remain in the present moment far more than I would if I were upset," says author Richard Carlson. "Being patient allows me to keep my perspective. I can remember that what's before me isn't life or death, but simply a minor obstacle that must be dealt with. Without patience, the same scenario can become a major emergency complete with yelling, frustration, hurt feelings, and high blood pressure. It's really not worth all that."

When you think about it, what are the real emergencies? In any daily routine, they are, in fact, rare. But we tend to inflate small dilemmas into insurmountable problems. A glitch throws off your morning routine: You find that the car has a flat tire. The kids will be late to school and you will be late to work. You have an important meeting at nine o'clock, which you simply cannot miss. The stress mounts. You break out in hives, your stomach churns, the kids are whining. STOP. Relax. Think about your options, then take positive action to remedy the situation. Call a tow truck; call your boss; put the kids in front of the TV until the problem is resolved.

Now that I am so self-sufficient, I find it hard to believe I once actually cried when a raw egg fell out of the refrigerator and broke on the kitchen floor during the usual morning rush. But I did! Nowadays even the news that my car has been stolen cannot elicit a reaction like that. I have become more resilient to life's setbacks. It took a divorce, uprooting myself and my children, starting over from scratch, being laid off six jobs, and the death of a close friend to teach me that life is a seesaw. Sometimes you're up, sometimes you're down. And even when you are down, you will be headed up soon enough. Emergencies come and go like rain clouds on a summer day. You will survive.

The trick is not losing the serenity you have worked so hard to master.

It's also important to pick your battles wisely, as the expression goes. Every day we have the opportunity to make a big deal about something—at home, at work, on the road, while shopping, with friends—anything. If you realize that very few things are worth getting upset about, you stand a much better chance of maintaining a calm, clear-minded approach to life in general and to being blindsided when you least expect it.

Many people argue, confront, and fight over practically anything, turning their lives into a series of battles over relatively small things. There is so much frustration in living this type of life that you lose track of what is truly relevant.

It is much easier to accept the fact that life is not always the way we want it. If you want to lead a stress-free life, learn to *let it go*. You don't always have to be right, or have your way. Once you begin to relinquish that need to control, you will begin to find peace of mind.

> The real troubles in your life are apt to be things that never crossed your worried mind, the kind that blindside you at 4 P.M. on some idle Tuesday.
> —MARY SCHMICH

■

The expression "Less is more" makes perfect sense if you want inner peace and harmony. Our lives are cluttered with obligations and commitments, many of which we do not enjoy. We say "Yes" when we want to say "No." Then we feel angry that our precious time is being used so unwisely.

At the core of all Buddhist teachings is the idea of simplicity.

"When we relinquish, or renounce, the extraneous, we are left with the essential," says Lama Surya Das. "When we stop clinging to ego attachments, we lighten our load and learn who we truly are. That's the magic of simplicity."

For Westerners, this lack of attachment to time, energy, money and things is difficult to comprehend. We tend to translate all problems into frustration, stress, and worry. But if you can learn to adopt the essence of Zen, which is being in the moment, your life will be simplified automatically. When you allow yourself to *be*, the mental chatter slows and eventually stops. You can step outside your beehive of activity and observe the world as though from afar. How much of your routine is necessary and how much is busywork that prevents you from getting in touch with your inner self? Slow down. Smell the roses (or whatever flowers are at hand). Take a deep breath. Take a walk. You don't need a destination or company. Meander. Go around the block, see where your journey will lead you. Observe the sky, the frantic pace of the people around you.

Says Lama Surya Das: "All the sages of all the ages have said the same thing in a million ways: We lose God, meaning, and our very selves in complexity. When we get caught up in the many, we lose the one—we lose sight of the essence. As spiritual seekers, we want to be able to sort through the clutter on our desks, in our lives, in our hearts, and in our minds and find what we're looking for."

We are weighed down with so much emotional baggage, we are overburdened with so many attachments, it seems impossible to unclutter our lives. It can be done, however, by chipping away at it, slowly peeling away the distractions and obligations and, yes, even people.

A few years ago my friend Sari found she had no time for herself. A wide group of friends and acquaintances called her day and night, dropped in for unexpected visits, and even tried to tap into the money she had recently inherited. I recall a visit during which the phone never stopped ringing and two people knocked on her door.

To take her life back, Sari stopped answering the phone. She lets her machine take all calls. Then she cut back on her activities and told a few people—including a woman with whom she had grown chummy—to please not call her any more.

"It was hard to do," Sari admitted to me. "But I had to. They were sucking me dry. I didn't have a minute to myself; everybody wanted something, until I had nothing more left to give."

Sari has retained her closest friendships and let go of the rest. "I have reclaimed my sanity," she adds. "Life is too short not to be able to sit back and enjoy it."

For peace of mind, step out for a walk with God.
—LINUS MUNDY

■

Westerners may find the idea of Prayer-Walking more comfortable than meditation. If that is the case, take a stroll with this ancient fitness plan.

"This combination of activities lets us keep moving, keep acting and doing on the outside while we slow down, quiet down and center ourselves on the inside," says Linus Mundy, author of *The Complete Guide to Prayer-Walking*.

Connecting prayer with our body rhythms lowers blood pressure, relieves stress, lowers the heart rate, improves breathing, boosts mental health and well-being, builds muscles, and brings a sense of tranquility.

"It prompts a calming effect known as 'the relaxation response,'" says Herbert Benson, president of the Mind/Body Medical Institute at Harvard Medical School. "Focused walking is associated with reduced anxiety and diminished negative thoughts."

You can use any short prayer when you stroll outside. Walk at your own pace. Start with the right foot and use these tips:

- Breathe consciously. Take four steps per inhale and count 1-2-3-4, then 1-2-3-4 on the exhale.
- Switch to meaningful words, such as "Breathing in, I calm myself; breathing out, I smile."
- Stay in the present. If worries intrude, let them go and return to your prayers.

- Use all your senses. Look around, breathe deeply, feel the ground, see the beauty around you, smell the fresh air.
- There is no right or wrong way to prayer-walk. As long as you feel at peace, you're doing fine.

**No one has power over you and your feelings
unless you give it to them.**
—NANCY O'HARA

■

Actress, singer, and talk-show hostess Queen Latifah says that at one time her life was in complete turmoil. She sold and used drugs, had sex for money, smoked and drank until she passed out. Every day. She became so depressed she wanted to crawl under a rock.

In her autobiography, *Ladies First: Revelations of A Strong Woman*, she says, "To get to the point of true contentment with who I am, I had to go through a whole bunch of years of being something other than myself."

For a while she ran wild, she hated her body, she did drugs and wanted to die. "I've been to these dark places," she admits. "And I will never go back to them. It's a fool who doesn't learn from mistakes."

She points out that too many women can't seem to fix their mistakes.

"They stay right there. They wallow in that point and never move on. They beat themselves down so much they don't get up ... The pain and lowness—and loneliness—of all of my mistakes have made me want to change. At some point you must get up, or else you'll stay right there," she warns.

These seven pointers should help you break the cycle of worry, self-abuse, guilt, and stress that rob you of your peace of mind.

1. Pray or meditate each day.
2. Forgive others and seek to be forgiven.
3. Renew relationships, particularly with family members, even if they are difficult to get along with.

4. Respect life and confront death.
5. Honor your elders and remain civil at all times.
6. Reach out to those in need, especially those who are unloved and unwanted.
7. Smile. It spreads cheer.

AFFIRMATIONS

These daily reminders may help you find a way to achieve peace of mind, body and spirit. They can be used as reminders or mantras.

- I will live in the moment.
- I will simplify my life.
- I will realize that if I am not at peace I cannot be happy.
- If I am at peace, those around me will also be more peaceful.
- I will begin to think of myself as a peaceful person.
- I will avoid confrontations and arguments.
- I will stop criticizing others and myself.
- I cannot change anyone but myself.
- I will be kind whenever possible.
- I will practice being patient.
- If I cannot find inner peace, I will find someone to help me.

Remove all blame from your vocabulary.
Catch yourself when you find yourself using your past history
as a reason for your failure to act today, and instead say,
"I am free now to detach myself from what used to be."
—OMAR KHAYYAM
■

RECOMMENDED READING FOR FINDING PEACE OF MIND

Anthony, Robert, Ph.D. *How to Make the Impossible Possible.* Berkley Books.

Das, Lama Surya. *Awakening to the Sacred.* Broadway Books.

Dyer, Wayne, Ph.D. *Your Sacred Self.* HarperCollins.

—.*Real Magic.* HarperCollins.

Freke, Timothy. *Zen Wisdom.* Sterling Publishing Co.

Goulston, Mark. *Get Out of Your Own Way.* Perigee Books.

Kabat-Zinn, Jon. *Full Catastrophe Living.* Delta paperback.

Kim, Grandmaster Tae Yun. *Seven Steps to Inner Power.* New World Library.

Mundy, Linus. *The Complete Guide to Prayer-Walking.* Crossroad Publishing.

Queen Latifah. *Ladies First: Revelations of a Strong Woman.* William Morrow & Company, Inc.

Seaward, Brian Luke, Ph.D. *Stand Like Mountain, Flow Like Water: Reflections on Stress and Human Spirituality.* Health Communications, Inc.

Sher, Barbara. *I Could Do Anything, If Only I Knew What it Was.* Delacorte Press.

Turner, Tina. *I, Tina.* William Morrow & Co.

Wegscheider-Cruse, Sharon. *Girl Talk.* Health Communications, Inc.

Four

IF LOVE IS WHAT YOU'RE AFTER

Men aren't a necessity.
Women have proven we can get along by ourselves.
—LAUREN BACALL

■

*T*HE AIR IS filled with songs of love. They are played on the radio day and night, they are used in television shows and movies and theater productions. We grew up on lyrics like "All you need is love," "Love makes the world go round," "You are the love of my life," and "Addicted to love."

The assumption is that we cannot be happy and fulfilled unless we love somebody and are loved in return—that true love is necessary for ultimate happiness.

Here's the lowdown: We don't really NEED love. Love and romance are not essentials, like food, water, and the air we breathe. Many men and women live their lives without the companionship of a life partner and they enjoy themselves immensely. And yet four out of five adults rate love as being important to their happiness. So they get married—and divorced: a whopping fifty percent!

What is going wrong? And what can be done to make it right?

"People who tumble into love tend to discount any problems in a relationship, and they're overly optimistic about love's lasting forever," advises David G. Myers, author of *Feeling Good*. "And newlyweds beware: Don't take a successful marriage for granted. The odds are you will NOT live happily ever after."

The truth is that before you can truly love someone, you must first love yourself. How can you hate yourself and expect a man to adore you? It doesn't work that way. If this is what you are expecting, you are placing the burden of your happiness on him. Perhaps that is one reason the divorce rate is soaring.

Actress Halle Berry says she considered suicide after her much-publicized split from baseball player David Justice. Now she is content to be alone.

"I've spent the last three years of my life really just getting to know myself and really appreciate who I am," she says. "When I stopped looking for love from everybody else and when I loved myself enough, I stopped caring about what people thought about me. If you like me, great, if you don't, so sorry, but my train is still going on."

> No man or woman really knows what perfect love is until they have been married a quarter of a century.
>
> —MARK TWAIN

■

What, exactly, is love? It's intangible and subjective. It cannot be measured or defined. Yet it makes us feel wonderful all over. It's no wonder we *want* it so desperately. In this chapter we will explore the ups and downs of love, marriage and the importance of communication, but first, a tale of lasting love.

Handsome Paul Newman and lovely Joanne Woodward tied the knot on January 29, 1958. Most Hollywood insiders said it wouldn't last. He was a blue-eyed movie heartthrob who liked fast cars and cold beer. She was a serious actress who preferred horseback riding and ballet. Yet more than forty years later, their love is stronger than ever.

"I can't imagine my life without Joanne," says Paul, now in his mid-seventies. "Without her I'd be nowhere, nothing."

Because their hectic schedules often keep them apart they savor each others' company, and are often spotted strolling hand-in-hand around the Connecticut town where they make their home, or dining at local restaurants—talking with quiet intensity—or cuddling in Paul's pickup truck at the beach.

"Taking time to be with each other is the best thing for our marriage," confesses Joanne, now in her mid-sixties. "We have dinners, drink champagne, watch movies in bed, and get romantic."

But they also give each other space and respect.

They met in 1951, when a talent agent introduced a hardworking boy from Shaker Heights, Ohio, to a poor girl from Thomasville, Georgia. He was shy and conservative. She was modern and independent. He was married to Jacqueline Witte and had three children. She was single and not hot to date a married man. He was smitten. She was cool.

But their paths crossed again two years later when they worked together in the Broadway play *Picnic*, and their mutual attraction was undeniable. Five years later, after Paul's gutwrenching divorce, they became husband and wife in a Las Vegas chapel.

To avoid divorce-cursed Tinseltown, they bought a 200-year-old Connecticut farmhouse and, with their three daughters, lived a life of their own, far from the hustle and bustle of moviemaking.

Being married to a Hollywood hunk wasn't easy for Joanne. Paul had gorgeous, sexy costars who flirted with him shamelessly, and acted in steamy bedroom scenes that left his female fans breathless. But in spite of temptation, he remains loyal. "Why go out for hamburger when you can have steak at home?" is his famous quip.

While Joanne's had her share of jealousy, so has Paul. He was particularly bent out of shape when Joanne, a ballet buff, began spending time with Dennis Wayne, director of a dance troupe she was backing. And, again, when she cast Dylan McDermott, now starring in the TV hit, "The Practice," in several plays she was directing.

"During one rough stretch, I packed up and walked out," Paul admits. "I was gone fifteen minutes, then turned around and came back."

What makes their love endure?

Respect and passion. He whisks her away for romantic holidays, and offers spontaneous demonstrations of love. "Sometimes I'll impulsively buy her a bracelet or necklace," he says. "It's my little way of showing her I'm still as attracted to her as I was forty years ago."

Says Joanne: "We spend a lot of time talking. As my grandmother said, 'Marriage isn't about romance or being swept off your feet. It's about being able to imagine talking to the other person at the breakfast table every morning for the next fifty years.'"

During their four decades together, the two have become grandparents as well as Hollywood legends. He has made dozens of movies and has been nominated eight times for Academy Awards, winning for *The Color of Money* in 1986. Joanne has been a serious actress since her career-launching role in *The Three Faces of Eve*, for which she won an Academy Award. She has also had three other Oscar nominations and has been awarded two Emmys. While they could rest on their laurels and take it easy, they have instead branched out and expanded their horizons.

Joanne earned a B.A. in fine arts from Sarah Lawrence College in New York in 1990. Paul founded Newman's Own food company in 1982, marketing salad dressing, popcorn, pasta sauce and other food products. Together, they've donated millions of dollars to charity.

"We've lasted because we built our relationship on the foundation of friendship," says Joanne. To which Paul adds: "Plus lust, respect, forgiveness, and persistence."

Well-married a person is winged; ill-matched, shackled.
—HENRY WARD BEECHER

■

Paul Newman and Joanne Woodward are not the only Hollywood couple to have made it through hard times. The marriage of Charlton and Lydia Heston has passed the 55-year mark. The basic commandment, according to the man who played Moses in *The Ten Commandments*, is that you need a basic commitment and a certain degree of tolerance and flexibility.

Dolores and Bob Hope have had 65 years of wedded bliss, yet they still treat each other like newlyweds.

Carl Reiner isn't joking when he says, "Marry somebody who can stand you." Apparently his wife Estelle shares his sense of humor. They've been hitched 56 years.

And *Murder, She Wrote* star Angela Lansbury has been married to Peter Shaw for half a century—through his triple bypass, her hip replacement, their daughter's liver transplant and the ups and downs of their children's drug abuse. "We've been through the worst and we're still here," says Angela. "When the going gets tough, you work it out."

These couples know that relationships are like gardens—they must be tended and nurtured to grow and flourish.

Don't be reckless with other people's hearts.
Don't put up with people who are reckless with yours.
—MARY SCHMICH

■

WHAT'S HOLDING YOU BACK?

Language has created the word loneliness to express the
pain of being alone, and the word aloneness to express
the glory of being alone.
—PAUL TILLICH

■

More than sixty years ago, the revolutionary anarchist Emma
Goldman said: "Love is the strongest and deepest element in all
life, the harbinger of hope, of joy, of ecstasy." Then she asked:
"How can such an all-compelling force be synonymous with that
poor little State and Church-begotten weed, marriage?"

Goldman, who died in 1940, thought the institution of marriage made a "parasite" of a woman. "It incapacitates her for
life's struggle, annihilates her social consciousness, paralyzes
her imagination, and then imposes its gracious protection, which
is in reality a snare," she wrote.

Either Goldman was a cynic at heart or times have drastically
changed for the better. New research now indicates that marriage is *good* for you. It boosts confidence and contributes to
longevity. In addition, a National Institute of Aging survey
found that married people end up with almost twice as much
money as never-marrieds, partners heal faster after surgery or
illness, sex is more fulfilling and more frequent and married people—in most cases—take better care of their bodies.

So what's the problem? If you are alone and don't want to be,
the problem may be you.

Love, marriage, and good feelings about oneself should not be
lumped together. They are three separate entities and must be
treated as such. Women who feel they must have love to be fulfilled, who must be married to be validated, and who can't feel
good about themselves until they are "happily married" are in
for a sad awakening.

If you think that being loved is as crucial as breathing, and that without a significant other you are basically unworthy, the message you are sending out to the universe is: "I don't like myself. I need your approval to feel worthwhile." No wonder guys turn and run the other way.

There is a big difference between being lonely and being alone, as psychiatrist David D. Burns, explains: "If you are lonely and dependent, your anger and resentment stem from the fact that you feel deprived of the love you believe you are entitled to receive from others. If you are independent, you have the capacity to feel happy when you are alone. Your moods will not go up and down at someone else's mercy."

Marjory Stoneman Douglas was one woman who chose to live alone—but she was not lonely. She was a young idealist when she married her husband in the 1920s. But before their first anniversary, he was sentenced to a jail term for swindling. Not willing to waste time brooding, Douglas hightailed it south to Miami, Florida, at the time nothing more than a pile of sand with a few buildings perched along the edge of the mighty swamp called The Everglades. The only thing Douglas kept from the marriage was her last name, and with it she built a legacy for herself and for ecology.

As a journalist she became a tireless crusader against greedy developers who planned to drain the Everglades and build condos, and against the sugarcane-field owners who polluted the land. She dubbed the Everglades "the River of Grass" and founded a society to help preserve and protect it. Until her death in 1998 at the age of 108, she used her time, energy and love of the land to create a national park.

> Husband and wife are like mirrors. If you reflect your spouse and
> find an ugly image there, you cannot blame him or her, because
> that ugliness is projected by your own thought.
>
> —MASAMI SAIONJI

■

Relationships are complicated. First you must find someone you like well enough to share time with—someone who will make you feel good about yourself and not drain you emotionally, physically, or financially. Then the two of you will waltz around until you find a comfort level of togetherness. Settling down is a whole other ball of wax. Do you live together first or get married? Are both of you ready for the commitment?

"In a relationship, men and women have their own rhythms and cycles," says noted author John Gray. "Men pull back and then get close, while women rise and fall in their ability to love themselves and others."

Gray describes men as rubber bands—they pull back then spring forward—while women are more like waves. When a woman's wave rises she has love to give, but when it falls she feels empty and needs filling.

It is important to realize that nobody can appreciate everything about you all the time. Men may not be affectionate at times, possibly when you need it most—when you are "bottoming out." That is why it is important for you to love *you* first and foremost.

"If you learn to love yourself, you will have a far more dependable and continuous source of self-esteem," says Burns. "Love is not an adult human need! It's okay to *want* a loving relationship. But you do not *need* that external approval, love, or attention in order to survive or experience maximum levels of happiness."

If you are pining away for that special person to step into your life and make everything perfect, it might be helpful to realize that no marriage is ideal: Millions of men and women who are married are also miserable.

"Happily married husbands and wives get depressed, fight, lose their jobs, struggle with the demands of the workplace and the crises of children and sexual problems," say authors Judith Wallerstein and Sandra Blakeslee in *Good Marriage: How and Why Love Lasts*. "People cry and yell and get frustrated."

Many experts warn that the first two years are the most difficult. This is when the power struggles in the relationship get worked out. It's also when minor problems seem magnified. You may even be unsure that you married the right person. The first flush of erotic excitement begins to subside and romance takes a back seat to reality.

Even if you make it past the early stages, marriages change. They evolve, as do the partners and the family itself. As Gray puts it, "When a man loves a woman she begins to shine with love and fulfillment. Most men naïvely expect that luster to last forever. That's like asking the sun to shine every day."

Often a man who is attentive at first, bringing flowers and small gifts or sending schmaltzy cards and notes, will eventually stop. A woman's natural reaction is that she has done something wrong. She may press for answers or become clingy. But they may not be the kind of answers she's looking for—it may just be that the man, as men do, needs his space. They do not react to problems like women do. Women talk about problems and get input from others—in other words, they go to the well. Men like to be alone—they retreat to the cave. Not taking their silence personally is a huge hurdle to overcome. We'll talk more about this a bit later.

Communicating on different levels is only one of the many problems that make relationships so complex. Experts say that the best way to clear up misunderstandings is to be direct. Men often have trouble interpreting what a woman is saying. So tell him in clear and concise terms exactly what you want.

In addition to the verbal netherworld in which men and women live, the lack of emotional understanding between the sexes often causes friction that takes a deeper understanding to resolve.

In *Men Are from Mars, Women Are from Venus,* John Gray says: "Love often fails because people give what they want. Because a woman's primary love needs are to be cared for, understood, and so forth, she automatically gives her man a lot of caring and understanding. To a man this caring support often feels as though she doesn't trust him.

"Then, when he doesn't respond positively, she can't understand why he doesn't appreciate her brand of support. He, of course, is giving his own brand of love, which isn't what she needs. So they are caught in a loop of failing to fulfill each other's needs."

Making a marriage last takes hard work and commitment from both partners. The ideals that float through your mind when you exchange vows may come to pass. But major adjustments will usually be needed.

> Bogie didn't tell me not to work. He wanted me to go on
> location with him and not go on location away from him.
> I did what he said, and I'm damn glad I did. Now that I'm alone,
> I can be as selfish as I want.
> —LAUREN BACALL

■

When Teresa Masters met James George Janos in 1974, she never dreamed she would end up the wife of Minnesota governor Jesse Ventura. She was only eighteen, working as a receptionist, when she spotted a broad-shouldered, six-foot-four-inch hunk with ice-blue eyes.

"Our eyes met, and it was just like they were locked there for a good minute," she recalls. Jesse was enrolled at a community college and he told Terry he wanted to be a pro wrestler. "He was a person who would never live a boring life," says Terry, who admits she knew they would get married some day. He proposed ten months later, over the phone, and they had a one-night honeymoon in a fancy motel before Jesse struck out for the road on the amateur wrestling circuit.

He quickly rose in the ranks to become one of the World Wrestling Federation's favorite players. Clad in shiny spandex, with hair dyed vibrant colors, his flamboyant persona inspired a Jesse-The-Body action figure. Big bucks rolled in. He bought a red Porsche. Together he and Terry purchased a 32-acre ranch, where she set up a horse-training business.

But into each happy marriage a little rain must fall. In 1983, after eight years of marriage, their daughter Jade was born.

She was a pretty baby, but she had such severe epilepsy that the seizures caused brain damage. The doctors told the Venturas that their baby should be institutionalized. Instead they enrolled her in a special school for children with disabilities. Extensive physical therapy to improve her motor skills and reflexes helped Jade acquire the coordination she needed to attend a public elementary school. Through this Jesse was on the road much of the time, but he tried to make it home so the family could attend church on Sundays. Terry managed her business and helped their daughter learn to play the flute and the piano. She also cared for their son, Tyrel, now 19.

Jesse decided to seek political office back in 1990, but it wasn't until the fall of 1998 that he was elected governor. Terry, who is painfully shy, says the first few months as Minnesota's first lady were a time of "stark-raving fear and terror." But she is adjusting. Today, they have been married 24 years and they are still committed to each other.

The solid union of Jesse and Terry Ventura shows that any long-term relationship requires a give and a take. Each partner must allow the other to have his or her interests, be supportive of the other and stay positively focused. When the unexpected happens—when tragedies arise or when things don't work the way you plan—it is time to re-evaluate the ties that bind instead of abandoning ship.

You may have been married or in a committed relationship that did not last. You may now be fearful of trying again. Perhaps your parents had a terrible marriage. You may be afraid of being hurt. Who isn't? Because everyone is entitled to the joy that love can bring, it's a pity if you think you are too ugly, too fat, too plain or unlovable.

Terry's mom told her: "Be yourself. Don't try to live up to other people's expectations." That excellent advice rings true for anyone, in any situation, especially where love is concerned. Be yourself.

True to her husband, and true to herself, Terry attended the gubernatorial inaugural ball wearing a black leather jacket, a black suede miniskirt, and knee-high boots. "This is the way I dressed before, and I'm not changing," she said.

There is somebody out in the universe who will love and respect you for who you are—just the way you are. And that person will walk into your life when the time is right. But first you must embrace yourself. Take a look at this questionnaire to see what's holding you back.

> Marry, and with luck it may go well. But when a marriage
> fails, then those who marry live at home in hell.
>
> —EURIPIDES

■

Reprinted with special permission of King Feature Syndicate.

LOVE QUESTIONNAIRE

Answer these questions honestly for some insights into what kind of partner you are looking for and what you expect from a relationship.

1. Do you love yourself?
   Yes_____No_____
2. Do you think you are worthy of someone else's love?
   Yes_____No_____
3. Can you have fun while waiting for Mr. Right to come along?
   Yes_____No_____
4. Are you willing to go out with anyone who asks you?
   Yes_____No_____
5. Are you willing to settle because you feel unworthy?
   Yes_____No_____
6. Do you fret and worry that you'll never meet Mr. Right?
   Yes_____No_____
7. Do you need a partner to be happy?
   Yes_____No_____
8. Are you waiting for someone to fulfill your life?
   Yes_____No_____
9. Do you expect a man to read your mind?
   Yes_____No_____
10. Do you make him guess at your needs and wants?
    Yes_____No_____
11. Do you get mad when he is clueless?
    Yes_____No_____
12. Do you call your partner at work and expect to be with him all the time?
    Yes_____No_____
13. Do you get mad when he wants to be with his guy friends?
    Yes_____No_____

14. Do you think he should pay more attention to you?
Yes_____No_____
15. Has the romance gone from your marriage?
Yes_____No_____
16. Would you like to get it back?
Yes_____No_____
17. Do you allow him to yell at you?
Yes_____No_____
18. Do you yell back?
Yes_____No_____
19. Does he hit you?
Yes_____No_____
20. Do you allow it?
Yes_____No_____

KEY TO ANSWERS:

If you answered No to questions 1 to 3, you lack confidence.

If you answered Yes to questions 4 to 11, you have unrealistic expectations about love and romance.

If you answered Yes to questions 12 to 14, you need to get a hobby or find and outside interest. Men need their space, and so do you.

If you answered Yes to questions 15 to 20, you might want to consider marriage counseling.

FINAL QUESTION:

Are you willing to compromise your values just to be with someone?

Yes_____No_____

POSITIVE STEPS FOR FINDING LOVE

A commitment requires daily renewal. A promise kept, an action
taken, over and over and over and over again.
—GREGORY J. P. GODEK

■

Romance can be a frustrating and confusing experience. What
does he want? What do you want? If they are not the same
things, can you click? Sometimes opposites attract, sometimes
they don't. It's a matter of chemistry, timing, and playing it
smart.

We all have expectations of how a perfect partner should act.

"One of the surest ways to destroy a relationship is to enter it
with a lot of expectations," warns Gregory J. P. Godek, author of
1001 Ways to Be Romantic. "It's okay to have value expectations—
to expect your partner to be honest, compassionate and loving—
but it's not okay to have behavior expectations—to expect your
partner to act in a certain way."

It boils down to this: Love is simple. But people are complex.

When we're fortunate, a kind of alchemy bubbles inside a marriage, creating a fuel that powers women—and men—in their confident course through the world.
—FRANCINE PROSE

■

When my parents split up back in the 1960s after twenty years
of marriage, I became acutely aware of the change in my family's new, and unspoken, status. My standard answer to people
who asked about my dad's absence was: "He's on a business
trip." Amazingly, it wasn't until my twentieth high school
reunion that I learned the parents of a friend were also divorced.
That's how secretive we were in those days.

Today divorce is not a dark and dirty secret. And marriages are more celebrated than ever. Today, couples consider themselves lucky to pass the five-year mark. Twenty-fifth anniversaries are a time for joyous celebrating. The reward for sixty years of marriage is diamonds and hearty congratulations. Now imagine being hitched for eighty years!

When I interviewed George and Jessie Shephard in 1998, their names were being submitted to the Guinness *Book of World's Records* for the longest-married couple in America. He was 99, she was 98.

"I didn't like him at first," admitted Jessie, who attended West Seattle Central High School with George back in 1918. "He sat in front of me in study hall and used a mirror to look at me over his shoulder."

She complained to her mother, who made matters worse by teasing: "Oh, that red-haired George Shephard, he'll probably marry you."

George pursued Jessie on his motorcycle as she rode the trolley to her job as a sewing teacher, waving as he sped by. Little by little he "grew" on her. While swinging in a hammock on a sunny afternoon, he proposed. She accepted.

But George's boss didn't want him distracted by marriage and fired him ten days before the wedding. The couple started their married life with $37.50, an electric hot plate and a couch in a 10-by-12-foot shack in her parents' orchard.

"Parts of life were rough," he confessed, referring to the Great Depression and the death of a daughter. "We struggled, but we were lucky to have good friends to help us out. And we had many wonderful times."

Together they raised their son, Willis (now in his mid-seventies and himself married fifty years). George's job as a salesman took the family around the world and the Shephards now reside in Milton, Washington, where they are still madly in love. Although their eyesight and hearing are failing, they still go out for dinner every night.

"We started off on a wild lark," said George. "And we're very, very happy to have ended up as well as we have."

The marriage spirit is a current of unselfish love that flows through every strong and healthy union.
—EVELYN MOSCHETTA
■

Human beings need acceptance, respect and appreciation. Conversely, we fear rejection. Incredibly, within the first minute of an encounter we decide if we like and trust the person we are meeting. Subconsciously, we wonder whether this person will like us. There are ways to connect even before any words are exchanged.

"By matching a person's nonverbal behavior, you become similar to him," says California psychotherapist Jonathan Robinson. "To do this, simply notice how a person talks, sits, or stands, and attempt to mirror his or her behavior. If, when you first meet someone, you talk at about the same speed and hold your body in a like manner, you'll already have something in common. On a subconscious level, the person you just met will feel a mysterious rapport with you. It works like magic."

You need not imitate every move, but by matching body position and voice tone, you create feelings of acceptance and trust.

When Elmer Gildersleeve spotted a young woman in a crimson dress with brass buttons strolling across the deck of a cruise ship back in July 1940, he felt the urge to approach her. There was something about the familiar way Arlene moved that made Elmer want to know her better. They were bound from New York to San Juan, Havana and Haiti, but Elmer wasted no time on his quest to meet the woman in red. The second day out he found her sitting with his friend near the pool.

"I came up to say hi and she asked me the time," recalls Elmer, now 88 and living in Florida. That question led to a kiss later that night and before the cruise returned to New York, Elmer had proposed. Arlene promptly accepted. They spent their honeymoon skiing in Quebec, then settled down in Connecticut where Elmer worked as a salesman for the Diamond Crystal Salt Company.

Although Arlene, now 81, suffered a stroke six years ago and is wheelchair-bound, they both feel at home sitting near the beach watching the waves roll in. "We plan to enjoy the view of the ocean," says Elmer. "After all, that's where we met."

> People think love is about a man and a woman. But love is about loving, respecting and caring for yourself—and being the best you can be, whether you are alone or in a relationship.
>
> –JANET LIFSHIN

■

Nobody likes rejection. Perhaps that has prevented you from reaching out. Or perhaps you become defensive, thus inviting the very thing you dread. Facing rejection may be the most important survival skill you will ever learn—not only for creating a special loving bond, but also for making your way in the world.

This is especially true when you first meet a guy. You have a date, you have a terrific time. Maybe you fall into lust or into bed. He says, "I'll call you." But he doesn't. You blame yourself. "There's something wrong with me," you tell your friends.

Not necessarily. He may simply not be interested in pursuing a relationship and does not want to hurt you, suggests Paul Wanio, a psychotherapist who practices in Boca Raton, Florida.

"People have strong fantasies, which generate strong feelings," says Wanio. "Men can, in the blink of an eye, fantasize and feel the power of physical intimacy and then desire it immediately. For the man it's having sex. For the woman it's making love. Both are mistaken. Sex is an intimate act, but does not create love."

Wanio adds that love is not created in bed. It takes much sharing, understanding, commitment, respect, and growing together. Jumping into bed quickly is impulsive, and evidences a lack of integrity and self-respect.

"There is no love at first sight, because love takes time," he says. "You cannot love what you do not know and to genuinely know someone takes time—much time."

There are two other reasons a guy may not call, even when there is a loving relationship: (1) He may have something else on his mind—in other words, he's in the cave. Or (2), he may not feel it is necessary to call. He cares and he assumes you know it. His silence is not a lack of emotion or respect, instead it's a form of reverence. Some men are more sensitive than you may realize.

Another major problem can arise with timing. A few years ago I was waiting for a date to call and becoming more agitated with each passing day. In response to my lament, a friend offered these pearls of wisdom: *"Nobody is on your time schedule."* You might *want* a call back today. But you might not *get* it for a week.

Likewise, a friend complained for months that her boyfriend had not yet said those three precious words: "I love you."

"I'll give him until our first-year anniversary," she threatened. "Then I'll go looking somewhere else."

"Nobody's on your time schedule," I told her. "He will say it when he's ready—when he means it—not simply to please you." Naturally, he did. Then he couldn't stop saying it. Patience is a virtue when it comes to romance. Everything happens when it is supposed to: the proposal, the wedding, starting a family. However, you also have to know when you're heading up a blind alley without a road map. In other words, when it's time to bail out. Like Jill, who waited six years for her beau to propose. He gave her a ring, they moved in together and set a wedding date. Then he got cold feet, asked for the ring back, and took off running.

> We may go to bed mad, but even if we're still upset, we always say,
> "I love you" and kiss good night.
> —MARGARET RUSH

■

Getting past the basics—the awkward stage where you want to get to know him better—can be frustrating and discouraging.

How fast should you move? How hard should you push? Or should you let him take the lead? Relationship experts offer these simple tips.

- *Make him work.* Don't give yourself away. Men like the chase. By coming on too fast or too strong, you may cause him to back off.
- *Show him you have a life.* You don't always have to be available: It tells him you have nothing better to do. This also applies when you are together: Have your own interests, hobbies and friends.
- *Know how to laugh.* A good sense of humor goes a long way.
- *Keep the complaining to a minimum.* He cannot be expected to solve your problems—and he may have a slew of his own.
- *Be interested.* Guys like gals to listen, so pay attention.
- *Have fun but stay sober.* If you are intoxicated or drugged, effective communication is impossible and your judgment is impaired. You might act in a way you will later regret.
- *Be real.* No use pretending to be something you're not. He'll get the picture soon enough. Be you and be proud of it.

Each person has different rules or laws as to what true love is.
—JONATHAN ROBINSON

■

Once a guy is interested, you will have your ups and downs before getting together on a permanent basis. Communication is a top priority, not only during the initial phases of a relationship but also throughout a committed union—whether or not you are married. Studies show that in today's society, couples spend an average of 15 minutes a day talking. And of those few precious minutes, children, chores and emergencies are often topics of conversation.

Susan Scott, an interior decorator, has been in a serious relationship with Jack for seven years. Having been divorced once, she has a better understanding of what it takes to make a long-term relationship work.

"It gets easier with time," says the fifty-two-year-old mother of two. "First of all I trust Jack to do the right thing and I give him plenty of space. We spend time together on the weekends and in the evenings, but when he does something that bothers me, we sit down right away and talk. Bottling up bad feelings only leads to trouble. I try to understand his point of view and when we don't agree we both try to compromise."

Most couples who are already experiencing relationship troubles have little or no ability to speak effectively to one another, much less resolve problems.

"They are either very self-centered or so emotionally distraught that they can no longer listen or empathize. They cannot have effective or intimate conversations," advises Paul Wanio.

The dynamics in any union of two people—or more if there are children or in-laws involved—are complex. However, experts agree that the key to getting along is talking.

Ellen Kreidman, author of *The Ten-Second Kiss*, says: "A relationship is only as deep as its level of communication. Unless you can share your deepest fears, pain, hopes and dreams as a couple, your communication will remain on the surface."

Kreidman has devised a four-step formula to help couples confront their frustrations and communicate more effectively:

Step 1: Describe the situation that is making you
           uncomfortable.
Step 2: Describe how the situation makes you feel
           emotionally.
Step 3: Ask for what you want in a positive way.
Step 4: Stop talking and give your partner a chance to
           respond.

Remember, in a relationship nobody is blameless and neither party is completely guilty. Marriage is a two-way street. It's not a matter of who is right or who is wrong—it's about being open. Don't expect your partner to be a mind reader and don't expect to find answers if arguing is your idea of sharing.

If you see yourself in this picture, you need to learn communication skills. That takes practice as well as an understanding of how your partner is hearing you.

In his books, John Gray stresses the fact that men and women speak different languages.

"Men and women seldom mean the same things even when they use the same words," he explains. "To fully express their feelings, women assume poetic license and use various superlatives, metaphors and generalizations. Men mistakenly take these expressions literally."

For instance, when a woman says "I want more romance," the man usually responds defensively, with something like, "Are you saying I am not romantic?" A woman says "We never go out," and the man responds, "We went out last week."

Here's an example of one of my own faux pas. I have been dating a terrific man for the past three years. He's a computer whiz and I admire that. But, I'm ashamed to admit, one evening I blurted out, "You're always fooling around on the computer."

We were on our way to a party, but that "fooling around" statement undid us for the evening. With those unthinking words I dismissed all the time, energy, and brain power that goes into understanding the complexities of computer technology. Luckily there were no long-lasting repercussions. We were able to move past that blip—and I learned a valuable lesson: Think before you speak.

"Unclear and unloving communication is the biggest problem in relationships," says Gray, who adds that the number one complaint women have is: "I don't feel heard." And even that complaint is misunderstood and misinterpreted!

If men really understood what women were saying, they would argue less and be more supportive. Clearly, effective communication is by far the most important part of making and keeping a loving connection.

Since women typically share their problems, they imagine the worst when men shut down. They feel rejected, unloved, and insecure. Gray points out that when a man is upset or stressed he will stop talking and try to work things out by himself.

"No one is allowed in that cave, not even the man's best friend," he says. "Women should not become scared that they have done something terribly wrong. They need gradually to learn that if you just let men go into their caves, after a while they will come out and everything will be fine. But it is important for women to *not try* to get a man to talk before he is ready. Men really do need to be alone or silent when they are upset."

This is a difficult lesson because women are more talkative and supportive of each other when problems arise. So a woman wants to act that way with her man. Don't. While your intentions are good, it is not what he wants or needs.

Jeanie Wilson, a writer who has been married twenty-one years to the same man, says that even a devoted and helpful husband cannot take the place of your best girlfriend. "Most men aren't as communicative as most women would like them to be. Speaking as the wife of the Original Macho Man of Few Words, I can assure you that a man's moody silences rarely have anything to do with you."

Columnist Dave Barry wrote a hilarious essay a few years ago about men and women. He used this example to point out how conversations go awry: You're both riding in the car and your guy is silent. You, of course, think that you've said something to offend him. You start to apologize, but he has no idea what you are talking about. Why? Because he was thinking about the last time he changed the car's oil. Then, when you get upset, he makes a feeble attempt to get back into the conversation, but he's at a loss since he was completely tuned out.

We women tend to take ourselves too seriously at times. Often, when a man remains silent, he has either lost track of the conversation and is embarrassed to admit it, as Dave Barry points out, or he might not want to offend you by disagreeing. For example: One night my boyfriend and I were driving home and I asked him four questions in a row: Did he want to come over for dinner? Did he want to take a walk after dinner? Did he want to go for a bike ride the following day? And could we go dancing the next night? To which he said nothing. I ruminated on that for a while, started to get upset with his silence, then realized I was planning every minute of the next few days. In effect, I had made all the plans and had left no room for spontaneity. He did not want to reject me by saying no to my proposals, nor did he want to commit himself by saying yes. So he said nothing.

We drove for a few miles in silence and finally I said, "I get it, I get it." That opened the floodgates and the discussion continued long after we arrived at our destination. Believe me, now I am very careful about proposing plans, either long-term or short. Sometimes it's better to just let things happen. Or, as they say, go with the flow.

During those times your guy is out of his cave, here are some practical pointers for opening the verbal portals for a better understanding of each other.

- Talk about topics other than the house and kids.
- Don't whine or shout; talk in a modulated tone.
- After you speak, give your partner a chance to reply.
- Don't pose a question for which there is no practical answer.
- Don't fire off several questions in a row without giving your partner a chance to reply.
- When the answer comes, listen with an open mind. (And don't be surprised if there is no answer.)
- Laugh at appropriate remarks; never laugh *at* someone or poke fun.
- Listen to *what* is being said, not *how* it is being said.
- Try to speak without placing blame.
- Avoid hostile words like "always" and "never."
- Try saying "I'm sorry."

Though all humans need both intimacy and independence,
women tend to focus on the first and men on the second...
as if their lifeblood ran in different directions.
—DEBORAH TANNEN

∎

A committed relationship is about sharing space and giving your partner enough room to do his thing.

"Essentially, marriage should offer freedom, not restraint," says author Masami Saionji. "One ought to be far freer in marriage than when alone. This is real marriage. Because people don't understand this, many marriages fail. The two people must share more freedom than before with each other, and continue to give more freedom to each other. Each partner must value his or her own freedom, and equally respect the other's freedom."

Since no two people are alike, trying situations may arise when they live together. In addition, people change. Are you the same person you were five years ago? Second by second, we evolve. If you are expecting your spouse or partner to be the same person he or she was when you first met, you are in for a surprise—perhaps positive, perhaps negative. All humans constantly renew themselves.

Love does not consist of gazing at each other but in looking
together in the same direction.
—ANTOINE DE SAINT-EXUPÉRY

∎

Keeping a relationship alive and well is a full-time job. Some couples inflict hurt and pain, each partner playing out old grievances. Others enjoy the happiness fostered by warmth and love. To keep your connection on the upswing instead of the downslide, experts offer these Dos and Don'ts.

Things To Avoid:

- Don't stalk off if your partner wants to talk
  (unless he is yelling).
- Don't be inflexible.
- Don't have the kids around during serious discussions.
- Don't accuse, belittle, name-call or threaten.
- Don't take an "I'm right" attitude, even if you believe
  you are.
- Don't adopt a superior attitude.
- Don't interrupt.
- Don't judge, criticize, or minimize your partner's
  position.

Things To Do:

- Find a quiet place to talk, and allow adequate time.
- Listen actively.
- Accept responsibility if you're wrong.
- Give your partner the benefit of the doubt.
- Respect your partner's position.
- Maintain eye contact and physical closeness.
- To avoid a misunderstanding, repeat back what's
  being said.
- Hug and kiss when you're finished.

> **A man is already halfway in love with**
> **any woman who listens to him.**
> —BRENDAN FRANCIS

■

When you learn how to speak effectively and share differences of opinion, you will learn to appreciate each other more.

Few couples agree on everything. That's what makes life so interesting. Acknowledging and accepting your partner's opinions and preferences builds trust and a common bond between you, which will, in the long run, enrich your love.

"We need to make a better effort to get to know our partners for the unique individuals they truly are," suggests love guru Gregory J. P. Godek. "We need to stop treating each other as stereotypes."

On any given day, there is at least one reason to hug your mate.
—ELLEN KREIDMAN

∎

Evelyn and Paul Moschetta have not only been married for twenty-three years, they have also saved countless marriages with their book *The Marriage Spirit* as well as through their monthly column in *Ladies' Home Journal*.

These New York marriage counselors say: "Our marriage has enriched us as individuals, has deepened our love, and was a help in carving out a satisfying family and professional life." After more than twenty-six years advising others on how to get along, the key word that sums it all up for the Moschettas is "unselfish."

As Evelyn explains: "That's the part of us that comes from some higher place and not from our everyday egos."

Here are their seven suggestions for making a relationship work for you.

1. *Rediscover each other.* Bring back that loving feeling by reflecting on special moments and discussing the positive things you bring to each other.
2. *Become your best self.* Think before you act. Stop before you say hurtful things. When the selfish side of you comes out, call upon your higher self to overcome the temptation to act selfishly or thoughtlessly.
3. *Be nonjudgmental.* Eliminate old stereotypes or notions. Try to see him from a new perspective. Remain open to different experiences. Be spontaneous.
4. *Defuse anger.* Pay attention to your moods, especially during stressful times or when you are PMSing. Allow those strong emotions to pass through you without acting on

them. This will prevent those spontaneous outbursts from damaging your relationship.

5. *Create a strong bond.* Trust your mate and trust that you have made the right choice of partners. Have confidence that he will not hurt you intentionally. Nourish the romantic side of your union.

6. *Do the right thing.* Put aside your ego and try to work harmoniously to explore the values of truth and goodness. Don't get caught up in chore wars or a tit-for-tat mentality.

7. *Have faith.* Provide physical, emotional and spiritual nurturing to your partner and turn a deaf ear to critics who try to tear you apart. Find strength in each other and those people who support you.

Lynne Mitchell remembers her husband, John, when he was a tearful first-grader who missed his mom. They grew up only a few houses apart in Boca Raton, Florida, but didn't pay attention to each other until they met again in junior high school. She says he was the class clown. They began dating in high school, but not seriously. During their college years, Lynne says: "We dated other people but we'd always wind up back together on vacations home."

During Christmas break in 1968, John realized they were meant to be together. He proposed. But just weeks earlier, Lynne had begun to feel an odd numbness in her legs. By that February she required hospitalization and was diagnosed with multiple sclerosis.

"When he came to visit I told him he didn't have to marry me now that I was ill," she says.

John says his decision was a "no-brainer." He had already decided to marry her that summer. They wed in August 1969.

Over the years, their dedication to each other has deepened. When Lynne falls out of her wheelchair, John, now fifty-two, is right there to help her. What is the secret behind their long standing romance? After spending thirty years together and raising two grown sons, they say it's hard work.

"It's just like a good garden," says John. "You have to keep working at it. You get out of it what you put into it."

Keep your old love letters. Throw away your old bank statements.
—MARY SCHMICH

∎

AFFIRMATIONS

Whether you are in a relationship or not, these daily affirmations will help you get a better understanding of what love is all about. And they will help you cherish yourself, so you can cherish others.

- I will make an effort to love myself.
- I will be selective about the men I date.
- My happiness and sense of self-worth does not depend on others.
- I will be with a man only if he makes me feel good about myself.
- If a man makes me feel guilty, unhappy, or unlovable I will call it quits.
- Anyone who hits me is not worthy of my love.
- I will not put anyone on my time schedule.
- I will be more attentive and less defensive when I listen.
- Even if I am alone, I am worthy of being loved.
- I will have a good time whether or not I am with someone.
- I will keep my mind open and my voice gentle.
- I will put some fun and flirtation in my life.
- I will laugh more.
- I will make the one I love feel special and appreciated.

If you would be loved, love and be lovable.
—BENJAMIN FRANKLIN

■

RECOMMENDED READING ON LOVE

Burns, David D., M.D. *Feeling Good*. Avon Books.

Godek, Gregory J.P. *Love: The Course They Forgot to Teach in School*. Casablanca Books.

Gray, John, Ph.D. *Men Are from Mars, Women Are from Venus*. Harper Collins

Kreidman, Ellen. *The 10-Second Kiss*. Renaissance Books.

Moschetta, Evelyn and Paul. *The Marriage Spirit*. Simon & Schuster.

Robinson, Jonathan. *Communication Miracles for Couples*. Conari Press.

—.*Shortcuts to Bliss*. Conari Press.

Saionji, Masami. *The Golden Key to Happiness*. Element Books.

Tannen, Deborah, Ph.D. *You Just Don't Understand: Women and Men in Conversation*. Ballantine Books.

Five

IF POWER IS WHAT YOU WANT

I long to speak of the intense inspiration that comes to me from lines of strong women.

—RUTH BENEDICT

■

*I*N TODAY'S SOCIETY, women can be anything—from mommies to CEOs. Some of us have babies early then return to school to get high-school, college and postgraduate degrees, well into our seventies and even eighties. Career-minded women begin climbing the corporate ladders right out of college and put off long-term relationships and children—or they opt not to raise a family at all.

No matter which path you have chosen, it's important to feel that you can accomplish your dreams no matter what obstacles block your way and regardless of what people think or say.

It means you must feel empowered.

"The concept of power still carries negative connotations for women," says Priscilla V. Marotta, a motivational speaker and behavioral psychologist. "As a woman who went back to college at age thirty-five and became pregnant at forty, I personify a woman juggling many roles. But when a woman attempts to activate her power she experiences a level of discomfort, which complicates her attempt to balance a multifaceted life."

Transforming those negative ideas into a positive mindset is the major challenge of women facing the millennium.

> **Even if it is not fully attained, we become better by striving for the higher goal.**
> —VIKTOR FRANKL

■

One of the most powerful women in America today is Oprah Winfrey. With the words "Oprah's on," millions of viewers worldwide hurry to their TV sets to catch the pearls of wisdom offered by this incredibly talented woman—a woman who made her own fame and fortune and who uses her power for the good of humanity. Oprah's frightful beginnings make her story even more remarkable.

Oprah Gail Winfrey was born on January 29, 1954. Her mother, Vernita Lee, was single, eighteen years old, poor, black and living in Kosciusko, Mississippi, deep in the segregated South. Oprah's father, Vernon, was a twenty-year-old soldier who didn't even know he'd had a daughter after his brief fling with Vernita.

Unable to cope with a baby and no husband, Vernita left Oprah with her mom and moved north to find a better life. For her first six years Oprah lived with her grandparents on a small pig farm with no indoor plumbing. Her strict grandmother disciplined her with a stick.

At age six she was sent to live with Vernita and her half-siblings in Milwaukee. "We weren't a family with lots of hugs and touching," says Oprah. "Nobody ever said 'I love you.'"

Even without love, Oprah was able to cope—until she was raped by a cousin at the age of nine and her world went into a downward spiral. Sexual abuse by other relatives and family friends continued until she was fourteen. She told no one. Instead, she stole money from her mother's purse and tried to run away.

Unable to control her wild child, Vernita sent her daughter to Nashville to live with her father, Vernon, and his wife. Soon after arriving, Oprah gave birth to a baby boy who died within a week or two. That was the turning point in her life—she had been given a second chance.

"The experience was the most emotional, confusing, and traumatic of my young life," admits Oprah, who has been incredibly forthright about her horrific early years.

Vernon, a barber, took charge of his wayward daughter and set high goals. He made her read books, memorize vocabulary words and behave respectably. "He saved my life," says Oprah.

In spite of dabbling with cocaine in her early twenties, she managed not only to survive but also to thrive. Oprah excelled in school and won a scholarship to Tennessee State University, where she majored in speech and drama. An excellent speaker, she gave dramatic recitations of poetry and Bible passages. At age nineteen, she was hired by a CBS affiliate in Nashville as a reporter and anchor, becoming the city's first black TV newscaster.

In 1976, she moved to Baltimore to co-anchor the evening news. The makeover that the station insisted she undergo made her hair fall out in patches. Trouper that she was, she shaved her head and went on air with her head wrapped in a scarf. Her hair grew back, but she was dropped as a newscaster for becoming too emotional—often weeping as she read tragic news bulletins. Luckily, ABC had the foresight to pair her with a male co-host for a morning chat show called "People are Talking." Under the relaxed interview format, Oprah blossomed.

Six years later she was hired for a struggling Chicago talk show called *A.M. Chicago*. Incredibly, one month after she became the show's first solo host, it went to number one. Not only did Oprah reinvent the TV talk show, they renamed the program *The Oprah Winfrey Show.*

And a star was born.

Since 1985, the Queen of Talk has consistently kept audiences enraptured. The admiration she receives is tangible: 32 Emmys and a Lifetime Achievement Award from the Academy of Television Arts and Sciences, and she was named one of "The 100 Most Influential People of the Twentieth Century" by *Time* magazine, the latter honors both in 1998. Only three women in history have owned their own production studios: Mary Pickford, Lucille Ball and Oprah, who runs Harpo Productions.

When Oprah talks, people listen. She asked for donations to her Angel Network's piggy bank for college scholarships, and more than $1 million in donations poured in. Oprah's Book Club has been a raging success; when she recommends a particular title, it becomes an overnight best-seller. The American Library Association credits Oprah with "single-handedly expanding the size of the reading public."

When she asked for volunteers to help Habitat for Humanity build houses for the disadvantaged, over 15,000 viewers responded. The books written about her diet and fitness regime have sold millions of copies. At age forty-five, she is a movie mogul and a power player. She is single and happy and has no plans to marry longtime beau Stedman Graham.

"I have a position of power—I speak to millions of people every day," she says. "My black ancestors would never have imagined that a colored girl could have the life that I'm having right now."

But it wasn't always this way.

At one time Oprah was so insecure and eager to please that she removed the seeds from her boyfriend's watermelon slices. "I was a doormat," she admits. She tracked down viewers who didn't like her to find out why.

"Nobody had any clue that my life could be anything but working in some factory or cotton field in Mississippi," says

Oprah. "I feel so strongly that my life is to be used as an example to show people what can be done. But I don't think of myself as a poor deprived ghetto girl who made good. I think of myself as somebody who, from an early age, knew I was responsible for myself, and I had to make good."

And, girl, has she made it good.

Oprah's net worth, according to Forbes magazine, is $675 million. Harpo Production Company is a $20 million facility that takes up an entire Chicago city block. There are 135 people on staff and Oprah is the chairman and CEO. She has no outside investors or board of directors. She's the whole kit and caboodle, and she keeps a firm grip on the company.

In Oprah's own words: "I want to be a woman who lives without fear. I want to reach the highest vibration of humanity possible. I want my life to shine so brightly that others will be attracted to it and compelled to shine as brightly. I want the truth in the universe—to seek it, to stand for it, to be it."

Although there is only one Oprah, you, too, can be empowered. Power is not bullying or controlling others, nor is it a "guy thing." You have more power than you realize. The trick is to combine some practical steps with positive thinking and right action.

Janet Lowe, who has chronicled the life of Oprah Winfrey, says Oprah's life is in a state of flux as she transforms herself. "She's constantly seeking, questioning, changing, looking for her place and her power. On the wall of her luxurious Chicago apartment is the classic line from *The Wizard of Oz*, spoken by Glinda, the Good Witch: 'You don't need to be helped any longer. You've always had the power.'"

In Oprah's own words, these are the 10 commandments that have guided her amazing rise to the top.

- Don't live life to please others.
- Don't depend on forces outside of yourself to get ahead.
- Seek harmony and compassion in your business and personal life.

- Get rid of back-stabbers—surround yourself only with people who will lift you higher.
- Be nice.
- Rid yourself of your addictions—whether they be food, alcohol, drugs, or behavior habits.
- Surround yourself with people who are as smart or smarter than yourself.
- If money is your motivation, forget it.
- Never hand over your power to someone else.
- Be persistent in pursuing your dreams.

I believe you can have it all. You just can't have it all at one time.

—OPRAH WINFREY

■

WHAT'S HOLDING YOU BACK?

One of the things I learned the hard way was it does not pay to get discouraged. Keeping busy and making optimism a way of life can restore your faith in yourself.

—LUCILLE BALL

■

According to the dictionary, power is the "ability to do or act; might; a person who possesses or exercises authority or influence; energy, force or momentum; to inspire, spur, sustain."

Power is the ability to achieve.

Empowerment is feeling confident to act on your own authority.

"Acting with confidence, having control over your life—this is use of power," says Priscilla V. Marotta. "Power is the energy you emit to achieve goals in your life. A powerful you has thoughts, feelings and accomplishments to share. For years women have feared that to be powerful was to be unlovable. The opposite is the reality."

What holds us back from being empowered are the subtle messages that women receive during childhood and adolescence.

According to Marotta, these are the basic power-robbers that prevent us from achieving any form of power in our lives:

- *People-pleasing.* This dangerous behavior puts your own needs behind the needs of others; when people respond unkindly, you take it personally, thus lowering your self-esteem.
- *Not wanting to make mistakes.* Deep-seated fear of failure causes you to be your own worst critic, and your own worst enemy. But mistakes are part of the learning experience.
- *Needing security from others.* Seeking the external company of others—especially a spouse to protect and guide

you—can prevent you from taking control of your own life.

- *The need to be polite.* Women are trained to be deferential. By holding back and waiting for others to take the lead, you not only waste time but also limit your opportunities.
- *The need to act like a lady.* Outrageous, rule-breaking decisions may lead to incredible success.
- *Taking the blame.* Women are conditioned to accept responsibility for anything that goes wrong. The key to effective behavior is accepting the fact that others, too, should be held accountable.
- *Not wanting to make waves.* Edith Bunker was told to "stifle" herself. Stifling yourself is power-draining behavior. Women resist speaking out, but top leadership requires voicing your opinions. Allow your input to be heard.

When singer Madonna learned that director Alan Parker planned to pass on her for the lead in *Evita*, she sent him a long, handwritten letter saying she alone was meant to play Eva Perón. It worked for Madonna. It can work for you, too. Next time your boss isn't sure you are ready for that big project he has in mind, go to the mat to prove your worth.

Your own inner voice may have hit on an unbelievably lucrative idea, but you will never know unless you listen to it.

Press on. Nothing in the world can take the place of persistence.

—RAY KROC

■

Apology and powerlessness have been woman's lot since the beginning of time. Her traditional role has been dependency and submissiveness.

"Women have been expected to react rather than act, to have decisions made for them, rather than make decisions for themselves," say Stanlee Phelps and Nancy Austin, authors of *The Assertive Woman.* "What women deserve is the power to determine the course of their own lives without apology, to make their own decisions, and to be free from the absolute authority of others."

Yet personal power—while women need it—has traditionally been denied. When we are told that it's not natural or feminine, we have swallowed hard and buried our anger and frustration and disappointment. We have ridden the wave of guilt and defended ourselves and made apologies. With the advent of a new century, those old behavioral patterns are bound to change.

These days women can compete with men for success, money, prestige and authority.

"Power as a positive, creative force helps you choose for yourself, gives you a feeling of worth and purpose, and fosters a strong conviction to overcome feelings of anxiety and hopelessness," add Phelps and Austin.

I always thought of myself as a dumb blonde. Now I know better.
—ANN ZONDERMAN

■

Ann Zonderman from Jacksonville, Florida, with almost twenty years of experience in the nursing field, experienced firsthand the recent changes and cutbacks in the health care field. She understood that her career—as she had always known and loved it—was coming to an end. Ann says: "The hours were longer, the pay was shorter, the work was more intense and the patients were sicker. Every time I tried to advance, the management would take the highest-paid employees and let them go. Then the hospital I was working for was bought out by a large corporation and I lost my job."

Ann tried to find a women's support group to help her cope with the devastating changes. At age fifty, she was ready for a new career, but didn't know what direction to take.

"I didn't even realize I had the power within myself to change until I reached my forties," says the mother of two. "Then I discovered I had more strength than I had given myself credit for."

With the help of an intense weekend retreat run by a program called Understanding Yourself and Others (UYO), Ann determined that she would have a high degree of stability with a degree in law. Undaunted by the prospect of three highly concentrated years of study, Ann enrolled in Florida Coastal School of Law, a new institution which opened its doors—as though by magic—just as she was ready to enter. At our fortuitous introduction in Tallahassee during the summer of 1999, Ann was fifty-four and studying to take the Florida State Bar exam. She plans to focus on health-related legal issues.

"Women must pay attention to their needs and not dwell on the setbacks," she says. "Try to see the fortunate aspects of your life instead of the downsides. I always try to keep sight of the fact that I have the power within me to do what I want to do."

Would you have the power to change careers like Ann did? If the thought makes you weak in the knees, take a look at the questionnaire that follows to see how you hold yourself back and to determine what positive steps you can take to empower yourself.

> If one advances confidently in the direction of his dreams and
> endeavors to live the life which he has imagined, he will meet with
> a success unexpected in common hours.
>
> —HENRY DAVID THOREAU

ZIGGY AND FRIENDS, INC. Reprinted
with permission of UNIVERSAL PRESS
SYNDICATE. All rights reserved.

POWER QUESTIONNAIRE

Check off "True" or "Not True" for each of the following statements to see why you are preventing yourself from being empowered.

1. I feel inadequate.
True_____ Not true_____

2. I feel like a failure.
True_____ Not true_____

3. I don't want to make mistakes.
True_____ Not true_____

4. I don't want to upset others.
True_____ Not true_____

5. I want people to like me all the time.
True_____ Not true_____

6. I believe nice girls don't speak their minds.
True_____ Not true_____

7. I don't like to disappoint others.
True_____ Not true_____

8. I don't like to say "No."
True_____ Not true_____

9. I don't like to make direct requests.
True_____ Not true_____

10. I have trouble making decisions.
True_____ Not true_____

11. I don't want to make waves.
True_____ Not true_____

12. When I get what I want, I consider it luck.
True_____ Not true_____

13. I rarely get what I want.
True_____ Not true_____

14. My life is governed mostly by others.
True_____ Not true_____

15. I am afraid to take responsibility for my own life.
True_____ Not true_____

16. I fear I'll fail if I try something new.
True_____ Not true_____

17. I need to please those around me.
True_____ Not true_____

18. I put my own needs last.
True_____ Not true_____

19. I lack a specific goal.
True_____ Not true_____

20. I am content with what I have.
True_____ Not true_____

KEY TO ANSWERS:

If you answered True to more than half of these questions, you need a power-boost.

FINAL QUESTION:

I will feel empowered if I:

_____

_____

POSITIVE STEPS FOR EMPOWERMENT

> If something doesn't work, don't keep doing it.
> —NATHANIEL BRANDEN

■

"Now is the age of mastery," says Sharon Wegscheider-Cruse, author and therapist. "Women are learning to take control of their lives and become independent of their male partners. The result is that they are enjoying autonomy, freedom and economic security for the first time in history."

The first step toward empowerment is understanding that you have an enormous creative spirit within you; you have the ability to reshape your life completely. Your mind is one of the most powerful forces on earth. It can be your strongest ally or your worst nightmare.

In Chapter Three: If You Want Peace of Mind, you met Grandmaster Tae Yun Kim, who discovered at an early age that she wanted to learn a form of martial arts known as Jung Su Won. Everyone tried to discourage her, saying it was too hard, or it was not ladylike. Her parents said she brought them shame.

"The difficulties I encountered were enormous," she says, "not in the art itself, but in the resistance I encountered from people's belief that a woman couldn't do it and, furthermore, shouldn't be able to do it. My family was convinced there was surely something wrong with me."

But, she says, there are no obstacles you cannot overcome. And she has proven this fact.

"Others said it was impossible when I, a woman, attained a black belt in my martial art. Then (more impossible) I, still a woman, became a female Master. And then (absolutely impossible!) I became a female Grandmaster. Well, so much for what is supposedly impossible."

Kim explains there are six Silent Master images within each of us that will give us the power to overcome any roadblocks on our journey through life. They are:

> *Your Real Self*: the part of you that embodies the personality traits you developed while growing up, which expresses itself through your ideas and thoughts.
>
> *Your Life Force*: the power within you that makes your heart beat and allows you to become one with the universe—to be the best you can be.
>
> *Your Higher Conscience*: the force that combines your spiritual and physical sides and allows you to make right decisions.
>
> *Your Creative Self*: the source of your mental, emotional, and material energy, which you are free to use to shape the world around you.
>
> *Your Intelligent Self*: the innate insight, or that little voice inside your head, that can help fulfill your dreams, ambitions and goals—if only you listen.
>
> *Your Quiet Self*: the harmony, peace, joy and love residing within you that brings serenity when troubles or stress overwhelm you.

These six images can be used to empower you at any time. You may think you are a failure, but your Silent Master knows that you have the mental and physical strength to act and achieve. You may be fearful, but you have the power to overcome. It is already part of you. When you want to give up, your Silent Master will release the energy you need.

"The Silent Master has always been there," says Kim. "It is silent only when we are not aware of it. But when you make the decision to find your Silent Master, its power begins to unfold. Open yourself to receive it."

You have the power to change your life. It comes from within you.
It's about the work you put into it. Power is strength over time.
—OPRAH WINFREY

∎

You may have made limited choices in your life based on false premises about yourself and how women should or should not act. That is all in the past. Today a new age is dawning.

"No matter who you are, where you are, no matter what obstacles and limitations exist around you at this moment, you can change your life, your health and your state of mind completely," says Grandmaster Tae Yun Kim. "*You* can decide *who* you want to become."

Yet many women have trouble developing confidence in their own power.

According to Stanlee Phelps and Nancy Austin: "Becoming comfortable with power and enjoying a feeling of competence takes some practice. However it is possible to develop an assertive attitude and experience a feeling of being in control."

You should also have realistic expectations about what you want. If you are a big doer, it's fine to be a big thinker. If you are willing to learn from your mistakes without giving up, you are on the right path. You might not make it the first time, or the tenth. The trick is to prepare yourself mentally for possible failure and to stay positively focused.

Here are a few ways that you can stay on track.

- *Visualize what you want to happen.* Imagine how you would look, think, and feel as an assertive woman. Concentrate on this picture and fix it in your mind.
- *Meditate on the image you have fixed in your mind.* When you are relaxed and can give the idea your full attention, your inner wisdom will guide you. Trust yourself to be in control instead of controlled.
- *Affirm that you are taking charge of your life.* Be positive with your affirmations. Repeat them daily, or write them down. Affirmations are steps toward your goal. Don't expect miracles overnight. Every day will bring you closer to your dream.
- *Record your affirmations and your plan of action.* Repeat

them as you walk or wash the dishes. Or record them, put the tape into your car stereo and listen to it as you drive.

Draw a picture of what you want to achieve. If it's a house, draw that house or clip a photo from a magazine. Put it someplace where you can focus on it daily. Then spend a few minutes each day contemplating your picture—whatever it is.

> If you treat a long shot like a sure thing, it's a sure thing you will end up disappointed. But if you treat a long shot like a long shot and a sure thing like a sure thing, you are a good bet to get everything you deserve out of life.
>
> —DR. MARK GOULSTON

■

Air Force Col. Eileen Collins became NASA's first female space commander when the Space Shuttle Columbia lifted off the launch pad in July 1999. At age forty-two, Collins charted a new course for women. Not only was it the first time in 126 space shuttle launches that a woman was at the helm, but she also had four other astronauts, three of them older men, under her command. In addition, she was responsible for one of the priciest shuttle payloads ever with NASA's 25-ton, $1.5 billion Chandra X-ray Observatory onboard.

"You've got to have the attitude that 'I am confident enough to handle anything,'" says Collins, who has logged more than 5,000 hours in 30 types of aircraft. Collins, who touched down days later with a perfect landing, could certainly have taken a back seat and gone along for the ride. Instead, she found her style—a quiet staying power combined with a positive "can-do" attitude.

> I don't think my daughter Bridget knows that everybody's mother doesn't fly in space or command a space shuttle.
>
> —COL. EILEEN COLLINS

■

Although Oprah must have been distressed when the TV station took her off the news desk, she made the best of it. And, in fact, switching her to an informal chat format was the best thing that could have happened. The important point to remember is that Oprah used the lesson wisely.

Lessons come in many shapes and forms. Priscilla V. Marotta, Director of the Center of Psychological Effectiveness in Ft. Lauderdale, Florida, and president of Women of Wisdom, Inc., has these positive power lessons to help you be more assertive and in control of your life.

1. *Welcome mistakes.* Being defensive is not constructive. Learning is an ongoing process. Trial and error are the best teachers. Rather than being upset, use mistakes for growth and understanding. As Oprah says: "There is no such thing as failure. Mistakes happen in your life to bring into focus more clearly who you really are."

2. *Ask for what you need.* Once you know what your *own* goal is, you can implement a plan to get what you want. You'll find the shortest route is the most direct one. Don't beat around the bush. Ask and you shall receive—and if you don't, use that negative feedback to find another route.

3. *Use your time and energy wisely.* Setting priorities is a must. So is establishing good networking relationships. Find others with complementary skills and strengths that fulfill your needs.

4. *Be flexible.* Again, think of Oprah. She could have left the network and found another newscaster position. Instead, she gave the new format a try. You may even have to push the rules to get what you want.

5. *Engage in positive self-talk.* Guilt and self-blame are a trap to keep you mired in negativity. It's self-defeating behavior that must be broken before you can move forward. Positive talk encourages positive imaging. Set your mind on a forward track. Stop second-guessing yourself and criticizing yourself

for past behavior. Stay in the present and focus on the future.

6. *Make waves.* Everyone has a talent. Once you've found yours, speak out. Become a leader. Initiate changes.

7. *Step into the limelight.* Why take a back seat when you can toot your own horn? Acknowledge your accomplishments. It's not being egotistical, it's showing respect for yourself and showing others you believe in your own self-worth.

> Surround yourself with the best in other people, and don't be
> afraid of competition. Consider it a teaching method.
> —MARY TYLER MOORE

■

The female movers and shakers of today have a different approach to leadership. They are not women trying to act like men. Instead, they are expressing women's values and translating that force into behavior patterns that suit their new-found power.

For instance, they operate on a reward system and invite speaking out, instead of blindly demanding respect. Rather than act as drill sergeants, they motivate their employees and coworkers to think and to offer new information and ideas. Imposing discipline is out, valuing creativity is in. Most women in power don't have a bottom line. Instead they have a vision— or they ask for assistance in developing a future plan. They say, in effect, "How can I serve you?" instead of barking, "Here's what we're going to do." In other words, men see job performance as a series of rewards for services rendered or punishment for inadequate performance. Women leaders try to transform people's self-interest into organizational goals.

When Carole Black received her bachelor of arts degree in English literature from Ohio State University, she probably never dreamed that she would be the first female CEO of Lifetime, a major television cable channel. Yet at age fifty-four, she is just that.

Black, who is a divorced mother of one, began her career at Procter & Gamble promoting products such as Crest toothpaste and Head & Shoulders shampoo. In 1983, she moved to Chicago and sold "the softer side" of Sears to attract female customers. From there she was hired by Walt Disney Studios to target women for video sales; she moved up to vice president of marketing between 1986 and 1993. Although she had no TV experience, she was made general manager of NBC's TV station in Los Angeles. Within two years it was rated number one.

Again, with no cable TV experience, Black beat out twenty-five other hopefuls to become CEO of Lifetime in July 1999. She promptly began beefing up programming. Her vision is to broaden the base of women viewers.

"There's a whole group of women who have never even viewed Lifetime," she says. "Those are the people I'm going after." She also plans to expand into magazine and book publishing. "I think women understand women more than men," says Black, who is always up for the challenge. Her rise to the top is based on her unique brand of marketing that accentuates the positive.

Judy B. Rosener, a professor at the University of California's Graduate School of Management in Irvine, says the following traits are common to female leaders:

- They encourage participation.
- They share power and information.
- They enhance other people's self-worth.
- They get others excited about their work.

Every woman in power will find her own leadership style through trial and error. Studying the lives of other powerful and successful women is a good way to learn about new and unique approaches. Use what works for you and disregard the rest.

Employees at Saturn headquarters in Troy, Michigan, are already amazed at the way forty-six-year-old Cynthia Trudell is handing her new position as the first woman to head a major U.S. auto manufacturer. In a male-dominated industry she stands out not only because she is a female, but also because she is so approachable.

"She's very down-to-earth," says Dora Mack-Talley, Saturn's union liaison. "She talks *to* you, not *at* you."

Adds a worker from the Spring Hill, Tennessee, plant: "A lot of times people are leery about approaching someone in that capacity, but she came down here one day and people were amazed. They were saying, 'Wow, she's actually interested in what we're doing.'"

> The old style of beating on people to get things done does not
> work. People do better when they are happy.
>
> —GRACE PASTIAK

■

In 1995, more than 40,000 women from 184 countries gathered in Beijing to discuss their dreams of a new world. By sheer force of their numbers, midlife women have the power to launch a new kind of social and corporate reform—a more compassionate and understanding way of running the show.

There is a difference, however, between being a powerful woman and being a confrontational feminist. Instead of taking an adversarial stance, you can deal with problems in a positive and creative way.

"When you are a feminist in thought, you do not see any discrimination or oppression, nor do you blame yourself," says Priscilla V. Marotta. "You recognize the limitations of others who try to hold you back. You possess a belief in your abilities and the wisdom of other women like yourself. You activate positive power for the goals you select. You are no longer represented as a victim, nor are you invisible. You are a powerful and talented woman who shapes your personal and professional world."

Women are the real architects of society.

—HARRIET BEECHER STOWE

■

Being empowered does not necessarily mean you want to be a CEO or own a business or run for political office. Empowerment can work at home with your loved ones, as in this case study from Nathaniel Branden, a Los Angeles–based psychotherapist.

A woman named Nadine called his office from Minneapolis. She was distraught. Nadine worked all day and at dinner time she wanted to walk into a clean kitchen, not a garbage dump with plates piled high and trash everywhere. Although her two teenage sons and her husband promised to clean up, they never followed through. Begging, cajoling, demanding and screaming had done nothing to improve the situation.

Branden instructed Nadine to walk out of the kitchen if she found dishes in the sink and the counter cluttered. The following evening, Nadine did as advised. Without saying a word, she curled up on the couch with a book until the kitchen was spotless. Then she cheerfully made dinner. The following night the kitchen was clean. The night after, it was a mess again. Nadine picked up her book, headed for the couch, and started to read. It took several weeks, including one final "test" by the males in the household to see if she would cave in "just once." She didn't.

"You need to change your behavior in order to compel them to change theirs," Branden told her. "The moral of the story is: When you hit a wall, look for new actions to take."

Without yelling, belittling or scolding, Nadine had empowered herself. She took charge of the situation and made it work to her advantage by acting in a positive and decisive way.

Judge Judy Sheindlin, star of TV's "Judge Judy" show empowered herself on the home front with these legal maneuvers. Her husband, Jerry, also a judge, was never satisfied with the way his shirts came back from the dry cleaner. He would complain bitterly and send Judy back to make things right. They had been through a dozen cleaners when she asked herself, "Are you some kind of an idiot?" Instead of reproaching Jerry, she let his shirts pile up on the closet floor until he got the message. Not only wouldn't she take his clothes to the cleaner, she refused to tell him where she was going so he wouldn't make a fuss and turn the new cleaning establishment against her, too.

And when it came to changing the roll of toilet paper, Judy's reprisal was swift and sweet.

According to Judge Judy, Judge Jerry was incapable of replacing the roll and would leave the cardboard with only one square of paper attached. So Judy squirreled away her own stash of TP and left the roll with the one square. When Jerry called out from the bathroom, she shouted back: "There's still paper on the roll, honey."

After twenty-two years of marriage, Judy Sheindlin says that if you start a relationship denying your own needs and desires, it will come as a shock to realize that you've been had.

"In relationships there is almost never an equal division of responsibilities," she adds. "It's never going to happen, so make your peace with it. Look at the good things you have together."

Empowering yourself is a long-term investment that will pay off handsomely and in many ways. You need not be passive and ineffective. You need not be victimized. Learn from your losses and your mistakes, take pride in your successes, let go of the toxic things and people in your life, move with confidence and accept the challenges that lie ahead. Know that you can be strong and affirmative.

> You can if you think you can! When your attitude is right, your
> abilities will always catch up.
> —Dan Clark

In 1983, Julie Golden was a twenty-one-year-old mail clerk from Iowa, with no dreams or ambitions. Her life was making enough money to pay the bills and giving her two-year-old son, Dallas, as much love as possible. Over the years it was just the two of them, forming a special bond. In 1991, they moved to the Seattle area and Julie enrolled as a part-time college student, while holding down a full-time job as an office manager. Julie and Dallas both studied hard and worked hard to become the best they could be.

Then, in June 1999, mother and son graduated and received diplomas—within two days of each other: Dallas from Lynnwood High School, where he was homecoming king, senior class president and a standout in football, wrestling and track; Julie from Central Washington University, with a bachelor's degree in business administration. "It's kind of surreal . . . it's like it's not really happening," said the thirty-seven-year-old single mom, gold tassel hanging from her mortarboard cap.

This is her advice: "Keep your head up, keep on moving and don't ever be ashamed of who you are."

In a 1999 issue of *Redbook* magazine, authors Mary Moore and Rose Martelli polled the experts for important habits that can empower any woman and came up with the following. Post these on your refrigerator for those times when you need a shot in the arm. Incorporate them into your daily living and feel the surge of power that these tips can bring.

1. *Make a great entrance.* First, make sure you are wearing something that fits you well and is appropriate for the occasion. Check your self-consciousness at the door and move steadily toward a destination without hesitation.
2. *Work the room.* Overcome your phobia of mingling. Imagine everyone naked, if you must. If you don't know anyone, approach a group, introduce yourself and ask if you can join them. It's a good ice-breaker.
3. *Wiggle gracefully out of social faux pas.* If you've forgotten someone's name, admit it. Don't try to beat around the bush. Honesty is the best policy.
4. *Remain poised at all times.* If you feel excited or agitated

before speaking to a group, do a few minutes of aerobic activity and then take three deep, cleansing breaths, letting the toxic air out through your mouth. Now smile.

5. *Ask for a raise early in the day.* Wear your favorite suit or outfit and ask your boss for a minute of his or her time before the day gets hectic. Outline your past and continuing contributions and ask if you would be considered for a raise. No demands. No specific numbers. No ultimatums. Allow the person time to respond by offering to wait a few days for a decision.

6. *Know the facts.* When making a major purchase, be an information warrior. The Internet is a veritable wealth of data; so are magazines such as *Consumer Reports*. Go armed with facts and *never* feel pressured to buy on the spot. *Always* be ready to walk away.

7. *Overcome fear.* Condition your mind to overcome fear by using visualization techniques and biofeedback. Breathe in and breathe out until the body is relaxed and the mind follows.

8. *Don't be intimidated.* When you find yourself in a negative situation, visualize pushing the other person far away from you and imagine him or her being very small. Make sure your heads are on the same level. If the other person is standing, you should stand, too. Allowing someone to tower over you allows you to be bullied. And remember, you don't have to win. You simply have to come out of the encounter with your dignity intact.

People buy things from and listen to people who smile at them.

—VALERIE ADAMI

∎

AFFIRMATIONS

For women like Julie Golden—or for anyone who needs a power boost—here is some positive self-talk that you can use to maintain your focus.

- A mistake is an opportunity for new learning.
- I will acknowledge my shortcomings and limitations.
- If something does not work the first time, I'll try a different approach.
- I will ask for help when I need it.
- I recognize my talents.
- I will be persistent in pursuing my goals.
- I will remain flexible.
- If an opportunity arises, I will seize it.
- I will invest my time and energy wisely.
- I will be discriminating in my associations.
- Attitude is everything. I affirm myself daily.
- I will create success and happiness for myself.

Life is a series of problems.
Some want to moan about them and some want to solve them.
—M. SCOTT PECK, M.D.

■

RECOMMENDED READING ON POWER

Aburdene, Patricia, and John Naisbitt. *Megatrends for Women.* Villard Books.

Borysenko, Joan, Ph.D. *A Woman's Book of Life.* Riverhead Books.

Branden, Nathaniel. *A Woman's Self-Esteem.* Jossey-Bass Publishers.

Burns, David, M.D. *Feeling Good.* Avon Books.

Kim, Tae Yun. *Seven Steps to Inner Power.* New World Library.

Lowe, Janet. *Oprah Winfrey Speaks.* John Wiley & Sons.

Marotta, Priscilla. *Power and Wisdom.* Women of Wisdom, Inc.

Phelps, Stanlee, and Nancy Austin. *The Assertive Woman.* Impact Publishers.

Six

IF SUCCESS IS YOUR GOAL

> Don't be afraid of taking risks or being criticized.
> If you don't want to be criticized, don't say anything,
> don't do anything and don't be anything.
> —MARIAN WRIGHT EDELMAN

■

AH, THE SWEET smell of success . . . or so they say.

The truth is that success takes hard work, dedication, commitment and a positive attitude. Instant prosperity is rare. And even those baby-faced celebrities who pop up overnight like mushrooms, have, over the years, paid their dues. Although Latin heartthrob Ricky Martin—who rocked the world with his hot, hip-swiveling performance at the 1999 Grammy Awards—seemed to appear out of nowhere, he actually started in show biz at the age of twelve as a member of the teen group Menudo.

Minnie Driver, Oscar nominee for the Academy Award–winning movie, *Good Will Hunting*, says she was performing in school plays from the time she was seven. In fact, the acting bug bit her so hard she skipped college and headed straight for Hollywood after high school.

And Carleton Fiorina—the new CEO of computer giant Hewlett-Packard, one of the top Fortune 500 companies—was a secretary and an English teacher in Italy before putting in 19 years of hard work at AT&T. Although destined for a career in law, she dropped out after only one term, which prompted her father, a federal judge, to remark: "I don't think you're going to amount to anything."

At AT&T Carly, as she likes to be called, found her niche in global sales. She was an innovator, an explorer and a road warrior, often spending sixty percent of her working hours traveling to Europe and the Far East—where corporate executives often refused to talk with her simply because she is a woman. Nevertheless, she pulled in billions of dollars for the company.

At age forty-four, the first female chief executive at HP, she says: "Both of my parents had a huge influence on me, encouraging me to be the best I could be. I truly grew up with no sense of limits."

Success takes years. So if you are expecting it overnight, be prepared for a long evening.

Helen Gurley Brown, who wrote the blockbuster book *Sex and the Single Girl*, started her career as a secretary for $6 a week. She admits she was not a deep thinker and didn't have a goal when she began working, but she had drive. She wanted to make a difference. Sixteen secretarial jobs later she was hired at an advertising agency, where her boss recognized her talent and let her write copy for Sunkist radio commercials. After she'd been his secretary for five years, he gave her a full-time copywriting position. She was thirty-one.

"You do not have to know early in life what you want to do in terms of a career," says Brown, the formidable editor-in-chief who transformed *Cosmopolitan* into the slick, glossy magazine it is today. "Talent emerges only when you're already in the work world, getting paid for what you do."

One of America's most controversial entertainers had no problem sweating her way to the top. From the time she was in grade school, Madonna knew she wanted fame and fortune. She also knew she would do anything necessary to grab the brass ring. When she burst onto the music scene in 1985, she was an oddity—a cheap theatrical act that looked as though it would burn out. However, by cleverly marketing herself and constantly reinventing her image, networking with influential people and immersing herself in all aspects of the music business, she has made her name a household word. Whatever fears she may have had, Madonna did not let them interfere with her single-minded ambition.

Madonna attended St. Andrew's parochial school in Rochester, Michigan (a suburb outside of Detroit), where she was an average student. But getting noticed was her intent when she entered the fifth-grade talent show as a baton twirler. As she innocently stepped on-stage, the audience gasped. She appeared to be naked. Actually, she wore a bikini and was covered from head to toe with fluorescent green paint.

"It was my one night to show them who I really was and what I could really be," she recalls. "I just wanted to do totally outrageous stuff." This highly personal, modern approach has continued throughout her entire career.

Madonna left home in 1978 at the age of nineteen with $37, a suitcase and a dream. New York was her destination, and she was determined to break into show biz. After bouncing around in small bit jobs, she realized the only product she had to promote was *herself*.

"I'm tough, ambitious, and I know exactly what I want," says the woman who now commands more than $1 million per performance! "And I always want more."

Dressed in beads and lace, with teased hair, garish lipstick, and punk attitude, Madonna hit the music charts with "Like a Virgin." Her tacky tactic worked. The trashed look was in and so was she. Suddenly millions of preteen girls were Madonna wannabes feverishly buying anything in leather and lace. She was twenty-six and on her way to the top.

Two years later the "Material Girl" arrived with sleek, bleached-blonde hair à la Jean Harlow. In 1989 she was a brunette with tailored suits and a whopping bank account. Her albums soared off the charts. In 1990 she struck a pose with her Blonde Ambition tour and a multimillion-dollar market for bustiers was born. "Amazingly, women began wearing their underwear on the outside," says Philadelphia-based fashion expert Eileen Hammel.

In 1994 Madonna reinvented herself once again, wearing lingerie-like clothing in "Bedtime Stories." In the film *Evita*, she evoked the fashions of the 1940s. And in 1997 when baby Lourdes was born, Madonna learned to balance motherhood with her career, which was still going strong. At age forty she released "Ray of Light" and snagged three Grammy awards.

In between her incredible musical hits she made the movies *Desperately Seeking Susan, A League of Their Own,* and *Dick Tracy,* and toured the world several times over. She married and divorced Sean Penn and had numerous well-publicized affairs. Now she's reinventing herself again—to the tune of $6.5 million—to pitch the new Gold line of Max Factor cosmetics.

Biographer Christopher Anderson says, "She's obsessed with career—analyzing her mistakes and plotting every move."

"I'm a workaholic," she admits. "I have insomnia. And I'm a control freak. That's why I'm not married. Who could stand me?"

There has never been anyone like Madonna. She is not just the number-one female pop star, she consistently grabs the public's attention by breaking one taboo after another. She makes waves. She's not afraid to be heard. She is impossible to ignore. Her impact on our culture is undeniable. And Forbes magazine once proclaimed her as "the smartest business woman in America." In 1991 alone, she earned over $65 million! Now that's success.

> Thoroughbreds wear blinders; they don't look at other horses.
> They run their own races.
> —DANNY THOMAS

■

WHAT'S HOLDING YOU BACK?

There is a lesson to be learned from Madonna's intense drive and ambition. She is positively focused. Are you? Or do you picture yourself a failure? Interestingly, while many women crave success, they fear it at the same time. Experts say that both men and women hold themselves back from the very thing they want the most.

David Rottman, president of the Careers Counselors Consortium, says surveys show that the fear of success outweighs the fear of failure by at least five to one. "It's often a relief for people to discover that there are reasons—very good reasons—why they haven't been able to achieve the success they desire so much."

Those unexplored fears act as powerful hidden stumbling blocks that work against your best interests. There are numerous reasons why women fail to achieve success, even if they are completely qualified. These are three common fears:

1. *Fear of Social Isolation.* When a woman is promoted, she can become an outsider to the group she feels most comfortable with. Take Felicia, a secretary in a law firm, who was very popular with her peers. The attorneys thought her popularity would make her the ideal candidate for the job of office manager. So they promoted her. Instead of being "one of the girls," however, Felicia had to mediate conflicts (often between two of her friends), dish out difficult assignments or tell her coworkers they had to work overtime. Suddenly, she was not asked out for lunch; conversations stopped abruptly when she walked into the coffee room. Felicia was no longer included in the social set that had made her job so enjoyable.

2. *Fear of Raised Expectations.* Promotions to higher positions invariably bring more demands. Sadly, some women feel

they don't have what it takes or they don't want the responsibilities that go with the upgraded position. Suzanne was an editor's assistant on the photo desk of a midsized newspaper. She was also a young mother of two. When an art director's slot opened up, she was offered the job. Suzanne knew it entailed longer hours, which would take time away from her family. Although the job was tempting, she feared with young children at home she would not be able to give the art director's position 100 percent of her attention. Instead of risking failure, Suzanne turned down the opportunity. "I made the right decision for me," she says. "Perhaps I'll have another chance when my kids are grown, but for now I have no regrets."

3. *Fear of Disorientation.* When success comes quickly, it can be frightening and perplexing. Imagine going from student to CEO within a one-week time frame. How would you feel? How would you dress? How would you act? Who would your new friends be? The shift of self-image could crush your self-esteem. It did for Collette Dowling, author of *Perfect Women,* who went to work for *Mademoiselle* magazine after college. Suddenly she was expected to write interesting stories, but she admits she didn't have a clue. So she wrote nothing—not even a paragraph—for four years. "I compared myself with everyone, and I lost in the comparison," she admits. "I hated my betters for bettering me and I remained locked up tight until I entered a state of paralysis."

Overnight success may appear gratifying, but gradual and steady increases are easier to adjust to. Which brings us to a few additional factors that make success so elusive for some.

I tried to block out all negative thoughts. I kept reading books that tell you to just keep exercising your faith and continue to believe.
—JACKIE JOYNER-KERSEE

Several major factors contribute to not achieving success. One is lack of self-confidence. Many women fear that if they don't achieve their goal, they will be seen as losers. They do not want to hear "I told you so," or "What made you think YOU could do that job?"

"Some people appear to be victims of a cruel world where they never have a chance to succeed," says psychologist Robert Anthony. "In essence, they feel powerless, and this becomes their reality. The cycle becomes self-destructive because their belief keeps creating their reality."

In psychological terms it is called a self-fulfilling prophecy. The very thing you fear most becomes your reality. That's a good reason to stay positively focused, even when your goal appears unattainable.

Another fear—and a realistic one—is that even greater needs will be placed on your resources by others. You might feel you cannot meet those expectations; you might be unwilling to put in the time and effort the job demands, as Suzanne mentioned above. Turning down an opportunity for advancement does not mean you are not worthy; it may be that the timing is wrong.

Another success-robber is fear of taking a risk. Significant changes in life—perhaps starting your own business, or reaching for a promotion—spark feelings of doubt, anxiety and hesitation. You wonder if you can handle it, and what will happen if you cannot. These feelings are not always job-oriented. They can spill over into relationships, parenting, or even taking up a new sport.

Dr. Mark Goulston, Assistant Clinical Professor at the Neuropsychiatric Institute at UCLA, says that by caving in to such thoughts we end up settling for less than we deserve. "If, instead, we accept that a certain degree of tension is necessary to keep our minds and senses alert, we can rise to the occasion and respond effectively to whatever comes along."

He notes that even though world-famous athletes and actors have anxieties before performing, they convert their nervous energy to motivation and effective action.

> Taking charge involves taking full responsibility for your success
> or failures, whether they be at home, in the boardroom,
> or in the bedroom.
> —BARNET MELTZER, M.D.

∎

When I was downsized from a full-time writing job almost four years ago, I went into business for myself. Hard work and successful networking have allowed me to prosper. But freelance writing is a feast-and-famine adventure. Sometimes the jobs roll in and I'm frantic with deadlines. At other times I wonder how I will pay my mortgage.

Does it make me nervous? You bet. Does it cause anxieties? Absolutely. And, yet, somehow I manage to survive.

Problems befall all of us. To achieve success in any field of endeavor, try to view obstacles as learning tools. Avoid hanging onto misery and making excuses; let go and move on with your life. This is the first step in freeing yourself from negativity. Plant the seeds for success, prosperity and wellness with a positive mental attitude. Condition your mind to expect the best—not the worst. Remember, *thoughts create actions*.

Layoffs, downsizing and losing one's job are part of life. Instead of despairing over the rotten hand that fate has handed out, get over it and move onto bigger goals.

Jacki Keagy was laid off her job as a management trainer for a defense contractor in 1986. Today she's the manager of a career-consulting service in Minneapolis. These are her tips on how to survive in the workplace.

- *If you lose your job:* Assess your strengths, update your resume, then start job-hunting as soon as possible.
- *If you are reprimanded:* Listen to what's being said without being defensive. Take the information, digest it without anger, and come up with a plan to change your behavior.
- *If you have not received a raise:* First, find out if there's a salary freeze and inquire about salary plans for the coming year.

Request an early performance review and talk to your supervisor about your accomplishments. As a last resort, explore other options.

- *If you haven't received a promotion:* Ask why you were passed over, but don't dwell on your disappointment. Network with people within the company who can help you at the next opportunity.
- *If you get no recognition:* Learn to toot your own horn. Tell your boss and your coworkers what you have accomplished. Don't be shy.

The experts agree that you are accountable for the things that happen to you. Similarly, you are responsible for your own successes and failures. If you want make it happen, you can and you will.

"Determine the conflicts that exist in your life," says Barnet Meltzer, M.D., author of *The Ten Rules of High Performance Living*. "Take the necessary steps to resolve them. Now take charge! Realize that you have the mind power to transform your life through solution-oriented choices."

Taking charge means creating positive self-worth, a healthy body image, and a strong mind/body connection. Accept and love yourself, know you are worthy, and believe in yourself. Nobody is perfect. We are all perfectly imperfect.

Each of us is a unique and whole person with the freedom to seize an opportunity when it is presented. Taking control is something only *you* can do. When you are upset or angry your power is diminished. When you are confident, joyful, and compassionate, your energy expands.

"Taking charge teaches you that you can choose to be the hammer rather than the nail," says Meltzer. "The purpose of taking charge of your life is to empower you with the tools to live out your dreams. Your beliefs, a positive mental attitude, clear thinking, and self-determination will be the key instruments in your tool kit."

Failure is not the falling down, but the staying down.

—MARY PICKFORD

∎

The three most powerful negative factors that hold you back are fear, guilt, and a sense of unworthiness.

Success can be overwhelming. The pressures can be frightening and fear of failure may prevent you from pursuing your dream. Nobody wants to flop, especially at the top. But when you settle for mediocrity you have undermined yourself, and this can create a vicious cycle:

- Fear of making mistakes prevents you from taking action.
- Not taking action keeps you in a rut.
- Staying in a rut because you fear failure can be immobilizing.

However, "failure" is a relative term. It is determined by the rules you have established defining "success" and "defeat." If you change your definition, your vision of success also changes.

Turning down the position of art director was difficult for Suzanne, yet she realized the pressure and stress of the new job would entail more time and energy than she could handle, or was willing to give. So she said "No," and preserved her integrity, dignity and opportunity for future advancement. Even though the refusal was based on performance anxiety, for someone in her situation—with youngsters at home—it was a positive decision.

Thinking yourself unworthy can also thwart success. Self-worth is determined by your feelings about yourself, which in turn translates into how you act and how others perceive you. If you do not feel worthy of being recognized for who you are, what you can do and what contribution you can make, you will never take the first step toward achieving success. Having a negative opinion of yourself invites rejection and failure. Your life is diminished and your chances of success are decreased. Thus, a negative self-image obstructs your ambition and becomes a barrier to fulfilling your goals. For those of you who have lacked success in losing weight, not having a positive self-image may be the very thing that keeps you from reaching your goal.

Another success-robber is inaction.

"People often have excellent ideas that they consign to the impotence of daydreams—never taking action in reality to see them realized and implanted," says Nathaniel Branden, a therapist specializing in self-esteem.

Intelligence and creativity are not at issue here. Consider two women, both with bright ideas. One of them takes her ideas seriously, develops them and fights for their implementation. The other woman does nothing. The difference is commitment.

"I don't expect to be taken seriously," is the lament of many women—too many women. So they quit before they start.

Branden adds: "When we doubt our minds, we tend to discount its products. If we fear intellectual self-assertiveness, we may mute our intelligence and suppress the best within us."

That does not mean you should spin your wheels for every bright idea you have. Some projects take more energy and resources than we have available. Other issues, however, like losing weight, can never be successful without the commitment. Even if you have tried before and failed, even if nobody believes that you can shed the pounds, the power of success lies within you—and *only you*.

> Whatever happens in the workplace, you have to get over it. If you
> don't you won't succeed in your next opportunity. In fact, you won't
> even find one.
> —AMANDA FOX

∎

And, finally, certain baggage or bad habits that we may not even be aware of can short-circuit opportunities for advancement. Poor on-the-job conduct can work against you. If you see yourself listed below, or if you think any of these negative habits apply, ask a coworker whom you trust to tell you.

1. *Chronic lateness.* Lateness breeds resentment. It shows that you are inconsiderate of your coworkers and implies that you don't care enough to arrive on time. Do whatever is necessary to arrive on the dot—or before.

2. *Defensive behavior.* Making excuses or crude remarks when being offered constructive criticism is a warning sign to employers. Chips on the shoulder are generally not acceptable. Instead, take responsibility for your actions and smile instead of scowling.

3. *Procrastination.* You might be afraid of making mistakes. Or you may be lazy. Or you may be such a perfectionist that nothing ever gets done. If you feel overwhelmed, break large assignments into smaller tasks and set a time frame for getting them done.

4. *Nervous behavior.* Gum-chewing, hair-twirling or -flipping, foot-tapping and fidgeting with jewelry makes it look as though you are out of control. Madonna plays with her jewelry when being interviewed. It makes her appear as though she is not interested and would rather be somewhere else instead. It's hard to break these habits, but once you are aware of them you can.

5. *Acting crude.* Telling vulgar or racist jokes, talking about personal hygiene or using coarse language does not endear you to anyone. It is neither charming nor funny and it's only a matter of time before you embarrass the company— or yourself. Hint: Tone it down.

6. *Lack of attention.* Flitting from project to project and conversation to conversation like a butterfly makes you look like a flake. Instead, stick to one or two projects at a time and take them to completion. If you are talking to a colleague, finish your conversation before starting another one, or else excuse yourself politely.

7. *Lack of writing skills.* Unless you work on an assembly line, chances are you will have to generate letters, memos and e-mail. There is no excuse for poor grammar, punctuation or spelling. Always run a spell-check and always re-read the hard copy. Before sending something out, have a friend or coworker read it over if you doubt your own writing abilities.

In the next section we will take a close look at positive ways to implement your ideas for success, but first, one more example of how women hold themselves back.

> **When a woman experiences that she has no effect on her environment, she often develops a general feeling that what she does does not matter.**
> **—MARTIN SELIGMAN**

■

Woman's traditional role has been to marry, have children, and enjoy the fruits of her husband's success. But this stereotype of the typical homemaker is becoming as old-fashioned as hoop skirts as we move into the new century. Yet many women still voluntarily relinquish their power and serve up their will to their husbands, to be used or abused. Too many women allow their mates not only to provide financially, but also to take care of the myriad details involved with running a household. The woman who does this gives up her power and, in the worst-case scenario, suffers at his hands.

Even if your spouse is a wonderful loving husband, you may suddenly find yourself alone through death or divorce. You may be devastated to learn that you have no means of support and no skills to make a living.

During marriage a woman with a fine home, a luxury car and recognition within the community may be considered by her peers as a "success." With death or divorce, that social status may vanish overnight and she may find herself like a ship without a rudder, floundering in rough seas. She will have a rude awakening when she realizes that her triumphs were not her own, but had been provided by proxy through the accomplishments of her husband and/or children.

If you see yourself described in this section, it's not too late to change. Everyone has a talent for something, an interest or a desire. Whatever it may be, now is the time for some serious introspection to determine what the future may hold for you. If you are lucky enough to have a spouse who can support you while you explore your options and discover your talents, be grateful. There are many of us who are on our own with nobody to fall back on except ourselves.

Answer the questions in the section that follows. It should help pinpoint areas in which you show pessimistic thinking and ways in which you hold yourself back.

> True success means material and financial wealth—and enjoyment
> of life's journey . . . continued expansion of happiness . . . and the
> progressive realization of worthy goals.
>
> —DEEPAK CHOPRA

SUCCESS QUESTIONNAIRE

Answer these questions honestly to see what's preventing you from achieving the success you want.

1. Do you believe in yourself?
   Yes_____ No_____
2. Do you have faith that you can succeed?
   Yes_____ No_____
3. Do you want it all?
   Yes_____ No_____
4. Are you willing to work hard to get it?
   Yes_____ No_____
5. Do you make things happen?
   Yes_____ No_____
6. Do you use positive words such as "success," "energy" and "can-do"?
   Yes_____ No_____
7. Do you have a plan of action in motion?
   Yes_____ No_____
8. Do you dwell on the positive?
   Yes_____ No_____
9. Can you visualize your success?
   Yes_____ No_____
10. Do you wait to see what will happen?
    Yes_____ No_____
11. Do you spread yourself too thin by taking on too much?
    Yes_____ No_____
12. Are you in a job with no opportunity for advancement?
    Yes_____ No_____
13. Are you waiting for the right moment to make your move?
    Yes_____ No_____

14. Are you constantly comparing yourself to others and mea-
    suring your success by theirs?
    Yes_____ No_____
15. Do you complain, criticize and blame others?
    Yes_____ No_____
16. Are you stuck in a rut?
    Yes_____ No_____
17. Are you fearful of making mistakes?
    Yes_____ No_____
18. Do you associate with people who are not ambitious?
    Yes_____ No_____
19. Do you let others decide what you should do?
    Yes_____ No_____
20. Do you use negative terms such as "impossible," "unreal"
    and "too risky"?
    Yes_____ No_____

KEY TO QUESTIONNAIRE

If you answered No to more than half of questions 1 to 9, you
are not goal-oriented.

If you answered Yes to more than half of questions 10 to 20,
you have all the excuses for not succeeding.

ONE FINAL QUESTION

Am I afraid to aim for success?

Yes_____ No_____

POSITIVE STEPS FOR SUCCESS

I claim to be no more than an average man with below average
capabilities. I have not the shadow of doubt that any man or
woman can achieve what I have if he or she would put forth the
same effort and cultivate the same hope and faith.
—MAHATMA GANDHI

■

Mary Higgins Clark always considered herself a storyteller,
but becoming a best-selling author was another matter entirely.
She received her first rejection letter from *True Confessions* magazine when she was sixteen. When she married, at age twenty-
two, she left her job as a flight hostess and signed up for writing
courses to learn the craft.

"Some of the editors wrote rejection slips that were more creative than anything I had written," admits Clark, who now commands a cool $12 million per book.

One rejection from *Redbook* included a handwritten sentence
that read: "Mrs. Clark, your stories are light, slight, and trite,"
and her first novella earned a note that said: "We found the hero-
ine as boring as her husband had."

Instead of driving Clark to despair, these turndowns fueled
her determination to get a book in print. *Aspire to the Heavens*
soon rolled off the presses—and right onto the remainder rack.
At that point, knowing how much she loved reading suspense
novels, she thought that was the tack she should pursue.

While Clark is heaping huge rewards now, her life was not easy.
She gave birth to five children in eight years, coped with the sudden death of her husband, made a salary writing scripts for radio
shows, put herself through college and handled plenty of rejection. Now, seventeen novels later—many of them topping the
New York Times best-seller lists—Clark knows that to succeed you
must try and try again. And you must believe in yourself.

"Those rejection slips only whetted my appetite, produced a just-wait-and-see-pal response in my soul," says Clark, who started a women's writing group that has endured for 40 years.

> You may be disappointed if you fail,
> but you are doomed if you don't try.
> —BEVERLY SILLS

■

If you sincerely want success, the first thing you must do is turn negative thinking into positive action. Before moving on to a list of practical steps for achieving success, let's take a look at how you can get rid of those three rubber bands that hold you back: fear, guilt, and a sense of unworthiness.

Instead of fighting your fear or trying to get rid of it, neutralize its power by accepting it and taking action. That means plunging into the very thing that you are afraid of. Playing it safe gets you nowhere fast.

Dr. Mark Goulston contends that the inclination to either play it safe or take risks can usually be traced to childhood. Kids are naturally curious and adventurous. If they get hurt or do something wrong and are chastised by their parents, they are likely as adults to play it safe. Their inner voice says "Take a risk and you'll be sorry." If, however, their parents said, "Get out there and try again," they are more willing to test the unknown.

"Those who are comfortable taking chances don't shy away from surprise; they might even seek it out," adds Goulston. "They know the best way to grow is to reach beyond their grasp."

Childhood trauma is another obstacle to overcome. Remember falling off that bike? Get back on. Standing up to fear and taking action does not mean that you will fail again. It's normal to retreat into a protective shell when life has thrown you a curve. But the sooner you resume living, the less likely you are to become a casualty and the quicker you will achieve your goals.

To conquer fear is the beginning of wisdom.
—BERTRAND RUSSELL

■

Guilt is the emotion that keeps you bound to the past. It is the inner feeling that you must pay a price for any and all mistakes you have made during your life. But guilt serves only to make you feel bad about your current thoughts and actions. It is strictly negative thinking, without any redeeming qualities.

Author Wayne Dyer tells us that the inner self thrives on guilt. Your psyche serves up a plate of guilt—over anything and everything—and it wants you to gobble it hook, line and sinker. However, your higher self knows that you should be forgiven. So instead of whipping yourself with a wet noodle when you do not succeed the first, second or third time, use the opportunity to learn from your mistakes. Release feelings of anxiety and fear and trust that you can do better next time. Remember, without courage, the process cannot begin; without perseverance, it cannot be completed.

As long as you believe in yourself and your own vision, you have something. When you give that up, you are personally bankrupt.
—OLIVIA GOLDSMITH

■

The biggest blocker of them all is the feeling that you are unworthy. If you don't feel you deserve success, you will push it away. It's the equivalent of deciding that you will fail. A woman may insist that she is entitled to success for all her hard work; yet on a deeper level, if her self-esteem is weak, she will expect something to go wrong—thus setting herself up for failure.

Nathaniel Branden says: "You may be aware that success ignites some measure of discomfort in you, yet you are not driven to drastic self-sabotage. You may not undercut yourself completely; you may only retard your progress, holding yourself down to a lower level of achievement than is possible."

And all the while you wonder what is holding you back.

The truth is, *you are entitled to success earned by your own effort.* And it may take tremendous courage to accept this.

"When we see ourselves moving toward success and anxiety kicks in, we must learn to do nothing, that is, keep out of our own way," advises Branden. "We must learn to identify the ways in which we tend to self-sabotage so that we can make a conscious effort to abstain from doing those things."

> You can fail your job, or a test, or your finances can fail, or
> your business or a relationship. But that's not YOU.
> You can never fail as a person. Any problem can be corrected.
> Separate YOU from what you do.
> —ROBERT ANTHONY

∎

Now that you're ready to move forward with your blueprint for success, let's see how others have done it.

Joan Lunden was crushed when she was dumped after seventeen years on *Good Morning America*. But she is not looking back. Instead, she enjoys getting up with the sun rather than at 3:30 in the morning. She goes to bed late and spends quality time with her three daughters and her beau, Jeff Konigsberg.

She believes transition is a good thing. "Your purpose is to find your gift, perfect it and give it back to others," says this multi-talented lady. "Take the ups and downs of life in stride." These are her tips for everlasting success:

- Don't burn your bridges when you leave a job.
- Eliminate obstacles with perseverance.
- Know what you want from life, then go for it.
- Choose your profession wisely.
- Be flexible in times of change.
- Keep your options open. Try new experiences.
- Be passionate about what you do.
- If you don't like the way life is unfolding, rewrite the script.

Steven K. Scott, author of *Simple Steps to Impossible Dreams*, has studied winners such as Steven Spielberg, Henry Ford and Helen Keller. He says no matter what your background or how you rate yourself, your talents, and your abilities, starting right now you can effect extraordinary accomplishments—whether it's shedding fifty pounds, or enjoying a rewarding career or running a household (or a large company)—while providing emotional and spiritual foundations for your children.

Simply stated, every successful venture begins with a Dream Conversion Process that looks like this:

1. Define your dream in writing.
2. Convert that dream into specific goals.
3. Convert each goal into specific steps.
4. Convert each step into specific tasks.
5. Assign a projected time or date for completion of each task.

Some experts may tell you to set realistic goals—goals that are achievable, so you won't get discouraged and frustrated. This makes perfect sense. On the other hand, Scott says setting realistic goals is a severe limitation to your program. Imagine if Madonna had said, "I just want to sing in nightclubs in New York; I'll be happy with that." But her dreams were larger than life. Way back in high school, when she was taking dance lessons, she supposedly told her instructor he could be in her first video. He laughed at the notion. Who's laughing now?

Think about Thomas Edison, Henry Ford, the Wright brothers. Where would the world be without their grandiose plans? In every instance, shoot for the moon.

Although I write small informative booklets that can be found in every supermarket and discount store in America, my dream is to have my novel in every major airport. Or have this book become a number-one bestseller. It may be a long shot—but that's how I will measure my success. If I don't make it, I won't consider myself a failure. My books are out there to prove that I am a successful writer. I simply want more.

There are no easy shortcuts to success. As one celebrity put it, "It's taken me years to become an overnight sensation."

> Most people want to win. They want the rewards, glory, and satis-
> faction of achievement. Yet, tragically, few people take it to the
> next level and actually plan for that success.
> —CYNTHIA KERSEY

■

Persistence pays off, as this story illustrates.

The Great Depression was still echoing down Wall Street when Anne Scheiber, then thirty-eight, decided to invest $3,000—which represented a major portion of her life savings—in stocks. She entrusted the money to her younger brother, Bernard, who was just starting out as a broker. He picked good issues for her and things looked promising. But his firm suddenly went belly-up and she lost it all.

Anne was furious. That hard-earned cash had been accumulated a penny at a time by skipping meals, wearing frayed clothing and walking to work to save bus fare. Instead of giving up, Anne tried again—with a vengeance—and in 1944, ten years after her big loss, she was back in the investing game with a $5,000 account at Merrill Lynch Pierce Fenner & Beane.

Dressed in the same black coat and hat every day, she plowed every dime back into the market. Relying on her own research and analysts' reports, she invested in new companies that specialized in drugs, beverages and entertainment, rarely buying more than 100 shares at a time. In the early 1950s she splurged with 200 shares of Schering-Plough, which set her back $10,000. In 1996 that investment was worth $3.8 million. She rarely sold anything, refusing to pay brokerage fees and commissions; instead, she bought and held on tight.

Anne Scheiber died on January 9, 1995, at the age of 101, having never married. With no children to inherit her nest egg—which was valued at an astonishing $22 million—it was donated to Yeshiva University!

Opportunities come to those who pursue them;
don't wait for something to happen.
—JOYCE JILLSON

■

Spiritual guru Deepak Chopra, author Stephen Covey, and motivational speaker Zig Ziglar all have formulas for turning humdrum lives into success stories. As you read about others' secrets of success, you will probably notice that a certain pattern will emerge and that some steps will make more sense than others. Keep them handy. As you progress in your quest for success, you should be able to make all of them work to your advantage.

Deepak Chopra, author of *The Seven Spiritual Laws of Success*, has developed an approach that focuses on the mind/body connection:

1. *The Law of Pure Potentiality:* To tap into your potential, try meditation and silence to hear your true heart.
2. *The Law of Giving:* To allow wealth and happiness into your life, you must give to others.
3. *The Law of Karma:* Accept the fact that everything you do will affect the future, and everything you do is affected by the past.
4. *The Law of Least Effort:* Success does not require a struggle. Do less and accomplish more.
5. *The Law of Intention:* Whatever you concentrate on will grow stronger. Add intention and you will progress toward your goal.
6. *The Law of Detachment:* To acquire anything you must relinquish your attachment to it. In other words, concentrate on the process, not the outcome.
7. *The Law of Dharma:* Discover the talent in your life—your dharma—to achieve the deepest kind of success.

Chopra's vision of success can be seen in the story of Vanessa Singer, a pretty girl with musical talent.

At the age of twenty, Vanessa suffered a massive brain hemorrhage. Bedridden and under twenty four-hour care, she found comfort playing the guitar and writing songs while doctors solemnly pondered the slim chances of her survival. It was finally decided that the best option was an operation to remove a large portion of her left brain. After an eight-hour surgery and extensive rehabilitation, Vanessa was on the long road to recovery.

"One day I was writing a song," says the thirty-year-old entrepreneur, "and I was hearing a percussive sound in my head. I had a shaker, but I didn't have anyone to play that sound for me."

So she sliced open the shaker and wedged a guitar pick inside. And, in 1994, The Rhythm Pick was born. Although the dummy version did not sound as good as she knew it could, Vanessa took it to a store that sold guitars. The new-product advisor, Cliff Calabro, tried it and liked it. Vanessa says: "It took all my strength not to do cartwheels through the store."

Cliff and Vanessa started a fledgling company, Take Your Pick, Inc., and launched The Rhythm Pick at a trade show in Nashville a year later. Within two years they were pulling in an estimated $3 million in sales.

Vanessa credits her near-death experience with the impetus to move ahead with her dreams.

"We take life for granted," she says. "That's something I'll never do again."

You only have a few opportunities.
If people say you're crazy, put blinders on and ask
where that's coming from. Be around go-getters.
—PIXIE YATES

■

Stephen Covey, motivational speaker and author of *The Seven Habits of Highly Effective People*, says you can be successful beyond your wildest dreams. It's simply a matter of implementing a few basic habits—many of which we already possess.

Covey's extensive research of highly successful people boils down to these seven steps:

1. *Begin with an end in mind.* Clearly define what you want to accomplish.

2. *Put first things first.* Prioritize and organize your personal and professional life so the most important things are taken care of.

3. *Instead of merely reacting, choose your response to a situation.* In other words, listen carefully before you speak and choose your words wisely.

4. *Seek to understand, then be understood.* We tend to rush to fix a problem without knowing exactly what the problem entails. Instead, study what needs to be done, taking past mistakes into consideration. Seek the advice of others and then take corrective action.

5. *Value people's differences.* Don't seek to mold everyone into your way of thinking.

6. *Take care of yourself.* Your physical, spiritual, mental and social self make all other habits possible. Make sure you eat right, exercise and take time out for relaxation and meditation.

7. *Think win, win, win.* Keep your eyes on the prize and maintain a positive attitude about getting there. Do not let setbacks throw you off course.

Great works are performed not by strength but by perseverance.
—SAMUEL JOHNSON

■

After finding her talent as a fashion designer, Jennifer Barclay went from rags to riches in a few short years. Now, in her early thirties, she continues to pursue her dream of excellence. Jennifer is considered one of America's hottest fashion tycoons, with such celebrities as Cher, Meg Ryan, Oprah, Rosie O'Donnell, Courteney Cox and Goldie Hawn clamoring for her designs.

"As a teen, I never found anything in the stores that felt like me, that made me feel good about myself—that I even wanted to wear," says Jennifer, who earned the Outstanding Young American award several years ago. "So I made my own clothing."

As a seventeen-year-old entrepreneur with just $100, she began experimenting with block printing in the basement of her parents' home in Bucks County, Pennsylvania. She used old tablecloths, cutting them up and fashioning them into garments. While she was a student at Temple University Art School in Philadelphia, Jennifer took 60 samples of her clothing designs to a New York crafts festival. She returned home with 6,000 orders—and no clue as to how to manufacture or ship the product.

"I wasn't afraid though," says Jennifer. "The truth is, anything is possible."

Determined to succeed, she first learned about fabrics. Next, she used the Yellow Pages to locate a factory for rent, and she borrowed $4,000 from a bank with a loan co-signed by her dad. Then she buckled down to work.

Today Jennifer Barclay is the owner and president of Blue Fish, a clothing manufacturing company in Pennsylvania with retail outlets across America. She designs imaginative, free-flowing cotton garments and oversees 200 employees in a sprawling 60,000-square-foot factory.

"If you have a new idea, share it," she advises. "There is always a market for creativity. And only you can give yourself the power to succeed."

> I'd rather be a failure doing something I love
> than be a success doing something I hate.
> —GEORGE BURNS

■

If you want things to change—for the better—you must know how to change. That means having a plan. You might see the brass ring you want to grab, but it's so near and yet so far. So how can you get it? Do you wait until the merry-go-round swings past and make a wild grab? Pretty chancy, if you ask me.

Leaving too much to luck will not bring the rewards you so desperately desire. And it can make life a whole lot worse. For instance, a woman who wants a baby and settles for the first partner who comes along may find that she's picked herself a first-class loser who not only cannot provide but who abuses her as well.

People who vow to give up alcohol, drugs, tobacco or overeating are bound to fail if they do not have a plan. Altering destructive behavior takes more than just a wish or a prayer. You must have a goal and a scheme for getting there. You may go on a crash diet and you may peel off the pounds, but without a long-term plan to keep the weight off, you can end up weighing more than ever.

Says Dr. Mark Goulston: "An ounce of planning is worth a pound of luck. Wanting things to be different, without a strategy for making them different, will keep them the same."

An optimistic attitude should go hand-in-hand with your game plan. Being bright and focused can help you make contacts, get hired and promoted, win friends and influence people. And when those pink slips are being handed out, it can keep you from getting fired. Facing discouraging situations and overcoming hurdles while maintaining a positive frame of mind is a winning combination that is bound to be recognized in whatever field you have chosen.

Bright ideas are welcomed everywhere. However, there is a right and a wrong way of presenting them. For example: You have just been hired and you see an opportunity to make an improvement in the procedure. So you say, "I have a better way to do it." Although you mean well, this is a red flag for most employers. Get to know how things work before trying to implement changes. Even worse is saying, "We used to do it a different way." Whining, complaining, or criticizing your current work environment is the fastest way to fall into disfavor. So choose your words wisely and present them cheerfully.

Judith Thompson, CEO of Thompson Brooks, Inc., a San Francisco contracting firm, says: "Optimism includes respect, faith, vision, and commitment. I owe the success of my company to my own personal optimism and that of the people we've hired."

Optimism translates into motivation, hard work, and team spirit, which in turn translate to a positive attitude.

> **Never complain. Constantly smile.**
> **And if you're asked to walk ten miles, walk twenty.**
> —DEBBIE MATENOPOLOUS

■

From the time Cheryl Pruitt was five years old, her dream was to be crowned Miss America. The little girl from Ackerman, Mississippi, took piano and voice lessons and kept her eyes on the prize. But her quest for the crown nearly came to a screeching halt when she was eleven years old and a serious car accident left her physically challenged. Her family was told she would never walk again.

For ten months Cheryl wore a total body cast. When it came off, she walked with a severe limp and her face was marred by 100 stitches. It seemed certain that Cheryl's dream had come to a tragic end.

And yet, Cheryl persisted. She credits physical therapy and prayer with the successful healing of her legs. At the age of seventeen, she tried out for her first county beauty pageant—and lost. The following year she lost again. But she did not give up. On her third try, she won at the county level but lost by a landslide in the state competition. By the fifth year, she was crowned Miss Mississippi. She was twenty-two and still dreaming. In 1980 Cheryl made it to Atlantic City, where more than 75 million television viewers watched her walk down the runway as Miss America—our new beauty queen. Cheryl's heartfelt persistence and soulful pursuit of personal excellence were the dynamics that made her dream come true.

You should expect setbacks, strikeouts, and criticism. If your goal is to lose weight, there will be plateaus and weight gains. If your goal is to be a public official, there will be elections lost. If you want to be a school principal, you'll have to pay your dues first as a teacher or administrator. If I want that best-seller, I have to expect many, many rejections without becoming discouraged.

"When people around you begin to criticize and second-guess you, don't get defensive and don't look for others to blame," suggests Steven K. Scott. "Just ask them to put their thoughts and suggestions in writing so you can analyze what happened and see a little more clearly."

Clearly define what it is you want to accomplish.
—STEPHEN COVEY

∎

If your goal is to succeed in business, you must dress the part and know how to play the game. Correct image is the first step up the corporate ladder.

"While women need to dress for success, it is important to project the professional image," says Michele Bellisari, founder of Image Management Consultants in Boca Raton, Florida.

A professional image is not about designer suits. It's about self-esteem. Put a $700 outfit on someone who thinks she doesn't stand a chance of being hired or being considered for a promotion, and that's an outfit gone to waste.

"Image is your best asset," adds Bellisari. "It is about walking tall." Here are some of her tips for dressing and acting the part.

- *Dress appropriately.* Be well-groomed. Look the part. Make sure shoes and purse are clean and coordinated. Keep jewelry to a minimum.
- *When dining with a prospective employer or financial supporter, be decisive about ordering.* Don't salt your food before tasting it. You need not lick the plate, and never take home a doggy bag.

- *Learn corporate etiquette* and understand corporate culture, such as dress code, expected conduct and who is the power executive.
- *Learn about using e-mail.* Do not use it to vent hostile feelings or to disparage coworkers.
- *Know what is appropriate banter.* Stay away from politics and religion, and jokes or stories that are in bad taste.

> You can't do it all yourself. Don't be afraid to rely on others
> to help you accomplish your goals.
> —OPRAH WINFREY
> ∎

One of the most important resources for achieving your goal is networking with the right people—people who can boost you up the corporate ladder or help you get where you want to go.

"It stands to reason that the more successful you are in getting others to cooperate with you, and the more people you can solicit as allies, the greater your chances of achieving positive results," says Anne Boe, author of *Networking Success.* "Networking is getting together to get ahead."

Who you know can make all the difference when it comes to snagging a job, as this excellent example of networking shows.

Susan Peacock had moved from Indiana to South Florida and desperately needed a job. She had recently been certified as a registered dietitian, but the newspaper ads had not helped her find a position in her field. Susan is an avid in-line skater; to network she joined The Beach Bladers of South Florida for a Sunday-morning skate. I belong to that group and at lunch after the skate Susan and I found ourselves at the same table.

During the schmoozing that followed, I asked Susan about her line of work. "I'm a registered dietitian, but I can't seem to find work," she said.

Incredibly, my daughter Zena is also a registered dietitian and had recently been hired for a new job. I suspected that her previous position had not yet been filled. So I gave Susan my daughter's number and suggested she call. Within two days, Susan had been hired for the job!

When you vie with other applicants through the want ads, you are no better off than the next person. If you can get referrals, recommendations and direct connections, you increase your odds of beating the competition. Susan, who mentioned my daughter's name, was hired before the hospital had a chance to place an ad in the newspaper.

The empowering part of networking is that you do the selecting. *You* are in charge of your network and your feelings, and *you* are the one who controls your destiny.

Totally believe in your pursuit.
—CARL DESANTIS

■

Investor's Business Daily, a newspaper for serious investors, has spent years analyzing leaders and successful people in all walks of life. Here are their tips for turning dreams into reality.

- Always be positive.
- Think success, not failure.
- Beware of a negative environment.
- Write down your goals and dreams, then develop a plan to reach them.
- Don't be afraid to get started. Just do it.
- Never stop learning. Go back to school, read books, get training and acquire skills.
- Be persistent and work hard. Never give up.
- Learn to analyze details. Get all the facts, all the input.
- Learn from your mistakes.
- Focus your time and money. Don't let other people or things distract you.
- Be an innovator. Following the herd is a sure path to mediocrity
.

- Communicate effectively with people.
- Learn to understand and motivate others.
- Be honest and dependable. Take responsibility—otherwise, none of the above will matter.

> Don't be afraid to fail and confess. If you fail more than most
> even try, and learn why, you'll fail your way to success.
>
> —DAN JENKINS

■

Although the maxim "Don't talk to strangers" is a strict rule for children, it can be moderated for adults. Like the example above, positive networking often comes from strangers. Pleasant banter with people you meet at parties, in the supermarket, in restaurants and at the mall or any public place can be your ticket to success. Start with simple chatting and work toward creating an information exchange so you can get the other person to open up.

Anne Boe suggests approaching others in a natural, easy way. "A genuine smile is a great icebreaker. Have several conversation-generators in mind. Perhaps you'll find you have something in common." With luck, you will find one thing leading to another. And do not be afraid to make your requests known. Susan Peacock was forthright in saying she needed a job. Without that statement, I would not have volunteered the information about my daughter's vacated position. Another example: I was introduced to two literary agents by talking to several of my coworkers.

Speak up. You never know where it might lead.

Networking can include friends; however, your good friends are the emotional support you need, especially during difficult times. They are your safety net and your emotional base, allowing you to take risks, overcome fear of rejection and move toward your goals. Your network is only as powerful and reassuring as your relationships, so nurture your friendships well. These are the people you will fall back on when the going gets tough. And these are the people who will ask for your help when it is needed. Therefore, it is important that you pick your friends judiciously. Friends who are negative or needy are draining. They will deplete your energy and your resources. When you need help, they will not have the time or the means to assist you.

"People are divided into the givers and the takers," I told my daughters as they were growing up. "Takers will suck you dry and then move on. Givers are there for you when you need them, to replenish your spirit and even provide financial support, if that's what you need."

If you are to succeed, you must remove toxic people from your life. They are anchors, not buoys. Friends who are positively oriented and well-grounded will help you achieve your dreams by becoming your own personal cheering squad.

> **Will you help me? Those are the only words you need to say, and someone will help you.**
> **—TOM HARKEN**

■

A partner may also help you achieve your goal of success. But beware: A partner can be as much of a drawback as an asset. Author Steven K. Scott summarizes the attributes of a partner who can help you move forward, if this is the route you select.

- A partner should not be a carbon copy of you.
- A partner should compensate for areas where you are lacking.
- A partner should share your vision with the same excitement.
- A partner should have the highest ethical and moral principles.
- A partner should be totally committed.
- A partner should be a positive person.
- A partner should be someone who takes a hands-on approach instead of simply talking about what should be done.

And don't think that good friends always make good business partners.

Two women I know, whom I'll call Sally and Amy, decided to expand on Amy's successful upholstery business by adding a line of antique furniture and knick-knacks. They both put money into the pot and began buying and selling. But only a few months into the venture, Sally took over the operation, running things her way without Amy's input. Soon their small business venture was a veritable battleground.

Then one day Amy opened the door to her shop and found all the antiques had been removed, along with the fixtures. The bank account, into which she had just deposited $10,000, was closed, the money gone.

"I was wiped out overnight," she confided to me. "Who could have known it would end like this?"

Amy still has her upholstery business and she's a survivor. But it will take a lawsuit and plenty of hard work to get back what is rightfully hers. And the women's friendship may never be repaired. So if you are going into partnership, make sure you have picked the right partner.

> **Never stop believing! Never give up! Never quit! Never.**
> —JOAN RIVERS

■

Persuasion can unlock more doors than you can imagine. Persuasion is the art of guiding someone's mind through a field of ignorance, misinformation or misunderstanding so that a logical choice can be made. It is a skill that must be mastered if you want to succeed. Others must understand what you are saying and hear the passion in your voice. The scope of this book is not broad enough to encompass all the principles of effective communication and persuasion, however, there are excellent resources on the market. Local Toastmasters groups can also help you learn to be an effective speaker, as well as provide you with a terrific networking group. Find them in your local phone book or on their website.

Persistence is another quality of successful people, and you cannot go uphill without it. Although persistence is not an inborn behavioral trait, it can be developed. Thomas Edison had many, many setbacks and failures while working on his inventions, but it was always his broader vision that ignited his creative juices.

As Steven K. Scott says: "Persistence is not hitting the brick wall, dusting yourself off and hitting it again. That's stupidity. Persistence is hitting the brick wall, dusting yourself off and figuring a way to get over it, under it or around it. If need be, blow it up."

If Miss America Cheryl Pruitt could overcome such incredible odds, you can, too.

To accomplish your objective, you need short-term and long-range plans so you remain in control. Time management is essential. Planning and prioritizing will help you squeeze the most out of each and every day. If, however, you do not focus on the task at hand—if you procrastinate or budget your time unwisely—you will waste precious hours, days, weeks and even years—time that can never be recovered.

Most of us are in a time crunch. There never seem to be enough hours in the day or days in the week. And yet, we all have the same twenty-four hours a day at our disposal. Some people fritter it away, accomplishing nothing, while others manage to make the most of every minute.

Even if your day is hectic and you think you cannot squeeze in one more thing, you must make time for you.

Doreen Virtue, a time-management consultant, says, "There are methods for breaking free. I must emphasize the value of investing little chunks of spare time in goal fulfillment. Ten minutes here, thirty minutes there—these moments add up, like pennies in a piggy bank."

Here are Virtue's top time- and energy-wasters.

Procrastination	Conflicts
Not prioritizing	Disorganization
Overeating	Mindless media (too much TV)
Not delegating	Indecision and worry
Saying YES when you mean NO	

Here are effective ways that you can stay one step ahead of the game:

1. *Force yourself to focus on the task at hand.* Stay in the present.
2. *Take an inventory of your time.* How much of it do you waste in watching television or "shooting the breeze"? Block out the hours in a day and chart them on a graph to get an idea of where time goes.
3. *Make the most of your time* by budgeting it wisely for tasks that will get you closer to your goal.
4. *Delegate time-consuming activities to others.* Nobody said you have to do it all yourself.
5. *Identify those things that rob your time* (chatty friends, silly errands, waiting in lines) and take positive steps to deal with them. Cut conversations short, group errands together and do them during non-peak times. Whenever possible, make yours the first appointment of the day.
6. *Plan and prioritize your day before it starts.* Make a "to do" list and check off items as they get done.
7. *Execute your day as you planned*—or as close to it as possible. Emergencies are not avoidable, but a trip to the mall is.

I am the greatest. I said that before I knew I was.
Don't tell me I can't do something. Don't tell me it's impossible.
—MUHAMMAD ALI

∎

Above all, for success in whatever you do, *keep the passion alive.* Your dream—whether it is possible or not, whether you succeed or not—is *your* dream. It will keep you moving toward a positive goal. And the reward will be yours to keep—whether it's attaining your desired weight, making your first million, starting your own business, writing a best-selling book or starting a family.

"There is no secret to success," adds Virtue, "except having a strong desire to create the life about which you dream, and the determination to follow through. You can have anything you want, unless you believe otherwise. It doesn't matter what your life is like. No matter how time-consuming your job is, how many family obligations you have, what your financial status is, the amount of education or training you have, or what condition your body is in, if you want something badly enough, you *will* achieve it."

Before we get to the affirmations, there are a few more pointers from Helen Gurley Brown, who propelled herself to success at *Cosmopolitan* magazine, where she was a topnotch editor from 1965 until her retirement in 1997.

Once you reach the top, you want to stay on top and you want to be respected. These tips can help keep you flying high and in control.

- *Learn what the office structure is and stay with it.* Operate within your territory; do not cross the boundary into another executive's domain or boss around his or her employees.
- *Don't be cheap.* Being cheap is worse than giving nothing.
- *Spread the goodies.* Don't hoard the accolades and financial profits (even Christmas gifts) without sharing with your key people—the ones who make you look good.
- *Keep your priorities in order and never forget who you are working for.* If you are self-employed, you may find yourself working harder than you ever did for someone else.
- *Hire the best people you can,* then let them do their jobs.

- *Give clear and concise instructions.* Say what you want and when you want it.
- *Never pit employees against one another* or belittle them in public.
- *Praise your good workers.* Give credit where credit is due.

I always wanted to be somebody,
but I should have been more specific.

—LILY TOMLIN

■

AFFIRMATIONS

Success is attainable if you stay focused and work hard. Keep a positive mind-set and an upbeat attitude. And remember, you may not reach the stars the first time around or the second, but you cannot fail to succeed as a person.

- I will identify my dream and visualize a clear picture of it.
- I will set short-term and long-term goals.
- I will not let fear of failure stop me.
- I will use criticism as a learning tool.
- I will find the resources I need to achieve success.
- I will take control of my time by prioritizing and delegating.
- I will remain positively focused.
- I will avoid confrontations, arguments and other time-wasters.
- I will not procrastinate.
- If my mind can conceive it, I have the power to achieve it.
- Nobody can rob me of my dream.
- If at first I don't succeed, I will try, try again.

RECOMMENDED READING
ON SUCCESS

Anderson, Christopher. *Madonna*. Simon & Schuster.

Anthony, Dr. Robert. *How to Make the Impossible Possible*. Berkeley Books.

Boe, Anne. *Networking Success*. Health Communications, Inc.

Branden, Nathaniel. *A Woman's Self-Esteem*. Jossey-Bass Publishers.

Brown, Helen Gurley. *Having It All*. Simon & Schuster.

Butler, Pamela E. *Self-Assertion for Women*. Harper & Row.

Chopra, Deepak. *The Seven Spiritual Laws of Success*. Amber-Allen Publishing.

Clark, Dan. *Puppies For Sale and Other Inspirational Tales*. Health Communications, Inc.

Dowling, Colette. *Perfect Women*. Simon & Schuster.

Goulston, Mark, M.D., and Philip Goldberg. *Get Out of Your Own Way*. Perigee Books.

Kersey, Cynthia. *Unstoppable*. Sourcebooks, Inc.

Meltzer, Barnet, M.D., *The Ten Rules of High Performance Living*. Sourcebooks, Inc.

Phelps, Stanlee, and Nancy Austin. *The Assertive Woman*. Impact Books.

Scott, Steven K. *Simple Steps to Impossible Dreams*. Simon & Schuster.

Virtue, Doreen. *I'd Change My Life If I Had More Time*. Hay House.

Seven

IF YOU WANT GOOD HEALTH

The best way to fully enjoy your life and achieve lasting fulfillment
is to be totally healthy and fit in mind, body, heart and soul.
Life is a most precious gift.
—Dr. Barnet Meltzer

■

*D*O YOU TREAT your body like a temple or as a toxic waste
dump?

The answer to this question may help you understand how
you promote, or sabotage, your physical well-being. If you
smoke, drink, overeat, indulge in junk food or substance abuse,
and ignore warning signs of illness, you do yourself a grave disservice. If you disrespect your body, you will have a heavy price
to pay. It all boils down to how you feel about YOU.

The way you see yourself stems primarily from your childhood experiences. A negative sense of self does not necessarily
mean you are fat and ugly. Instead, you tend to dwell on unhappy childhood experiences, or to see yourself through the eyes of
others who are hurtful and fault-finding.

Some women are estranged from their bodies. They feel dis-
connected, as though their body is a foreign object. They see

themselves as weak and susceptible to illness, and they are not in touch with their sexuality or their strengths. Since they feel they deserve abuse, they allow it to happen. That is madness. No woman deserves to be treated poorly, by others or by herself.

Every woman is a goddess.
—SARI

■

Poor body image can lead to poor health. When a woman does not love her body, she does not take proper care of it. She may postpone dental appointments and eye exams, avoid exercise or skip routine gynecological exams, Pap smears, and mammograms.

Luckily, Olympic figure skater Peggy Fleming has a high regard for her body. It's her livelihood. She stands five-feet-four and weighs 110 pounds. This vision of health stays fit with aerobics and running. She is as lovely and positively focused at fifty-one as she was when she won the Olympic gold medal at Grenoble in 1968.

For Peggy and her husband, Greg Jenkins, fitness and good health have always been a top priority. She neither smokes nor drinks, and she has always treated her body well. So it came as a complete shock when she discovered a lump in her breast.

"I was putting on makeup and fixing my hair in front of the mirror," Peggy says. "I did a few stretches and I saw it. The lump was large enough to cast a shadow. I knew it wasn't normal."

Even though she had recently had a mammogram, instead of pretending the lump wasn't there Peggy hurried to the doctor. He referred her to a surgeon who scheduled an immediate biopsy. A lumpectomy was next.

"He said he got all of it and I would be fine," she says. "In fact, I felt great. I was going to Boston to perform in a TV special so he put in a few extra stitches to keep the wound closed. I felt really lucky."

While she was skating in Boston, her husband learned the crushing truth. She had breast cancer.

"It's like somebody takes a rug and yanks it out from under you," she admits. "I broke down and cried."

Her second surgery was on February 10, 1998—exactly 30 years to the day after her Olympic victory.

Surgeons carved out more breast tissue as well as several lymph nodes. Six weeks of radiation followed. "It was pretty rough going," she admits, but to date, there have been no recurrences.

"Athletes are often put on a pedestal as being the image of health," she says. "But this goes to show it can happen to anyone. Cancer's not a death sentence anymore. Early detection saved my life. Get regular checkups and mammograms and check yourself. Take charge of your life and your health."

> Optimism . . . is a mania for maintaining that all is well
> when things are going badly.
> —VOLTAIRE

■

The complex issue of women's health would require volumes to explain thoroughly—from eating right to menopause, and everything in between. This chapter will cover the basics so that by the time you are finished, you will know how you may be sabotaging yourself. Then you can take positive steps toward eliminating those problems so that you can enjoy optimum well-being.

First, let me ask you: Do you respect your body?

If you don't, the problem may stem from your outlook on life. Research now points to the fact that an optimistic lifestyle has been linked to good health; a pessimistic one to poor health.

An optimist says: "In uncertain times I usually expect the best."

A pessimist says: "If something can go wrong, it will."

What do you say?

Studies have found that robust, strong women take on stress-ful events as challenges and adapt more easily to life changes. They maintain their courage under fire and they learn to bend like the willow in a storm. When troubled waters rise around them, those who are more fragile find the world overwhelming; they tend to be more passive and despairing.

Facing problems directly is the healthy way to deal with life. It puts you in control instead of making you feel victimized. When you believe that your behavior will produce effective results, you feel better about yourself and the world. That kind of thinking boosts your immune system. And it works to your favor in other ways. People who aim for specific behavior changes—such as going on a diet or giving up cigarettes—know-ing they can stick to their commitment, promote their own well-ness both physically and mentally. In addition, people with this type of determination are better able to cope with stress. Research indicates that high stress adversely affects the immune system. It follows, then, that those who can control the level of stress in their lives will fare better, health-wise.

One way to relieve stress is interaction with a circle of friends, coworkers or family members in whom you can confide. Studies have found that loners suffer from a wide variety of ailments and emotional disorders. Their quality of life is diminished and so is their life span. They tend to drink more, smoke more, eat poorly and drive less safely. Without a friend or family member urging her to take care of herself, a woman living alone who finds a lump in her breast is more likely to ignore the problem. She may ask herself, why bother? Nobody cares.

Human beings are good for our health. A support system pro-vides emotional reassurance, tangible items such as money or food, advice, comfort in time of grief, a sounding board, and a physical presence in times of need.

If I can survive cancer, I figure I can do just about anything.

—MARY DIXON

■

Every woman thinks about breast cancer at some time in her life. An estimated 179,000 new cases are reported annually, and nearly 44,000 deaths. Unfortunately, too many women ignore the warning signs, thinking that the problem will go away. Or they may be afraid to hear the truth. Or they are ashamed that their body has failed them.

There is no shame attached to cancer—of the breast or any-where else in your body. Many celebrities have come forward with their stories: Peggy Fleming, Betty Ford, Olivia Newton-John, Shirley Temple Black, Sandra Day O'Connor, Jill Eikenberry, Diahann Carroll.

So has Mary Dixon, who was working in the White House Women's Office and gearing up to attend graduate school in New York when her life was turned upside down. One of the last things she did before leaving Washington was to get a physical checkup.

"The nurse-practitioner told me that she'd detected a lump in my left breast and that I should have a mammogram right away," admits Mary, who was only thirty-five at the time. "My first reaction wasn't fear but annoyance—another last-minute chore."

The mammogram was not conclusive so the doctor suggested an ultrasound test, which detected something abnormal.

She says: "I didn't panic at this news, maybe because I'd always taken my good health for granted. I ate well, didn't smoke, and ran regularly. I had little experience with medical problems."

The doctor scheduled a biopsy and the results were devastating: three lumps, all cancerous. Although Mary was stunned, she was determined it would not change her life. But when the doctor left, she admits she felt chillingly alone and, for the first time in her life, deathly afraid.

Telling her family was not an easy chore, but Mary knew she needed their love and support for the ordeal to come.

"The only way to get through it was to keep myself focused," says Mary, who put off plans to move to New York. "If I gave in to my fears and let myself get depressed, I wouldn't be able to take on the cancer with a vengeance."

Mary faced her options: lumpectomy, mastectomy, implants, reconstruction. She opted for a mastectomy, to avoid the cancer recurring, and reconstruction. The operation took eight long hours.

"I woke up freezing cold with tubes everywhere, and yet I was never more at peace," says Mary. "All my day-to-day worries no longer existed, and nothing mattered but getting through that first night."

One month after surgery she was back at her job, feeling weak but upbeat. Although it lacked a nipple (which was added a year later), Mary's breast had been reconstructed, and with the help of family, friends and supportive coworkers, her life slowly returned to normal. Mary became deeply involved with the National Breast Cancer Coalition and says that she used her cancer experience as a catalyst to get her life moving again.

WHAT'S HOLDING YOU BACK?

Health is wholeness and balance, an inner resilience that allows
you to meet the demands of living without being overwhelmed.
—ANDREW WEIL, M.D.

■

We live in stressful times. People feel trapped and unhappy.
Pollution, addictive behavior, dysfunctional relationships, and
nutritional self-abuse have—in too many instances—replaced
happy, healthy, fulfilling lifestyles. We are in such a rush that we
don't take the time to eat right. The profusion of fast-food joints
attests to that. We are "too busy" for a visit to the doctor, or we
do not feel we are worthy of treating ourselves to the best of
nutrition and the best in medical care.

Here are a few typical excuses that women use for their poor
habits: I don't have time. I like to eat. One cigarette now and then
won't hurt me. A few glasses of wine help me unwind. I haven't
the energy to exercise. I'm afraid to get a checkup . . . what if they
find something?

You can find a zillion excuses for abusing your body. But who
are you really hurting?

When you put yourself at risk, everyone who loves or cares
about you is affected. Too many women die young and need-
lessly, or spend their lives suffering with aches, pains and diseases that could have been avoided.

A new study has concluded that many women who undergo
heart surgery seem to think they are cured and do not bother to
exercise, eat properly or lose weight. Of the 130 female bypass
patients interviewed, most still had the risk factors that brought
them to the operating room in the first place. One year after their
surgery, 58 percent were obese, 54 percent had high blood pressure, 92 percent had high cholesterol. And of the 17 percent who
smoked cigarettes, 10 percent still had not given up the habit. A

spokesperson at Johns Hopkins University School of Nursing, where the study was conducted, says it was obvious that these women were not going to make the changes on their own.

Recent statistics indicate that more than one-third of all Americans are overweight. Being uncomfortable is not the only problem with carrying excess pounds. Obesity contributes to hypertension, diabetes, heart problems, and aching joints. Sure, blame it on a slow metabolism or a thyroid problem or bad genes. The sad truth is that most women do not eat right; they indulge in the wrong things for the wrong reasons, using food as a substitute for love or comfort or God. They then make themselves miserable on fad diets which don't work, and the pounds that have been painstakingly peeled off—plus a few extra—are put right back on. Since they feel they have failed, these people punish themselves by eating, and then eating some more. And gaining weight. And making themselves ill.

The answer lies in a lifestyle change and the knowledge that you are important. You are worth caring for. It goes back to loving yourself. And it means having a high-performance fitness plan.

> Every ten pounds you are overweight is like carrying a bowling ball wherever you go. If you are fifty pounds over, that's five balls. One hundred pounds is ten balls. No wonder it's hard to get around when you are fat.
>
> —JERRY MATHERS

The most important health issues facing women today are nutrition, reproductive health, sexually transmitted diseases, menopause, cancer, depression, heart disease, stroke, osteoporosis, and obesity. Women are living longer. But we are not living better.

"Some five million women in America over the age of 65 have disabilities and over one million are living in institutions," says Bernadine Healy, M.D., author of *A New Prescription for Women's Health.*

Now is the time to take action in your own behalf. Every woman needs someone to guide and encourage her to get proper medical treatment. You can be a medical mentor for others by learning, listening and staying informed of resources and new advances in medical technology. When health is on the line, you must be awake and aware.

The potential for expanding your life has never been better. You can look younger, feel better and have more energy than you did when you were a teenager. However, it means taking care that your immune system operates at an optimum level. That's not all that easy, you say, and you're right. Emotional stress, addictive self-destructive habits, negative thinking, bad eating habits, depression, and self-abusive behavior can, over time, destroy your immune system. However, the process is reversible. You *can* make yourself well.

Nobody but *you* can change your habits or self-destructive behavior. Whether you live a healthy, productive life or suffer from chronic discontent and illness is your choice entirely. Without self-care and self-discipline, managed care is the same as *no* health care.

> Walking is the single most important exercise you can do.
> Unless you buy a treadmill, it doesn't cost anything beyond a
> good pair of walking shoes.
> —CHER

■

Dr. Andrew Weil, the self-help medical guru, says that you can change. Everyone has the power within herself. And he proposes that you can make yourself better within eight weeks! That's only two months. If you live seventy years, it's a single drop of water in the pond of time. This tremendous challenge will require dedication, commitment, and hard work. Are you up to the task?

Weil says he was overweight, ate high-fat foods and drank alcohol and sodas, huffed and puffed climbing stairs and suffered from allergies, hives and migraine headaches when he was a medical student. His heart was not in good shape and neither was his body, which was rarely exercised. Yet he knew that if he wanted to be a doctor who healed others, he first had to heal himself.

Now, when patients come to him with tales of woe, his advice is: there are no magical cures, no quick fixes. The only path to wellness is to change one's eating habits, get regular exercise and learn to handle stress. Sadly, too many people would rather pop a pill or try a fad diet instead of seeking good health by changing their lifestyle.

"You can certainly medicate yourself regularly with painkillers if you are prone to headaches, or with antihistamines if you have allergies, anti-inflammatories if you have arthritis, or sedatives if you cannot sleep, but how much better it would be to solve those problems by modifying diet and patterns of activity and rest and by using natural remedies," advises Weil.

> A body at rest tends to stay at rest . . .
> A body in motion tends to stay in motion . . .
> —ISAAC NEWTON

∎

Inertia, passivity, laziness, lethargy, sloth. While you argue semantics, your body is getting fatter and flabbier by the minute. Getting up off the couch and into action is the hard part. But you are not alone. Millions of Americans are addicted to cocaine, cigarettes, chocolate, alcohol, coffee and food. With the proper motivation, these "drug" habits can be licked. But only if you *want* to stop. Your spouse, significant other, children, friends and family cannot make you change. Even checking yourself into a rehab center may not help: Once you're back in your old surroundings, you may also find yourself back at your old habits.

Case in point.

In 1986 Michael Hebranko weighed an incredible 900 pounds. But with the help of fitness expert Richard Simmons, Michael peeled away 700 pounds and, at a svelte 200, became a pitchman for TV's Deal-A-Meal plan. Then his father died and he went into a downward spiral. The gorging began again. By 1996 he was back up to 800 pounds with suffocating fat pressing against his heart and lungs, making it impossible to breathe. He could not stand or his fragile legs would snap. He was rescued from his home and hospitalized. He lost 300 pounds before he was sent home. In June 1999 he was rescued again, this time weighing an incredible 1,100 pounds—that's more than half a ton! He knows he will die if he cannot get a grip on his eating habits.

"I can make a list of excuses," says Michael, "but I'm responsible. Once I start eating I cannot stop. It's a disease."

Obesity is like any other addiction. And it can be cured.

Ex-smokers say cigarettes are the hardest habit to break. By now, studies have shown cigarette smoking to be potentially harmful to the health, and, in most instances, addictive. On the side of a pack of cigarettes, the Surgeon General of the United States warns: Quitting smoking now greatly reduces serious risks to your health. Yet those who find that smoking yields a feeling of well-being, no matter how fleeting, or that it improves concentration, if only temporarily, are unwilling to give it up.

When you finally decide that you want good health and you are willing to do anything to get it—and as you take control of your body and your life—you may find old habits dying easier than you ever imagined. Giving up chocolate was easy for me once I realized it was playing havoc with my blood sugar levels. Sure, I love the taste—but it gives me a rush, which makes me dizzy and hyperactive, then it drops me down and I feel sick to my stomach. Chocolate may be tempting but it spells danger, which makes it easy to avoid.

At one time Sue, a computer programmer from Boston, didn't think twice about grabbing a doughnut or two from the coffee room at work. Now that she has taken control of her eating habits, she says she is no longer tempted by the deep-fried sugary confections.

"For me, eating a doughnut is like a shot of heroin," says Sue. "They're poison for the body."

Did you know that a chocolate-covered doughnut can have up to 25 grams of fat? They go down so easily, they taste so good—and they are *so* bad for you.

What are your addictions and bad habits? And how can you improve your overall health? Take this quiz, then take a look at the positive suggestions in the next section.

Even if it is not fully attained, we become better by
striving for the higher goal.
—VIKTOR FRANKL

■

CATHY © 1999 Cathy Guisewite. Reprinted with permission of UNIVERSAL SYNDICATE

HEALTH QUESTIONNAIRE

Answer these questions truthfully to get a handle on what areas of your physical well-being could use some improving.

  1. Do you feel you are in control of your physical wellness?
     Yes_____ No_____
  2. Do you pay attention to what you eat?
     Yes_____ No_____
  3. Do you take vitamin supplements?
     Yes_____ No_____
  4. Do you use sunscreen?
     Yes_____ No_____
  5. Is your weight within the national guidelines for your height?
     Yes_____ No_____
  6. Do you have enough energy to get through the day?
     Yes_____ No_____
  7. Do you get regular physical checkups?
     Yes_____ No_____
  8. Do you smoke?
     Yes_____No_____
  9. Do you walk at least 15 minutes every day?
     Yes_____ No_____
 10. Do you work out at a gym or other facility?
     Yes_____ No_____
 11. Do you eat what you want, without regard to fat, sugar or salt content?
     Yes_____ No_____
 12. Is your cholesterol over 200?
     Yes_____ No_____
 13. Do you eat when you're lonely, sad or angry?
     Yes_____ No_____

14. Are you on more than one prescription drug?
Yes_____ No_____

15. Do you eat fast food more than once a week?
Yes_____ No_____

16. Do you have an excuse for not exercising?
Yes_____ No_____

17. Do you walk at least a mile a day?
Yes_____ No_____

18. Do you drink more than one glass of alcohol a day?
Yes_____ No_____

19. Do you worry that you are out of shape?
Yes_____ No_____

20. Do you WANT to improve your health?
Yes_____ No_____

KEY TO ANSWERS:

If you answered No to more than half of questions 1 to 10, you are endangering your health.

If you answered Yes to more than half of questions 11 to 20, you need to take better care of yourself.

FINAL QUESTION:

If you knew you would die prematurely because you overeat, smoke, and don't exercise, would you change your lifestyle?

Yes_____ No_____

POSITIVE STEPS FOR
A HEALTHIER YOU

Push aside the idea that beauty is everything.
Exercise will help you be everything that you can be.
—COVERT BAILEY

■

So you want to be healthy. That's a start. The question is: What are you doing about it?

There is no such thing as perfect health. Health is a temporary state of being which changes over time and under certain conditions. When the body breaks down, your healing mechanism kicks in so you can get back to a condition called "homeostasis," or equilibrium. Since a breakdown or health crisis may occur without warning, it is important to be prepared. When you are caught in the turmoil of a medical emergency, it is difficult to make informed decisions, to read up on the subject, find alternate healing methods, change your diet or give up addictive habits.

A few years ago Alice, an acquaintance from work, was hospitalized so doctors could determine the nature of a tumor they had found in her lung. When I visited her, she said, "I don't know how this happened, I gave up cigarettes five years ago." However, she later admitted that she had been a heavy smoker for forty years. "I thought it was too cool to have a cigarette in my hand when I went out on dates," she added. "If only I knew then what I know now."

Even though Alice made smart choices in her later years, those self-abusing decades had caught up with her.

Medical experts agree that the best offense against illness is a good defense. That means taking care of yourself in every way, keeping your immune system functioning at its optimal level and staying positive in your approach to life.

According to Dr. Andrew Weil, human beings are bodies, minds and spirits—all of which are connected. Conventional medicine addresses our physical bodies. And yet research is now showing the kinship of emotions and immunity—how our brain chemistry can help the healing process. So can prayer and other spiritual ventures.

In other words: *You are responsible for your level of fulfillment or your degree of suffering.*

The major complaint of most women is: "I'm tired. I just don't have the energy." This could be due to any of four major factors:

- You don't "eat healthy" or you do not have a program for healthy eating.
- You abuse your body with alcohol, tobacco or drugs.
- You don't exercise enough.
- You have a medical problem for which you have not sought treatment.

Yes, you may have a physical disability or a chronic medical problem. But for most women the four bullet points above hold true.

You know your body better than anyone—better than your mother, father, husband, lover or doctor. You know what makes you feel ill and what makes you feel good. When you put the responsibility for your wellness on a medical professional without making an effort to understand your own body, you have forfeited your own authority. You have, in effect, disowned your power and given it to someone else. This is a dangerous thing to do.

Only *you* can empower yourself to find the solution to your medical problems. Not long ago I began experiencing some very strange symptoms. As an avid tennis player and in-line skater, I have always counted on my body to support me during times of intense activity. I treat my body well; I don't smoke, drink or eat junk food. Yet suddenly I was dizzy a good deal of the time, I began experiencing a type of dyslexia which affected my writing, and if I exercised too strenuously I "bottomed out." In fact, some days I did not have the energy to exercise at all.

Fearing that something was drastically wrong, I began having anxiety attacks, which gave me digestive problems and hives. I was a mess, and I was frightened. So I hit the books and I began asking questions. In searching for answers, I found an interesting pattern of problems.

Not only was I going through the first stages of menopause (dizziness and fuzzy mental lapses), I had developed a low blood-sugar condition that was causing me to run out of energy. Since I don't respond well to medication, my aim was to regain my former state of wellness without prescription drugs.

First, I made an appointment with my gynecologist, who suggested I might not be producing enough progesterone. Instead of hormone replacement therapy, I began using an over-the-counter progesterone cream. The fuzzies stopped and my digestion improved.

I started to pay more attention to my eating habits, never going more than three hours without food, avoiding sugar and white-flour products and concentrating on protein and complex carbohydrates. I put Power Bars in my car, fanny pack, purse and tennis bag. The dizziness stopped. Now I consume more protein and eat regularly. As for the anxiety, I read that acupuncture works wonders; so instead of getting a prescription for Prozac, I became a human pin cushion for a single one-hour session. The results were remarkable.

Although my minor problems caused me a good deal of distress, I knew the symptoms were not life-threatening. That wasn't the case with Julie Pearce, a nurse and mother of two.

Julie left work one day thinking she had the flu. Five days later and still not better, she went to the doctor for some tests. They revealed a tumor in her pancreas. "The doctor's words hit me like a sack of lead," she says. "He thought it was malignant. I was going to die."

As a nurse, Julie knew that six months was the life span for patients with pancreatic cancer. She was numb, angry and incredulous. She didn't believe that she would not live to see her daughters grow up.

Before any kind of surgery or radiation therapy, Julie had more tests. Amazingly, they revealed no cancer. But the doctor still didn't know why she was sick.

"It's hard to say whether I was more relieved or angry," recalls Julie. "But at that moment a light went on inside my head: *I had to take charge of my own health.*"

Her hunch was that her gallbladder was somehow acting up again, even though it had been removed. The doctors soon discovered she was right. Her body was still producing a substance that interfered with her digestion and caused flu-like symptoms. By piecing together her medical puzzle, Julie realized that certain foods, combined with her hectic lifestyle, caused the attacks that made her ill.

To regain her homeostasis, Julie began bike riding and before long she was riding four times a week. She's lost twenty pounds and feels like a new woman.

"I'm free when I'm riding—it clears my head and helps me prioritize. I don't respond to everything as though it were a crisis," she says.

There's nothing more important than my health.
—JULIE PEARCE
∎

The health information you need is out there. The Internet is a superhighway of data for every illness under the sun, and there are excellent books available at the library or bookstores. In other words, there is no excuse not to be informed. Whatever problem you have, or suspect you have, help is available and support groups (even in online chat rooms) are out there. It is important that you *not* crawl under a rock and hope the problem will go away. Instead of ignoring it, face it, resolve it, take charge of your life and be grateful that we have such amazing technology available.

It was a different situation for Jerri Nielsen, a forty-seven-year-old female physician stationed at the Scott-Amundsen research station located at the South Pole, who discovered a lump in her breast during the winter of 1999. Outside temperatures hovered at 80 degrees below zero, it was dark nearly twenty-four hours a day and no planes could be sent to rescue her.

The credo "Physician, heal thyself" took on an ominous new meaning as Jerri had to perform her own biopsy and administer chemotherapy treatment. Just the thought of driving a needle into one's own breast to look for cancer cells might horrify most people, but a consultant on the case says: "I would assume that somebody who chooses to go to the South Pole is a tough person, a strong character."

In mid-October, with temperatures at a balmy minus-65 degrees and the winds light, two Air National Guard Hercules LC-130 cargo planes landed nearby to rescue her. Dr. Nielsen is now at home in the United States being treated for her breast cancer.

Unlike Jerri Nielsen, you don't have to perform your own medical procedures. But you do have the same bottom line: *You have the power to take control of your life. There is no such thing as being a helpless victim.*

> If you are unable to get out of bed for several weeks,
> something is wrong.
> —MARJORIE BRAUDE, M.D.

∎

In too many instances women's concerns have been brushed aside by male physicians. Recent studies indicate that medical complaints from women are not investigated as aggressively as those from men. Sometimes the description of a problem is no more than a general malaise, a feeling that "something's wrong." This is one reason it is important for you to learn about your problem. And do not rule out depression, which strikes one out of every ten Americans each year. Women are twice as likely to suffer from depression than men. Symptoms may include sad or anxious feelings, not wanting to get out of bed, a sense of emptiness, loss of appetite, sleeping too much or not at all and/or difficulty concentrating or making decisions.

Depression notwithstanding, there are certain physical symptoms that must not be ignored, no matter how trivial you or your doctor may think they are. If you cannot find satisfaction with one medical expert, try another. Be wary of doctors who say, "Don't worry about it" or "It's all in your head." That may be what you want to hear; however, your wellness is at stake. Please do not let a lack of medical insurance keep you from seeking adequate care. In the long run, it is less expensive to identify a disease early in its course. And, ultimately, a funeral is the highest price to pay.

Recently, "Lucky in Texas" wrote to Ann Landers that she was thirty-nine when she was diagnosed with uterine cancer. Her only symptom was a little bleeding after intercourse. A biopsy indicated nothing wrong and her doctor suggested that she had a cervical infection. He recommended a hysterectomy, but said "No rush; you can wait a year or two."

Lucky says she knew something was wrong and insisted on a hysterectomy immediately. The following week, during surgery, a malignant tumor was discovered. It had already progressed to the second stage.

"I went through all the radiation treatments, and luckily, it was caught in time," she wrote. "The doctor is not always right. If you have a gut feeling that something is wrong, it probably is. Listen to your instincts. And don't ever be late getting a Pap test. When I asked my doctor where I would be if I hadn't insisted on the hysterectomy, he replied: 'You would not be here right now.'"

Again, you know your body better than anyone. So these ten important warning signs must not be ignored—no matter what:

1. *Unusual fatigue.* To determine whether your increased tiredness is caused by illness, consider these other symptoms: stiff muscles or joint pain can be caused by arthri-

tis, lupus or Lyme disease; weight gain and sensitivity to heat and cold may indicate a thyroid problem; fever and swollen lymph nodes could indicate chronic fatigue syndrome; dizziness and nausea may be due to pregnancy or hypoglycemia.

2. *Sudden weight change.* Losing more than five percent of your body weight within three months without dieting, or gaining more than twenty pounds within six months without explanation, are cause for concern. Both could be linked with a thyroid disorder or adult-onset diabetes (also called type II diabetes). A large abdominal swelling may indicate a benign tumor, some of which have been known to grow to an incredible 300 pounds.

3. *Fainting or dizziness.* Occasional light-headedness can occur from standing too quickly, which lowers blood pressure; from exercising in the hot sun; or from becoming dehydrated. Dizziness can be the result of an inner-ear infection, Ménière's disease, or a virus that will clear up by itself. However, recurrent bouts of dizziness or fainting should be reported to your doctor. They may indicate an abnormal heart rhythm or an adrenal problem. Since the adrenal glands produce hormones that affect blood pressure, heart rhythm and other vital functions, it is important to make sure your endocrine system is working properly.

4. *Breast changes.* Performing regular self-exams can help you learn which lumps are normal—the benign lumps and swellings that come and go each month with your period—and which ones are potentially lethal. Think about Peggy Fleming, who had just gone for a mammogram when she found her lump. Do not wait. Prevention is well worth the price of an X-ray.

5. *Severe headaches.* Weather-related or tension headaches will usually clear up with aspirin or ibuprofen. More-serious headaches may be caused by high blood pressure, which can also cause blurred vision, shortness of

breath and chest pain. Other causes of severe or persistent headaches include meningitis, bleeding aneurysms and brain tumors.

6. *Chest pain.* Heart problems are the number one killer of American women. While it is rare for a woman in her thirties or forties to have a heart attack, more than 74,000 women between the ages of forty-five and sixty-four had coronary events in 1998. Key symptoms to watch for are shortness of breath, abdominal pain or pressure that does not ease up with a shift of position, pain that radiates to the jaw or neck or down the left arm, trouble breathing, a sick feeling in your stomach, sweatiness, nausea or anxiety. Get to a doctor pronto.

7. *Tingling or numbness.* While a stroke under the age of fifty is not likely, it can happen. If numbness is coupled with weakness, tingling, trouble swallowing or poor coordination and vomiting, get to the hospital at once. Tingling or numbness can also be a sign of a repetitive strain injury (such as carpal tunnel syndrome), an anxiety attack, multiple sclerosis or nerve damage. If the problem persists, seek help.

8. *Enlarged lymph nodes.* Before you get your period, the lymph nodes under your arms or in your groin may swell and hurt. The nodes in your neck may swell and hurt if you have an infection such as strep throat, a cold, the flu or mononucleosis. These swellings usually go away in a few days. However, if the problem persists for more than a few weeks it may indicate Hodgkin's or non-Hodgkin's lymphoma, a form of cancer. The sudden and painful enlargement of lymph nodes anywhere in the body may indicate a severe undetected infection. See a doctor immediately.

9. *Menstrual changes.* You know what your normal period is—how long it lasts and how heavily you bleed. Any change may indicate a problem. Spotting in between, missed periods, heavy discharge, two periods a month,

or intense pain that goes beyond usual cramps may all indicate trouble. Possible causes include fibroids, pregnancy, endocrine problems, endometriosis and endometrial polyps. If you also have pain during intercourse, tender breasts, nausea, lethargy, weight change or sensitivity to heat and cold, consult a doctor. Menopause is accompanied by its own set of difficulties including (but not limited to) dizziness, mental lapses, hot flashes, night sweats, anxiety attacks and digestive disturbances. There are numerous books on the subject, but it also helps to speak to your doctor about this complex time of life.

10. *Frequent urination.* This may be a symptom of diabetes—a disease that affects more than eight million American women, one-third of whom may be unaware they have it. Diabetes can lead to blindness, amputations, kidney disease, heart problems and stroke. A simple blood test can confirm whether or not you have it. Other causes of frequent urination include urinary tract infections and pregnancy. Both of those conditions also require medical care.

Finally, don't let this list terrify you. These are ways your body sends you a message; it's saying, "Uh, excuse me? Something needs attention here!" So if you notice any of the above happening to you, take your body's advice. See your doctor. The results may be better than you expect.

> If your car is getting more frequent checkups than you are,
> that's a danger signal. Don't dodge the possibility that you
> might need a little tune-up or surveillance from time to time.
> —MARIANNE J. LEGATO, M.D.

■

Dvera Berson from New York City began suffering chronic debilitating pain when she was fifty-four. The onset was the result of a freak accident when her adult son tripped and fell on

her. She subsequently developed rheumatoid arthritis, degen-
erative osteoarthritis, cervical spondylosis deformans and
osteoporosis. Dvera, once a model, was confined to a living
hell, existing on medicines, injections, hot-wax treatments and
physical therapy. She wore a cervical collar, back brace and
surgical corset, but nothing helped. She was in a state of
despair.

"I didn't care if I lived or died," she admits.

A friend suggested she spend the winter months in Florida.
The warmth made her feel less achy. Then one hot afternoon
Dvera slid into the pool, which looked irresistibly inviting. She
soon found that swimming relieved some of the relentless pain
she had been living with for so long. Encouraged at the relief,
she developed exercises that relaxed, stretched and strengthened
her weak, sore muscles. Instead of returning to New York, she
stayed in Florida and swam. Within nine months she was free of
pain and Dvera, who had taken charge of her life and defeated
the pain, wrote a book that could help others.

"My book, *Pain-Free Arthritis*, is not a cure, but the exercises
eliminate the pain and restore flexibility," says Dvera, today an
amazing 86 years young. "It's an alternative to medication, disability and surgery."

> I spent a long time being a mother and making sure everything
> was great with my family, but now I think I'm a better mom and wife
> because I take time out to take care of myself.
> —CARLA LINDER MAYER

■

Proper nutrition is an essential key to a well-balanced body
chemistry, which, in turn, means a healthy immune system and
a mind that functions at optimal efficiency. A high-performance
diet does not mean fast foods and empty calories. It means a
high-fiber, low-fat, chemical-free, whole-food eating program.
And it works for everyone, including babies, mothers, fathers,
grandparents, professionals, athletes, and homemakers.

An effective balanced eating plan includes:

- Fresh fruits, vegetables and juices.
- Plenty of complex carbohydrates from whole grains, pasta, potatoes and brown rice.
- Plant and vegetable protein, which are high in amino acids.
- Trace minerals and vitamins, in supplement form if necessary.
- Minimal intake of red meat, but adequate consumption of fish and fowl.
- Moderate intake of dairy products.
- Abundant antioxidants to fight free radicals.

Free radicals are chemical toxins that roam through your body looking for trouble. They result from ingestion of chemical-laden and artificially processed foods, including fast foods. When they are released into the bloodstream they cause incredible damage, including cancer, hardening of the arteries and arthritis.

Foods high in free radicals include: butter, dairy products, saturated fats, salt, beef, pork, caffeine, colas, junk food, and processed sweets. If these edibles are in your diet, you are looking for problems. Antioxidants include fresh fruits and vegetables, whole grains, legumes, beans, sprouts, nuts and seeds. Vitamin E is also useful for fighting free radicals.

Eating right is a matter of balance and moderation. The fact that dairy and meat cause the body to produce free radicals does not mean you have to become a strict vegetarian. A healthy body is the result of balanced nutrition, with a minimum of processed, salty and fried foods. The American Dietetic Association recommends a daily intake of approximately 50 percent carbohydrates, 30 percent protein and 20 percent fat.

Women should be especially aware of their bones, which will become more brittle and less dense with age. Osteoporosis will affect half of all women over 60—that's one out of two women! Osteoporosis literally means "porous bone," and it is often referred to as the "silent disease" because it has no symptoms and it is not diagnosed until a fracture occurs. It is also responsible for the disfiguring "dowager's hump," a variety of disabilities and even death.

With proper nutrition and exercise, bones continue to form, or increase their mass, until we reach our mid-thirties. As we age, our bodies take calcium from our bones, which causes them to become brittle. However, certain critical factors contribute to the likelihood of developing osteoporosis. They are: smoking, excessive alcohol intake, a family history of osteoporosis, lack of exercise, use of steroids and a diet low in calcium. You can have a simple bone density test to measure the health of your bones. But to help prevent bone loss later in life, orthopedic surgeons suggest the following:

- *Get enough calcium.* An adequate daily intake is three glasses of skim milk or two cups of low-fat yogurt or cottage cheese. Regular cheese is loaded with fat—in fact, it is the number-one source of saturated fat for Americans. For those who are lactose intolerant, there are lactose-free products or mineral supplements.
- *Exercise.* Stress on the skeleton helps make bones more dense. If you have arthritis or trouble getting around, try low-impact exercise or use wrist and ankle weights when you walk.
- *Get enough vitamin D.* A deficiency in vitamin D can cause poor calcium absorption. You can take supplements, eat foods rich in vitamin D, or get twenty minutes of sun per day.
- *Eat protein.* Protein—found in milk, meat, fish, eggs, beans and grains—builds strong bones.
- *Try hormonal replacement therapy.* It can increase bone mass up to two percent within a year.
- *Take bone-building supplements.* There are many products on the market that contain calcium in some form.

- *Eat enough calories.* When you crash-diet, your body looks for protein to burn to give you the energy to get through the day. Once the body depletes its supply of fat, it starts using muscle. Eat enough to stay healthy, but stay within the recommended weight guidelines for your height and bone structure.

> Dieting cannot work unless you care about yourself.
> It's about honoring your body and soul. Once you realize that
> you are a worthwhile human being, you will begin to treat
> your body with the respect it deserves.
> —WENDY HAMILTON

To eat or not to eat, that is *not* a question.

If you think you can save calories by skipping breakfast, or lunch, think again.

Fasting, or eating only one meal a day, encourages the storage of fat. Says nutrition expert Covert Bailey: "The body panics when food isn't provided on a regular basis, and it tends to save calories by storing them as fat. If 1,200 calories a day are spread out over five or six small meals, fewer of them will be stored as fat than if all of the 1,200 calories are consumed at one time."

Eating breakfast not only breaks the long fast you've been on through the night, it also improves memory and learning. College students who ate breakfast scored 22 percent higher in a word-recall test, compared to those who generally skipped the meal. Grade-school pupils also performed better, with higher math grades and better attendance. They were less hyperactive, less depressed and less anxious than their classmates who came to school hungry.

Breakfast boosts blood-sugar levels, which are needed to make the neurotransmitter acetylcholine, which is important for memory.

"Eating anything in the morning is better than eating nothing," says David Benton, M.D., of the University of Wales-Swansea in England. "Breakfast jump-starts your brain."

Incredibly, breakfast-eaters tend to be thinner than those who don't eat upon awakening. When you skip a meal, you may overeat at the next meal to make up for those lost calories. If you fast all day, you will gorge at dinner or, knowing you will not have food again for twenty-four hours, you will eat nonstop for the rest of the evening.

It's natural to reach for sweet things in the morning. Doughnuts, cake, waffles smothered in maple syrup and sugary cereals give you a jolt of energy. But you are doing yourself more harm than good. Simply put, here's what happens inside your body.

Calories are the units of energy that keep us going once they are digested. Carbohydrates—the most efficient fuel we burn—come either from starches (such as potatoes, rice, bread and pasta) or from sugars, including honey, molasses, table sugar (sucrose), fruits (fructose) and milk (lactose).

In our bodies, carbohydrates are broken down into glucose, which is a form of sugar that is burned for energy. Glucose goes into the bloodstream, where it drives the brain, muscles, nerves, and all of the body's life-sustaining activities.

Glucose is released into the bloodstream by myriad hormones that keep blood-sugar levels at a normal range—between 65 and 110 mg. Insulin, a substance secreted by the pancreas, is the key player. Its job is to assist in the transfer of glucose from the bloodstream to the cells, to make sure the body has an adequate supply of fuel at all times.

When you overload on carbohydrates or sweets you produce a surplus of glucose, which causes your blood-sugar levels to rise sharply. Your body must decide how much glucose it will use immediately, and how much it will store for future use. Insulin makes the decision.

When you have a sugar overload from too much pasta, cereal, candy, cake or other refined foods, your insulin rushes into action to convert part of that glucose to glycogen. Glycogen is a starch that is stored in the muscles and liver—to be used later, as needed. If all the glycogen storage areas in the body are filled, and there is still more glucose in the blood, insulin will convert the excess to fat.

It often happens that obese, diabetic and overweight middle-age people become insulin-resistant; that is, large quantities of insulin are secreted, but the body cannot use it properly. Since insulin is prevented from transforming glucose to glycogen for energy use, it coverts glucose to stored fat. That fat sits on your hips and thighs and around your middle. It hangs under your arms and forms double and even triple chins.

You want to slim down but your body has become a fat-producing machine!

To deal with the high sugar levels insulin is being secreted all the time, but it cannot do its job. It is overwhelmed by the amount of carbohydrates it must convert. In time, the insulin receptors that turn glucose to fat begin to wear out and you have the onset of adult diabetes.

If you think being overweight is merely a nuisance, think again. It is *downright dangerous*. Eventually, the overburdened pancreas may give up and shut down. With no insulin being produced, you would become insulin-dependent and need daily medication. Diabetes can be a life-threatening illness that increases the risk of heart disease and stroke. It also affects the eyes, kidneys, nervous system, skin, and circulation system, which often leads to amputation of extremities.

One of the early signs of adult-onset diabetes is the sudden unexplained loss of weight. While you might be delighted at first, the problem lies in the fact that blood sugar is no longer being converted into energy or body fat. If you suspect you have this condition, you must see a doctor immediately.

In 1995, Linda Mandel was a walking time bomb. At 210 pounds, the five-foot-five-inch former model was sick of being fat. She hated the thought of wearing anything other than tent dresses. At age forty-four, she felt and looked at least ten years older. Linda had tried every diet available but to no avail. She never peeled off more than five pounds. Food was her consolation whenever she had a bad day.

She says: "My first instinct was to soothe myself with potato chips, but my doctor's warning sprang to mind: 'You'll have to lose weight or you'll die.'"

Suddenly, something inside Linda clicked. She realized that what she needed was a healthy lifestyle. The diet books and miracle potions were dumped in the trash and Linda began walking every day. "After several weeks I was up to four miles a day," she says proudly. "In a year I lost 85 pounds and eight dress sizes."

Linda, who now weighs a svelte 125 pounds, adds: "For years I saw myself as the fat one. Today, I'm the one with the amazing body. I'll say it again—the only way to lose weight is to start exercising."

> Eating your way to wellness is an orderly, natural process. It naturally evolves from responsible nutritional decision making. On-the-go eating results in nutritional imbalance.
>
> —BARNET MELTZER, M.D.

∎

Carla Linder Mayer could barely walk five years ago, let alone run a marathon. At a whopping 288 pounds, the mother of three did not even like to be outside.

"When we'd go on family vacations, I would stay in the hotel or cabin," she says. "I was terrified of the whole world. My weight was a shell that kept me at a safe distance from people and from taking risks."

Weight was an issue with Carla from the time she was thirteen. She was taller than her classmates, standing five-foot-ten. And although at 145, her weight was just right for her frame, she began indulging in fad diets.

"I did the grapefruit diet, the egg diet, and the cabbage soup diet," Carla says. "I tried all the weight-loss plans that promised to burn fat quickly." Instead of slimming her down, the diets made her balloon to her heaviest weight ever.

She went on a well-known weight-loss program and dropped 100 pounds. But when she stopped eating their packaged food, she gained the weight back, plus some. So she stopped eating altogether and entered the terrifying world of anorexia and bulimia. Despite her bingeing and purging, the scale registered nearly 300 pounds.

"My sense of accomplishment was zero, my esteem was even lower," she recalls. Then came the wake-up call. Her brother died suddenly from a heart ailment at the age of thirty-two. Carla enrolled in Weight Watchers and started walking. Within a few weeks, the results were evidenced by her loose-fitting clothes and higher levels of energy. She added another day of exercise and started running. By the age of thirty-nine she had lost 120 pounds and was training for her fifth marathon.

Says Carla: "I'm just an average person going out and pushing myself beyond my comfort level. My success gives people the confidence to do the same type of thing."

Women with high cholesterol should be aware that if you keep your fat intake reasonably low, your cholesterol should automatically drop to an acceptable range. But did you know that two tablespoons of dressing can make your salad more fattening than a steak?

The best way to avoid blowing your dietary budget is to read food labels carefully. Note the serving size. If you buy a box of cookies and there are 3 grams of fat per serving, is that one cookie or five? It makes a huge difference. Also be aware that in reduced-fat or no-fat products the sugar content may be higher. There's a lot to learn about nutrition, but the information is readily available. The bottom line is that when you eat the right foods in the amounts that will keep you feeling satisfied, but not stuffed, you will thrive. But overeating and consuming low-quality toxic fuel will lead to fatigue, anxiety, depression and mental lethargy.

What goes in your mouth affects on your entire body chemistry. Without getting too deeply into this subject, here's what the most common food elements do inside you.

- *Sugar:* Refined white sugar weakens your liver and adrenal glands, overtaxes your nerves, depletes B vitamins and leaches the calcium from your bones. Sweets cause arthritis, tooth decay, bad skin, diabetes, hormonal dysfunction, hypoglycemia (low blood sugar) and added fat.
- *White flour:* Refined flour has no nutritional value. White bread clogs your digestion and puts on weight in the wrong places. It blocks your lymph system and plugs the filters in your liver and spleen.
- *Salt:* Salt damages your kidneys and causes water retention. Excess salt puts you at risk for high blood pressure and stroke.
- *Soft drinks:* Colas contain nothing of value for your body. They are corrosive and highly acidic; they damage your body chemistry with caffeine, sugar and artificial chemicals.
- *Meats:* Red meat is loaded with toxins fed to livestock to fatten them up faster. Red meat has been cited as a risk factor in rectal and colon cancer. It damages the nerves and joints and results in acid-residue toxins in the body.
- *Fats:* Fats block the flow of blood and lead to obesity, diabetes, stroke, hardening of the arteries and heart disease. Excess fat in your diet increases your risk of breast cancer, uterine cancer, gallbladder problems and may contribute to a hormonal imbalance. Plus it looks awful when you put on a bikini.

Interestingly, our ancestors ate better than we did. They dined on complex carbohydrates in rice, whole wheat grains, beans, fruits and vegetables. They garnished meals with herbs such as basil, parsley, watercress and dandelion greens. They used olive oil instead of lard. They ate fish instead of meat.

You, and *only you*, can make yourself hale, hearty and fit as a fiddle. For those you love, be good to yourself. Eat healthy.

> As women exercise, their body fat decreases automatically,
> and their new muscles hold everything in place in
> the most pleasing way.
> —COVERT BAILEY

■

Most women today operate on two fronts: in the workplace and at home. They carry the lion's share of responsibility for chores and for raising the children. They have less time for sports-related activities, in addition to which routine exercise is not a top priority—not when there are five loads of laundry waiting and shopping to be done.

One real problem facing women today is that they must carve time out of their already hectic schedules for regular cardiovascular activity. Research has shown that a woman can prolong her life, feel healthier and have more energy with only one-half hour of exercise a day. That's 15 minutes at lunch and 15 minutes after dinner. Sadly, too many women don't have the time, inclination or will power for even a minimal workout. Even worse is when they use valuable exercise time—health-promoting time— watching soap operas and other daytime television programs.

Interestingly, most inactive adults are the ones who were considered failures in physical education during their formative years at school. They were the last team members chosen and were often humiliated in the locker room or during class. Over the years that shame and embarrassment became the basis for a sedentary way of life. But as an adult—and knowing that your health depends upon it—you may find that it's time to slay those ancient dragons.

"The key to enjoying any activity is feeling successful at it," says fitness expert Joan Price. "And a moderate, realistic approach to exercise gets you in better shape than you were in high school."

She adds that although the past is gone, you should know that you weren't inadequate—the programs were inappropriate. The choices given to us as teenagers were wrong and since we didn't know any better, we thought it was our fault if we weren't the best ones out there.

Now, as an empowered adult, you can pick and choose your sport or your exercise regimen based on your likes and dislikes. No more rope-climbing or jumping rope or counting crunches. "This time you are free to choose your specific program and set your own goals," says Price. "And this time, you will be successful."

Here is the truth: *You can make excuses or you can exercise. You can't do both.*

A lifelong fitness program raises your self-esteem and can become genuinely pleasurable for its own sake.

—JOAN PRICE

■

It's too hot. You're too tired. The kids have the sniffles. The gym's too crowded. You have other things to do. When faced with the choice of whether or not to exercise, the world readily provides us with a million reasons for staying put. And yet the benefits of regular exercise far outweigh the cost when it comes to the investment.

Time-management expert Doreen Virtue says the major benefit for busy people is that after exercising you feel energized. Exercise for one hour and you will get additional energy for two more hours in return. Plus you will continue to burn fat long after you shower off.

For Ray Kybartas, the fitness trainer who has worked with Madonna, fitness is a religion. He says: "You must make the leap of faith."

Long-term goals are not popular in our society, he laments. We want immediate results, the quick fix, a prompt return on our investment—especially when it comes to being in shape.

"Fad diets, liposuction, drug-assisted weight loss, crash-exercise programs hold out the promise of instant results," he says. "But instant weight loss is not commensurate with health. With the long-term pursuit of fitness, weight loss—or more precisely fat loss—takes care of itself automatically."

If a car sits too long without having its engine cranked up, it will become "gunked" up inside and rusty on the outside. The same is true of people. Our bodies were meant to move. Kybartas lists seven major reasons why you should stop making excuses and start working out.

1. *It improves the quality of life.* People who exercise regularly, particularly past the age of forty, stand out from their peers who are unfit and unhealthy looking. Regardless of your age, you will be able to do physical things that most of your peers can only envy. Your attitude will be an inspiration to others.

2. *It slows the aging process.* The news is filled with articles of men and women in their seventies, eighties and even their nineties who are still skiing, parachuting from airplanes, running marathons and surfing. If you are strong, flexible and conditioned you will look younger, feel younger, and probably live longer.

3. *It improves your frame of mind.* Exercise and healthy living build self-esteem and boost confidence. People who are physically fit are less anxious, less depressed, less stressed and more cheerful. Activity reduces the adrenaline in the bloodstream and increases the endorphins, which give you a sense of well-being and calm.

4. *It provides consistent weight control.* Diets may peel away the pounds, but unless you institute a regular workout routine, the weight will return. By eating right and exercising, weight control is consistent and effortless. A healthy lifestyle is the best way to avoid the pitfalls of yo-yo dieting.

5. *It improves cardiovascular health.* Even if you reduce your cholesterol and avoid obesity, it does not guarantee that you are healthy. However, the joy and fun you derive from pursuing an activity will translate into a more positive attitude and a healthier heart. Whatever activity you choose, pursue it with gusto.

6. *It increases strength.* Muscles empower you—to open jar caps, for instance. If your muscles have gone slack, you have done yourself a disservice. Since muscle burns more calories than fat, every pound of muscle you gain increases your metabolism—which means you are burning calories even when you are not exercising. So you can eat more—without guilt or fear of gaining weight.

7. *It improves body chemistry.* Regular exercise changes the way your body processes the hormone insulin. People who are trim produce only half the insulin of sedentary folks, and this, in turn, decreases the risk of adult-onset diabetes. When your body uses insulin more efficiently, it stabilizes blood-sugar levels by drawing on stored carbohydrates. This means you will have a more consistent supply of energy and be less likely to store fat as adipose (or fatty) tissue.

> Too many people dive into a sport and overdo it. Then they stop
> because of sore muscles or a "bum knee" and figure since they
> skipped a week, they may as well give it up.
> —DOREEN VIRTUE

■

If you have not found a sport or form of exercise that you can enjoy, or if you feel that you will never excel at any sport, don't give up. Instead, simply walk. Walking, in fact, is the best exercise you can do. It needs no equipment, except a pair of decent support shoes. (A walking shoe is different from a running shoe. When you walk, your heel takes a beating, as opposed to the ball of your foot when you run. A walking shoe should have a cushioned heel, yet it should be flexible.)

You can walk rain or shine, during every season of the year, in the city or country. It requires no special training and you can walk at any speed, with or without music, alone or with company. It's a terrific way to bond with a child, spouse, friend or coworker. And you can do it for your entire lifetime.

If you take a brisk 30-minute walk, you will have burned 140 calories if you weigh 150 pounds. At 215 pounds you'll have burned 195 calories. If you do that two or even three times a day you will be on your way to a lifetime of fitness.

GARFIELD © 1999 Paws, Inc. Reprinted with permission of UNIVERSAL PRESS SYNDICATE.

Even if you do nothing but walking, it will boost your immune system, lower your cholesterol levels, improve your sex life and sleeping patterns, give you extra energy, relieve depression by sending mood-enhancing chemicals to the brain, reduce PMS symptoms, strengthen bones and reduce the risk of osteoporosis.

And now for the really good news: Scientists at the University of California School of Medicine say that exercise, including brisk walks four hours a week, for at least twelve years, can cut a woman's breast-cancer risk in half. If you didn't have a reason to walk before, this one may get you up off the couch and into a pair of athletic shoes.

Exercise can help a person slim down, but it may also strengthen the body's defenses against cancer, says Leslie Bernstein, author of a new study on the subject. And the sooner a woman starts, the better.

However, she adds, it is important to stay slim since the cancer benefits of exercise seem to be erased by the added risks brought on by weight gain.

"We think that women who are heavier have higher circulating levels of estrogen," she says. Estrogen, a hormone, has been linked to certain cancers and body fat is a way of feeding hormones to the body.

Instead of jumping into a marathon or high-impact aerobics class, begin with a modest goal, perhaps a half-hour, or even 15 minutes of any type of exercise. Build your endurance from there, so you don't get discouraged or hurt yourself and quit.

"To control weight you need at least 30 minutes of walking, at a speed of four miles per hour, at least four days a week," says Cher, a fitness enthusiast. "If you have never walked for speed before, you may want to set your initial goals lower—but advance toward a 15-minute mile. Set your own pace. Even if you're starting from zero and doing only five minutes a day, just add two minutes a day—it's consistency that counts."

Cher adds that with her tight schedule and high stress during the filming of *Mermaids*, she packed on fifteen pounds and lost muscle tone.

Afterward she gave herself three months to shape up before going on tour.

"I threw myself into a disciplined diet and exercise schedule," she adds. "I threw out my M&Ms but allowed myself a treat once in a while. I kept working out like crazy—and, yes, I got results."

If you take up a sport, invest in the proper equipment and get some instruction so you don't injure yourself. And you may find it easier to get started with a buddy. You'll be less prone to make excuses. If you join a club, you'll want to get your money's worth!

Never set your goals so high that you fall short and beat yourself up about it. The tendency is to throw yourself into it for a few days, see no change and say "The heck with this." Be patient. In the long run, the benefits derived will far overshadow the effort it takes and the pain you may experience. In time regular exercise will become as much a part of your life as eating and sleeping.

"Far too may Americans believe that the pursuit of health is a burden, an imposition on their overscheduled, fast-paced lives," says Ray Kybartas. "Yet maintaining a healthy lifestyle is not burdensome—it is liberating. After all, time and money are of little worth without health."

There is no one whose body won't change through exercise. And it's never too late to begin. No matter what your age or physical condition, the time to begin is now.

I believe that most bodies come with warranties for eighty years of productive, relatively trouble-free service, if basic requirements for preventive maintenance are followed.
—ANDREW WEIL, M.D.
■

The quest for physical fitness and better health means acknowledging your bad habits and modifying those behaviors. It means taking responsibility and adjusting your lifestyle. This book is about getting what you want out of life. The truth is that you must be vital, focused, enthusiastic and up to the challenge physically to achieve anything. Conquering your goals while intoxicated or stoned on drugs—yes, even some prescription drugs—is self-defeating. Then you reproach yourself and start on a downward spiral, while your quest for happiness, success, tranquility, respect, love or a stress-free life slip away.

Nurturing yourself means eating right, exercising, cultivating your spiritual side, meditating or praying for peace of mind and activating your plan of action. But first, you should rid yourself of those habits and behaviors that drag you down.

Admitting you have an addiction is the first step toward improved health. Habits such as excess alcohol consumption, overeating, smoking and taking drugs adversely affect the body, which is a finely tuned precision machine. They lower the body's natural immunity to disease and even contribute to a wide variety of diseases.

"Experts at the National Cancer Institute now estimate that 35 percent of cancer deaths are attributable to diet alone," says Dr. Andrew Weil. "And tobacco smoke is the most important environmental cause of cancer."

While one glass of alcohol may help you relax and unwind, alcohol is a dangerous mind-altering substance. If you drink to get happy, you may be surprised to learn that alcohol is a depressant. It works the way you don't want it to. Heavy alcohol use saps your energy by slowing down cell oxidation. Worst of all, it delivers only empty calories to your body.

"Excess alcohol consumption leads to serious health problems, including malabsorption of nutrients and the development of a fatty liver that can eventually result in cirrhosis," warns nutrition expert Richard Earle.

Alcohol can cause liver damage, impaired nutrition, insomnia, hangovers, peptic ulcers and gastritis, as well as contributing to cancers of the mouth, throat, esophagus and stomach. If you drink and smoke, a common practice at bars, you may be setting yourself up for cancer. Alcohol also damages the brain, destroys heart muscle and dulls the senses. Women should pay special attention to the warnings about alcohol and pregnancy, as well as the increased risk of breast cancer.

Overmedicating with prescription drugs can do more harm than good. Anti-anxiety pills and sleeping tablets can zone you out, not only at night, but during the day as well. Mixing and matching, especially prescription and nonprescription drugs can be deadly.

Sleeping pills will put you to sleep, cautions psychologist David Ryback, but their effect is reduced over time as the brain adapts to them. "They may affect your waking life as well, making your performance not as sharp. Eventually they build up in your system, significantly altering your brain and body function."

In addition to legalized drugs, illegal recreational narcotics take their toll on your health.

Any kind of mind-altering drug can cause fatigue, depression and intellectual impairment. Even marijuana can have a deadly effect. Cocaine can kill; so can heroin. If you use these drugs, you are endangering your body and preventing yourself from enjoying maximum health.

Nicotine is one of the strongest and most habit-forming drugs.

Some researchers say it's as addictive as opium. As you puff away, your blood pressure is rising, your heart beats faster and you breathe more quickly. While it may feel pleasurable for the moment, your body is starved for oxygen, and toxins are accumulating your bloodstream. Those toxins include nickel and cadmium, as well as nicotine, tar and other harmful additives.

Now know this: *Tobacco addiction is the most common preventable cause of serious disease in the world.*

Bryan Lee Curtis of St. Petersburg lay dying in a Florida hospital bed, bald, emaciated and looking old and skeletal at age thirty-three. He bravely let the media take photographs of his cancer-ridden body, showing how his 20-year-smoking habit had destroyed his body and his happy family. He died on June 3, 1999, two months after being diagnosed with a virulent form of lung cancer. Do you think this cannot happen to you? Well, it can. It happens to thousands of smokers every year.

Nobody can make you stop. But there are effective ways to give up nicotine, including the patch, hypnosis and anti-smoking gum. Or perhaps you need a good scare, like unremitting coughing attacks, constant sore throats or a spot on your lung. Perhaps you would like to be hooked up to an oxygen tank. If you are concerned with your health, know this: *Smoking is the single worst thing you can do to yourself.*

A lifestyle that includes taking life easy, going everywhere by car, not walking, eating the standard high-fat American diet and foods loaded with carcinogens, smoking, drinking and pill-popping are *not* the path to good health and well-being. You know what you are doing to harm yourself. And only *you* can take positive strides to correct those bad habits and put yourself on the path to improved health and a longer life.

Whenever you think you just don't feel like exercising, imagine
what your life would be like if you were physically incapable of it.
—JOAN PRICE

■

In 1979, Joan Price's car was hit head-on. Even though she was wearing a seat belt, her face was shattered, her wrist broken, her neck fractured, her heel crushed. As soon as she was released from the hospital on crutches, she returned to the health club to get back to her aerobics routine.

Incredibly, that terrible scenario repeated itself in 1995, when her car was hit head-on again. This time her right leg was shattered and her shin and ankle were fractured. But even before she left the hospital, she was exercising on crutches.

"Even on good days I never take for granted that my feet will support me, or my legs will move me," says Joan, who is back to teaching after four years of rehabilitation. "Yet I know the benefits of physical exercise. And I contend that there is nothing wrong with you, your body, or your willpower that stops you. It's all about attitude."

> **Beauty is superficial and fleeting, but health**
> **is profound and lasting.**
> —RAY KYBARTAS

■

AFFIRMATIONS

If Joan can overcome the odds not once, but twice, these affirmations should help you on your own road to better health.

- I will be good to myself.
- I will treat my body with respect.
- I will stop making excuses and begin exercising daily.
- I will eat nutritious foods and read labels.
- I will avoid empty calories and food that is bad for my body.
- I will not eat because I'm angry, lonely or depressed.
- I will stop smoking.
- I will consume alcohol moderately.
- I will seek medical care on a regular basis.
- I will keep my body healthy by any means possible.
- I will pay attention to my body and how it feels.

RECOMMENDED READING
FOR GOOD HEALTH

Bailey, Covert, with Lea Bishop. *The Fit or Fat Woman*. Houghton Mifflin Co.

Healy, Bernadine. *A New Prescription for Women's Health*. Viking Press.

Kybartas, Ray. *Fitness is Religion*. Simon & Schuster.

Meltzer, Barnet, M.D., *The Ten Rules of High Performance Living*. Sourcebooks.

Nelson, Miriam E., Ph.D. *Strong Women Stay Slim*. Bantam Books

Price, Joan, *Yes, You Can Get in Shape!* Pacifica Press.

Ryback, David, Ph.D., *Look 10 Years Younger*, Prentice-Hall Publishing.

The PDR Family Guide to Nutrition and Health, Medical Economics.

Virtue, Doreen. *I'd Change My Life If I Had More Time*. Hay House.

Warga, Claire, Ph.D. *Menopause and the Mind*. The Free Press.

Waterhouse, Debra, *Outsmarting the Midlife Fat Cell*. Hyperion Press.

Weil, Andrew, M.D. *8 Weeks to Optimum Health*. Alfred A. Knopf.

Wiatt, Carrie Latt, *Portion Savvy*. Pocket Books.

For information on breast cancer, call the National Comprehensive Cancer Network at (888) 909-6226 or the American Cancer Society at (800) 227-2345. Or try web sites www.nccn.org/ and www.cancer.org/.

Never Quit

Keep pressing on and never quit
It's what you want, that you will get.

Dream big dreams and don't forget
They will come true if you never quit.

Keep on smiling with you in your heart.
Let no one tear your dreams apart.

Keep moving on and don't forget
You will get what you want if you never quit.

—Flora Cousins

■

Eight

IF RESPECT IS WHAT
YOU WANT

All I need is a little respect when you get home, r-e-s-p-e-c-t, baby,
I don't want much, I just want respect wherever I go.
—ARETHA FRANKLIN

.

DURING MY CHILD-REARING years, whenever a birthday or
holiday approached and my daughters asked me what I
wanted, I replied with one word: "*Respect.*"

According to the dictionary, respect means *being held in high
regard*. Whatever your line of work—whether you are a homemaker or CEO—you are entitled to be treated with politeness,
courtesy, even admiration. While women have come a long way
over the past thirty years in terms of equality, in our culture
respect for females is still sorely lacking.

I learned more in two years sitting next to Barbara Walters
than I did during my entire education.
—DEBBIE MATENOPOULOS

.

One woman has blasted through the disrespect of her peers and earned admiration worldwide. Barbara Walters, now called "The First Lady of Television News," fought her way to the top in the course of an awesome career that has spanned nearly four decades. She has interviewed everyone from Fidel Castro to King Hussein, snagging interviews no one else could: Colin Powell, Christopher Reeve, Michael J. Fox as well as Monica Lewinsky, as co-anchor of TV's 20/20.

What makes Barbara so special?

As one journalist says: "She's an industry power player, a pervasive TV personality commanding a respect that, well, you gotta respect."

But it wasn't always that way. As a fledgling reporter, Barbara wanted to break into the male-dominated world of TV broadcast news. It was a daunting challenge for a woman with a speech impediment. Yet she was always gracious, standing her ground with quiet dignity, a classy lady. Although she stands five-feet-five, she appears much taller.

"I've gone through enough in my life," she confesses. "I am very aware of how hurt people can be. I know my reputation used to be for being very brash and very aggressive. And when you do a political interview, you still have to do that. But I know how tender people are. I don't have to anything to prove anymore."

Walters has achieved a level of prominence, both professionally and socially, that eclipses most of the celebrities she interviews. She appears in the society pages and on best-dressed lists; she is an A-list hostess and dinner speaker. Now in her late sixties, Barbara earns a reported $10 million a year.

Her father, theatrical producer Lou Walters, made scads of dough in show biz—and lost it all. Her mother, who lived well into her late nineties, provided a stable home environment for Barbara and her older sister, Jacqueline, who was born mildly retarded. Nevertheless, Barbara admits: "I didn't have a happy-go-lucky childhood."

When she was seven, her dad opened the Latin Quarter, a wildly popular nightspot during the 1940s and '50s. Suddenly they were rich and Barbara was sent to private school. But when she was twenty-three, Lou had a heart attack and lost it all. Says Barbara of her dad's debt: "They came and took everything. If there was a defining moment in my life that was it."

From the time Barbara was a kid, her motto was: *I have to succeed, I have no choice.* She was smart, not cute; she did not play coy games. She wanted to be accepted for who she was, and what she could offer.

Her career started with writing and producing segments for CBS's *Good Morning.* In 1961 she was hired to write occasional on-the-air features for NBC's *Today* show. Her big break came during the 1964 Democratic convention when she filled in on a trial basis following the departure of Maureen O'Sullivan. Barbara remained with CBS for twelve years, but it wasn't always easy. Anchor Frank McGee didn't like her. It wasn't until he died that she was promoted.

"They made me an anchor, literally over his dead body," says Walters, who was forty-three at the time.

In 1976 she was wooed with an incredible $1 million offer to co-anchor the *ABC Evening News,* as well as produce and appear in four prime-time specials. The problem this time was Harry Reasoner, who did not try to hide his discontent.

"I would walk out there and nobody would talk to me," recalls Barbara. "It was horrible. There were awful headlines every day."

Barbara-bashing was in vogue. She was attacked for everything from her gender to her pronunciation. "I was drowning without a life preserver," she says.

Quitting is not Barbara's style, nor is throwing temper tantrums. She did not make unreasonable demands, and she did not insist upon acceptance. Instead she worked her way through the trouble with quiet dignity and self-respect. She interviewed Fidel Castro and other international leaders with a professionalism that impressed everyone.

Says fellow newscaster Ted Koppel: "We were fully expecting her to be a royal pain in the ass, but she turned out to be great. She could take a lot of kidding."

But Koppel's admiration did not stop the media from disrespecting Barbara's decision to return to work after giving birth to her daughter, Jacqueline. At that time mothers were expected to stay home with their babies. But Barbara prevailed and triumphed. Today she holds no grudges, nor does she regret her three failed marriages. "I knew I'd never make the house-and-white-picket-fence scene," she admits.

Now, as busy as ever, Barbara has been called "a force of nature."

"She's in a class by herself," adds Koppel.

There is a valuable lesson in Barbara Walters' fascinating rise to the top. While you may not want to be a TV anchorwoman, you still want and deserve the respect that she has earned. So how can you get it?

No one is born with low self-esteem. We acquire it, often because we have internalized other people's faulty perceptions of us.
—DR. JOYCE BROTHERS

■

WHAT'S HOLDING YOU BACK?

If you spend your life deferring to someone else,
you lose yourself. It's a high price to pay to be liked.
—JUDGE JUDY SHEINDLIN

■

In real life people judge not only the merit of what we do and say, but also our worth as a human beings. But we don't have to buy into the faultfinding of others.

"Did it ever occur to you that if someone disapproves of you, it might be his or her problem?" asks Dr. David D. Burns. "Disapproval often reflects other people's irrational beliefs. There will, of course, be occasions when disapproval will result from an error on your part. But that negative criticism can only be directed toward a specific thing you did, not at your worth. A human being cannot do wrong things all the time."

Although we like approval far better than criticism, we cannot let our good feeling about ourselves be determined by others. Self-respect is essential before we can expect others to respect us.

By reacting to faultfinding with anger, a defensive attitude, harsh words, getting drunk, taking dope, quitting or lashing out, you project negative signals. Even worse is *believing* and *internalizing* other people's disapproval of you. It is far better to use criticism—whether or not you agree with it at the time—as a guide to excellence. More often than not, there is a nugget of truth to it.

One of the steps you must take to move ahead in life—no matter what your dreams or goals are—is to become more confident about yourself. This means being aware of your attitudes, actions and reactions—as well as the consequences they bring. If you have been submissive and now begin to behave with more assurance, you will be upsetting the social apple cart, so to speak. Friends, coworkers, employers, business associates, family members, neighbors and even your spouse may be unprepared for such changes. You may find yourself in uncharted territory and unprepared for the barrage of opposition that may occur.

One way that people lash out when they are unsure of themselves is to spit out labels. Labels can be especially demeaning. They are a quick and effective way of putting a woman "in her place" to prevent her from voicing her opinion, which might change the status quo.

For instance a woman can be labeled:

- A *bitch* when she suggests a better way of doing something.
- *Unfeminine* when she takes on a traditionally male role.
- *Rude* when she offers a critical suggestion.
- *Aggressive* when she pushes her point of view.
- *Selfish* if she puts herself first.
- *Ambitious* if she wants a higher-paying position or a promotion.

Other belittling labels include nag, ball-breaker, hag, egomaniac, bossy, shrew, domineering, pushy, shrill, hussy and gold-digger. There is no escaping the fact that women are often unfairly slammed with derogatory monikers for no apparent reason.

Barbara Walters, basically a successful woman in a male-dominated media, was considered pushy because she wanted to be a television journalist. The men around her couldn't sit back and allow their territory to be invaded without taking a stand. Fortunately, it didn't work, and the groundwork was laid for a succession of comely, talented women to make the nightly news more enjoyable and more interesting.

And actress-dancer-singer Jennifer Lopez, who began her career as a Fly Girl on Fox's *In Living Color* in 1990, had an inner voice nagging her to do more. So the media quickly labeled her too ambitious.

"People try to write about it as if it's a negative thing," she says, "but I don't see it that way. If I hadn't made it, I would still be trying to make it. I would just be working and working at getting there."

> Sticks and stones may break my bones,
> but names will never hurt me.
> —NURSERY RHYME

■

If only that were the case. In fact, names do hurt. Even worse, they can lead to negative self-labeling, as well as destructive behavior which, if we allow it to be, is turned against ourselves.

In the 1950s, Joan Rivers tried to break into the world of male-dominated stand-up comedy. She was fired from her first two jobs and her agent let her go. They said she was "too old," and that she wasn't "right" for television. Even her parents told her she was wasting her life. Now, who's laughing all the way to the bank?

Nancy Austin, a management consultant, explains that if you feel you are being impolite, bossy or bitchy when you assert yourself, you may inhibit your confident behavior and weaken your decisive stance.

"Other people's expectations of how you behave are being thwarted if you have been consistently passive with them and are now being assertive," she adds. "They will quickly label your behavior in an attempt to inhibit it, fearing they may have to change, too."

When labeled in a disparaging way, women react differently. Some allow themselves to become doormats for abusive men, feeling that they do not deserve better. Others set rigid limits on the way they react, expressing their opinions and feelings only under very restricted circumstances—the old "if this happens, then I'll speak up" scenario.

Still others take a defeatist attitude. Instead of voicing their ideas, they anticipate being shot down, ignored or discounted. So they say nothing. Others internalize the negativity, and this often leads to inaction and depression.

So how can this self-defeating self-criticism be turned around to gain the respect you want?

Be aware that belittling labels are *meant* to hold you down. Be attentive to how you let them interfere with your self-assurance. Then monitor any negative behavior that may result from those labels, and make a conscious effort to turn this behavior into a secure and positive attitude.

You might be asking what this has to do with getting respect. The answer is that developing an assertive attitude is an important part of becoming an assertive woman. And, labels or not, confident women *do* get respect.

Inner wisdom evolves out of trusting yourself in spite of what's happened around you.
—STANLEE PHELPS

■

Judge Judy Sheindlin, TV-star magistrate, became an expert on human behavior during her tenure on the bench in New York City's family court system. After observing hundreds of women who made foolish choices, she says the common denominator for stupid behavior is a lack of self-esteem.

"Women who lack self-worth put themselves in bad business situations and tolerate demoralizing and demeaning conditions," chides the author of *Beauty Fades, Dumb is Forever*. "They don't choose their mates, they allow themselves to be chosen. They stay in relationships that are untenable, with men who are physically and emotionally abusive."

She advises: "Set your standard and then wait for a man who has those qualities and treats you with respect."

When Judge Judy's first marriage ended after twelve years,

she was left alone with two young children and a mountain of doubts and fears. However, she had control of her destiny, which is all that really mattered. She says that, in a nutshell, is the definition of self-esteem.

When life is calm and on track, it's easy to be centered and guided by your inner wisdom. However, when turmoil arises, when life gets chaotic, we tend to become frazzled and upset. That's when it's important to remember that every obstacle is a natural and necessary step on the road to achieving your dreams.

Often women react to difficulties by becoming defensive, angry and hurt. Instead of dealing with a situation rationally, they either lash out (with hysteria, crying or temper tantrums), act in self-defeating ways (quitting or self-abuse), or retreat into themselves (refusing to talk or becoming passive).

The way in which you react to external stimuli usually stems from childhood. Too often women sell themselves short, or, when something goes wrong, they take the blame—although the fault lies with others.

David D. Burns says that if you grew up with constant disapproval and developed the bad habit of automatically looking down on yourself, that reaction is perfectly natural. "But," he adds, "it is your responsibility as an adult to think the issue through realistically, and to take specific steps to outgrow this particular vulnerability."

More women than you might imagine are prisoners of their own passive outlook on life. They do not believe they are valuable, so they allow themselves to be used or abused. They sell themselves short and do not speak up for themselves. And they get zero respect from others. The bottom line is this: *Self-esteem comes from within.*

Says Dr. Joyce Brothers: "You can become a woman who feels good about herself, a woman with a strong self-image and high self-esteem, a woman who is in charge of her life. It is the inner you that governs your perception of yourself."

If you are not the person you want to be, you can turn yourself into
the person you were meant to be.

—DR. JOYCE BROTHERS.

■

Garfield ®   by Jim Davis

GARFIELD © 1999 Paws Inc. Reprinted with permission of UNIVERSAL PRESS SYNDICATE.

RESPECT QUESTIONNAIRE

Answer these questions honestly to see how much self-respect you have and how you expect others to react to you.

1. Do you care about your appearance?
Yes_____No_____

2. Do you respect your body and keep it in shape?
Yes_____No_____

3. Do you respect yourself as a person?
Yes_____No_____

4. Do you feel you are a worthy person?
Yes_____No_____

5. Can you remain calm outside when you are angry inside?
Yes_____No_____

6. Do you expect others to respect you?
Yes_____No_____

7. Do you react to criticism with an apology?
Yes_____No_____

8. Can you let go of bad feelings in a short time (a few hours)?
Yes_____No_____

9. Do you have a sense of humor in difficult situations?
Yes_____No_____

10. Can you remain calm when others are in turmoil around you?
Yes_____No_____

11. Do you try to please others?
Yes_____No_____

12. Do you react with anger when others disapprove?
Yes_____No_____

13. Have you ever quit a job because of criticism?
Yes_____No_____

14. Are you critical of others?
Yes_____No_____

15. Do you react to criticism with anger?
Yes_____No_____

16. Do you lose your temper on a regular basis?
Yes_____No_____

17. Do you get drunk when things don't go right?
Yes_____No_____

18. Do you take drugs when you're upset?
Yes_____No_____

19. Do you express your anger by putting others down?
Yes_____No_____

20. Do you cling to bad feelings for a long time (a few days/weeks)?
Yes_____No_____

KEY TO QUESTIONS:

If you answered No to more than half of questions 1 to 10, you are defeating yourself.

If you answered Yes to more than half of questions 11 to 20, you need to get a handle on why you don't respect yourself and how you can improve your attitude.

FINAL QUESTION:

Are you a quitter?

Yes_____No_____

POSITIVE STEPS FOR
EARNING RESPECT

To become more tolerant and less controlled by your ego,
start practicing being satisfied with what is.
—DR. WAYNE DYER

■

U.S. Attorney General Janet Reno, U.S. Secretary of State Madeline Albright, astronaut Sally Ride, Paramount Studios chief Sherry Lansing, and TV's Barbara Walters are power players. They command the respect of their peers. They are hardy spirits—women who conquer fear, disappointment, fatigue and danger. They move straight ahead with a vision of where they are going. They take advantage of opportunities for advancement. They know that the road they have chosen is not easy.

They take responsibility and they don't condemn others. They use their self-respect to plow into uncharted territory (even into space, in Sally Ride's case) and learn from their mistakes. Women of this caliber do not give up and they do not place blame on others when things don't go right.

You can blame your partner for your lousy relationship; you can blame your boss for your miserable paycheck; you can blame your personality on your parents or your siblings; you can blame your appearance on genes; you can blame your weight on anything you want.

As Wayne Dyer says: "When you blame something outside of yourself for the circumstances you are experiencing, you give control of your life to that outer phenomenon. The alternative to blame is self-responsibility—becoming an inner-directed person. The key to you is always within. When you let go of blaming others and search within for the key, you will always find what you need."

Shirley Muldowney, a housewife from upstate New York, dreamed of racing big Formula One cars. But in the mid-1960s it was "men-only" and everyone told her it was impossible. Other drivers refused to race against her.

"Auto manufacturers refused to sponsor me; the National Hot Rod Association didn't take me seriously and hoped I would go away," she says. Even the governing board of the sport tried to prevent her from racing by declaring her license invalid. But Muldowney fought back with perseverance and dignity. She knew she was capable of fulfilling her dream.

"In 1970 I finally got my opportunity and competed at the U.S. Nationals in Indianapolis, where we missed qualifying by two one-hundredths of a second," she explains. "This showed that we were serious competitors." Six years later, she became the first woman drag racer ever to win an NHRA national event, controlling the awesome power of a 5,000-horsepower engine as she raced around the track at 300 miles per hour!

Shirley now holds numerous drag-racing records, including the World Championship, which she has won four times. She has also, by her persistence, won the respect of her male peers, the racing commission and the corporate sponsors.

Everything happens for a reason. And it happens when it is supposed to. Respecting the universe is the first important step in gaining respect from others.

Shed the fault-finding, suggests Dyer, and find the loving presence within you. Your ability to be self-reliant will overtake your habit of assigning blame.

Here are a few of his suggestions for freeing yourself of blame:

- When you feel the urge to blame others, say a prayer of thanks for the lesson. Appreciate the reminder.
- Feel thankful toward those who have angered you. Learn to respond from your center, rather than your sense of outrage. In other words, love 'em and bless 'em.
- Placing blame is futile. Instead, cultivate the inner knowl-

edge that everything in your life is divinely ordered.
- Learn to turn the negative into the positive.
- Know that you do not always have to be right.

If you have goofed up, it does not mean you are a loser. It is impossible to be wrong all the time or even most of the time. Think about the thousands of things you have done right.

Respect for yourself is the most important step to eliciting respect from others. Criticism and disapproval can upset you only if you buy into it.

And remember:

> The higher your self-esteem, the more disposed you are to form
> nourishing rather than toxic relationships.
> For nothing in life that is worthy is ever too hard to achieve
> If you have the faith to try it
> And you have the faith to believe
> —HELEN STEINER RICE

■

Ten years ago Melissa Sparrow of Baltimore, Maryland, was a runway model making $1,000 a day. She lived in Paris, where she was told what to wear, where to stand and how to comb her hair. "Other people made decisions for me," says Melissa, who appeared in TV commercials and clothing catalogues and on magazine covers. Tall, blond and photogenic, she began modeling at age fifteen. After graduating from high school, she moved to Europe and learned to speak French and German. But nobody in her business respected the fact that she was anything more than another pretty face. Although she was living the high life, she was miserable.

"I traveled constantly; there were no relationships," says the thirty-three-year-old mother of two. "I was not spoken to, and I did not talk. It was an empty existence. I was ready to try something absolutely different."

She retired at age twenty-four and was already "old" for her profession. She says: "As soon as you get a smile-line, it's all over. The glamorous world is there only because you're beautiful. And that's transient. In a flash, it disappears."

When Melissa returned America her fiancé, Ned, was waiting with open arms. They married and, after a year of teaching, she decided to explore the world of medicine.

"It's exactly the opposite of modeling," she explains. "You're not concerned with what's on the outside. You're concerned with what's on the inside."

Melissa was nine months pregnant when she took the entrance exam for medical school. In fact, her water broke during the exam and she was rushed to the hospital, where their son Russell was born. Daughter Marylouise arrived during a radiology exam a few years later. Melissa has recently graduated and is now doing her residency, hoping to become a pediatrician. She looks back on her former modeling days and recalls them as embarrassing.

"You have to be in love with your beauty," she says. "You have to think beauty is the most important thing in the world. But as a doctor, you have a relationship with a patient that's based on caring and mutual respect. At least you should. Those things are grounding. And they are real."

Kellie Lightbourn of Ft. Lauderdale, Florida, who has competed in dozens of beauty pageants, says there is more to a woman than her beauty and her long tresses.

"Although I never intend to practice law, I enrolled in law school so people would not think I was just a pretty face with nothing between my ears," she told me. "In order to get respect, you have to show people that you can set a goal for yourself and accomplish it—whatever that goal may be."

Being 60 is no different than being 40 or 20—what is important is that you've grown and developed as a person.
—DIAHANN CARROLL

∎

Dr. Laura Schlessinger made huge waves a few years ago when she penned *Ten Stupid Things Women Do to Mess Up Their Lives.* Her contention is that women do not respect themselves, so they make stupid choices in men and in the way they approach life.

Judge Judy Sheindlin has picked up the gauntlet Schlessinger has tossed down. From her highly visible perch as TV's authoritative dispenser of justice, Judge Judy says women must think smart. These are her rules for taking charge of your life and for earning the respect you want.

1. *Independence is the only path to happiness.* To ensure your long-term well-being, financial security and peace of mind, you must have a profession or vocation that makes you self-supporting.
2. *If you have talent, let it show.* Stop worrying that you might come on too strong, be too aggressive, or not be feminine enough. In other words, disregard the labels.
3. *Don't live in a state of denial.* Women stay in terrible situations because they fear being alone, or they pray things will get better. You may hope your life will get better, but you must be prepared if it doesn't.
4. *Be smart.* Men still control the workplace, and the higher a woman rises the more eager they are to knock her off her perch. To avoid a catastrophe, learn every aspect of what you do. Be assertive and aggressive, but with a light touch, mixing confidence with humor. Disregard labels, such as "bitch" and "ball-buster."
5. *Don't be afraid.* You can let your insecurities or the insecurities of others scare you away from your goal. Or not. Whatever job you tackle, make yourself *indispensable*, but *not subservient.* Demonstrate your worth, no matter what your position, then move forward with determination.
6. *Be firm.* This is especially true with children. You can be a disciplinarian as well as a friend to your kids. They want boundaries and, although they will challenge you every

step of the way, they will respect you if you *mean* "No"
when you *say* "No."

7. *Be non-judgmental.* It's easy to be critical and tell others
what to do. But imagine those comments coming to you
from someone else and bite your tongue. If you offer suggestions, always present them in a positive framework.

8. *Be a complete woman.* Too often, females feel incomplete
until they have mated. They hang in limbo, waiting for the
perfect man to make them whole. Instead of pining away
or settling for second best, opt for a sense of personal
accomplishment. Be the best you can be and the rest will
fall into place naturally.

No one can make you feel inferior without your consent.

—ELEANOR ROOSEVELT

■

Feeling sorry for oneself is a common practice. However, one
of the fastest ways to lose the respect of others is to wallow in
self-pity. The "woe-is-me" attitude consumes valuable energy
and prevents you from attaining your goals. Instead of being in
the moment and trying to create a better future, you become
stuck in the past, dwelling on what went wrong. Even though
you might be comforted by sympathetic friends and family
members, they will eventually grow weary and lose respect for
you.

"Self-pity feeds on itself," chides Dr. Mark Goulston. "When
you project a sorrowful image and lack of faith things tend to go
wrong, which only gives you more reason to feel sorry for yourself. If the cycle continues long enough, you run the risk of
appearing pathetic."

The best way to redeem yourself from this self-defeating trap
is to spend time with those who are truly unfortunate and
deserving of compassion. In other words, take the focus off
yourself. Volunteer at an animal shelter, read to the blind, hold

AIDS babies, visit a nursing-home resident, work with the hand-icapped. Or join a support group that can help yank you out of this negative space.

You need to make a 180-degree shift, from aggravation to appreciation, from grumbling to gratitude, adds Goulston. "Otherwise, your half-empty glass will empty completely."

Be content with what you have, rejoice in the way things are.
When you realize there is nothing lacking,
the whole world belongs to you.

—LAO TZU

■

Emme, the plus-sized fashion model, was selected to be in the 1994 edition of *People* magazine's annual survey of "The 50 Most Beautiful People in the World."

The magazine editors wanted to know three things: Would she be available for promotional purposes? Would she give a candid interview? Would she consider posing nude?

Emme says while *People* is not known for bare-all center spreads, she knew there was a chance they might ask if she agreed to the interview.

"I showed up for the shoot in a robe and a thong—hoping that I wouldn't have to reveal absolutely everything, but trusting the process," she confesses in her book, *True Beauty*. In fact, they *did* want her to take it *all* off.

Emme says: "I slipped out of my thong, took a deep breath and walked onto the set naked as the day I was born. Once I got into it, it really wasn't such an ordeal. It was all very dignified and I was transported to another time and place. I completely forgot that there were a half-dozen people milling about, worry-ing about the lighting, the set and the heaters that had been set up to keep me warm."

A situation like this could have been a great opportunity to make a scene or storm out or refuse to cooperate. Incredibly, although Emme had not planned on showing her bare body to everyone in the room, plus the tens of millions who would see it in hair salons and doctors' offices—and although at that moment she desperately wished her body was not quite as ample as it is—her high level of self-esteem got her through the photo shoot. When the issue hit the newsstands, the reaction was overwhelmingly positive. It produced an avalanche of letters from around the world, from people looking for a positive body image to which they might aspire.

"I decided to make a proactive effort to shake up some of our ideals, to challenge some of our widely held notions of what was beautiful and healthy and good," says Emme, who has since put together a presentation on body image and self-esteem for high-school students.

"The good news about self-acceptance is that you can work on it whenever you want to—all the time, if you like! After all, you're always available to yourself."

> **All that you are is a result of all that you have thought.**
> —BUDDHA

∎

How we feel about our bodies is reflected in the way we speak and act, and also affects the way others react to us. Emme admits that she might have felt more secure about the nude photo shoot had she been slimmer. However, she found a reserve of hidden confidence and ultimately found herself enjoying the experience.

Beauty standards in America are terribly rigid and confining. Is it any wonder that at any given time one-third of the population is on a diet? Cosmetic surgeons are staggering to the bank under the piles of money they are making from women dissatisfied with their appearance: they want to look younger, bustier, less flabby. While women should do what is necessary to feel good about themselves, cosmetic surgery is expensive. And not everyone is a successful dieter. This means digging deeper into the area of self-respect.

When physical appearance manifests itself as insecurity, many women go to extremes to portray themselves in a positive light. For instance, studies have shown most women will eat less in the company of a man than with other women or alone. A young woman I know would have a meal before going out to dinner with a date. Why? So she would appear to be a light eater.

When a woman's need for approval becomes so important that her own self-worth slips into oblivion, she sets a trap for herself. She subrogates her real self and pretends to be someone else—the person she feels will be accepted—which, in turn, perpetuates the underlying belief that her real self is unacceptable. *Her life then becomes an illusion instead of reality*, and she cannot live life to the fullest.

As Judge Judy says, don't wear your hair or makeup to please *him*, please *yourself*. "Look good to feel good—but do it for you, even if you'll be alone all day."

> Getting to know yourself is the best step you can take to reduce your need for social approval. When you get to know yourself— your values, goals, thoughts and feelings—you give yourself a firm foundation for handling challenging events.
> —JONI JOHNSTON

■

The proverb best known as The Golden Rule—"Do unto others as you would have them do unto you"—certainly holds true when anger is involved. Anger, whether it explodes at home, at the office, or the mall, or in the car, is one of the most difficult emotions to handle and one of the most destructive. Besides the damage it does to your own state of physical and mental health, it almost always sabotages the admiration and deference you seek.

When you are angry, one tendency is to sweep it under the carpet and not deal with it. But ignoring the problem will not make it go away and, ultimately, this will endanger your health.

Even daily, low-level hostility will eat away at you until it eventually explodes.

This morning's newspaper carried an article about Marcelle Becker, who was charged with assaulting and interfering with a flight crew in 1995. The widow of an insurance magnate, she was flying first-class from New York to Los Angeles with her Maltese dog. During the flight, the dog got loose and an argument with another passenger broke out. The crew said Becker became so hostile that she had to be tied to her seat with the animal's leash!

In the long run, animosity is harmful to your happiness, health, personal relationships, marriage and career.

Dr. Joyce Brothers says that anger is one of our most primitive emotions. "It is the descendant of the rage reflex that primitive man shared with lower animals."

Not all rage is the same. While Mrs. Becker's outburst may have been a knee-jerk reaction, the way we respond to irritating or maddening situations differs from person to person.

- *Hoarders:* "Some people hold onto their anger as if it were precious," explains Dr. Brothers. "They hoard every perceived injustice. Old grievances grow in importance almost as if they had been injected with a growth hormone. The suppressed anger becomes more virulent. And a time comes when relationships are poisoned by this anger that has flourished in the dark, like some giant toadstool."

  People who stockpile their wrath pay a high price in stress and stress-related ailments, including breast cancer, hypertension, heart attacks, asthma, diabetes, fatigue, immune-system disorders, and an unsatisfactory sex life.

- *Self-blamers:* When things go wrong at home or work, self-blamers take the rap. Instead of placing the responsibility where it belongs (on the boss, friends or family member they are reluctant to confront), they turn the anger inward. They consider muff-ups as their own personal failings. They, too, suffer from the litany of stress-related ailments listed above.

- *Exploders:* Like a volcano when internal pressure builds to the point of no return, explosions occur, even in otherwise quiet hoarders. Some people, by nature, are screamers. They yell at every opportunity, making no distinction between the trivial and the meaningful. At one time therapists believed letting go of anger was better than keeping it inside. Today we know better.

A study at King's College Hospital in London conducted interviews with 160 women as they were admitted to the hospital for a lump in the breast—before learning whether the lump was benign or malignant. The majority of women who had noncancerous tumors were found to have a "normal" pattern of emotional expression. However, the majority of women whose lumps were cancerous, had either a lifelong pattern of extreme suppression of feelings (mostly anger) or of suddenly exploding with emotion. Certainly, more study is needed to establish a connection between anger and illness. But this study's findings are definitely thought-provoking.

Anger begets anger. Letting loose is like throwing gasoline on a fire. The only healthy way to handle anger is to control it, and then either use it constructively or forget it.

Because anger is such a hair-trigger emotion, sometimes it erupts before you can get a handle on it. However, to gain the respect of those around you, it is imperative that you act professionally and with decorum at all times. That truth holds true for work, home life and friendships.

The only way to deal with rage is to *feel* it. While acting out may give momentary relief, or sense of power, the underlying emotion is still simmering. Whether you keep in it or let it out, hostility is self-defeating and self-destructive. Instead, you can learn to harness the sensation, unpleasant as it may be. Put some space around it by breathing deeply. Short-term fixes include: slowly drinking a large glass of water, counting to twenty, or going to the ladies' room. Driving is not recommended, but a long walk is. Breathe in and say: *I am angry now;* breathe out and repeat: *I can deal with it* or *I will get over it.*

Once your pulse rate is back to normal, you have to determine who is pulling your strings and why. Then you need a conditioning tool that will short-circuit those angry feelings and channel them into productivity and renewed energy.

These suggestions may be helpful for relieving anger-related stress:

- *Change your focus.* Think about something good in your life, winning the lottery, a trip to the mall, a new car.
- *Substitute new behavior.* Using the technique of visualization, imagine how you would react *calmly* to the situation that triggered your anger last time. Play that scene over and over until it becomes part of you.
- *Control the anger.* Animosity gobbles up energy and gives you nothing in return—except bad feelings. It can be all-consuming. To turn it into an asset you must decide what you will allow yourself to get angry about. In other words, pick your battles wisely and work on developing a greater tolerance for annoying situations. In time you will see that there are few issues worth getting steamed up about. A shrug of the shoulders can be the best response for everyone concerned.
- *Deal with the real issue.* Determine what made you angry and take action to ensure it does not happen again.
- *Recognize your "hot" buttons.* Certain things get us steamed. Once you know what they are, you can avoid them by thinking ahead. I use my first two initials to prevent snide comments about my given name. It may be cumbersome, but it works by disconnecting that particular "hot button."
- *Avoid name-calling.* By yelling back with labels like jerk, idiot or moron—or worse, with profanity—you make the other person your enemy. The repercussions may come back to haunt you.

- *Realize that no one but you can make you angry.* Again, you can place blame on the kids, the car, your boss, your husband. But the bottom line is that *you* generate your anger and *you* keep it going. Take responsibility and learn to control it.

"Being able to lower our voices and calm down is essential," says Scott Wetzler, a clinical psychologist and professor of psychiatry at Albert Einstein College of Medicine in New York City. "In the heat of battle, we lose control and say things without concern for the damage we might wreak, and this loss of control devastates our built-up store of trust and security."

Finally, disarming an angry person is another useful technique for gaining respect and making life more stress-free. You may want to go nose-to-nose and yell back. Obviously, this accomplishes nothing, since no meaningful dialogue is taking place. Or, like me, you might want to turn and run. Or you may burst into tears. When this occurs, nothing is resolved.

Instead, try saying, "I hear you. I know you are angry." Sometimes this works to calm the person yelling so you can discuss the issue at hand. If this does not work, try saying, "I want to talk to you about this, but I can't when you are screaming. As soon as you are calm, I will be happy to talk to you."

If the tirade continues, you have the right to leave. To stay and battle it out is masochistic, unnecessary and a guaranteed ulcer-maker.

On the other hand, simply listening to someone, allowing them to blow off steam, sometimes defuses a situation enough that the matter can be discussed and solutions found.

> Ideally, an argument does not have to be hurtful; instead it can
> simply be an engaging conversation that expresses our
> difference and disagreements.
> —JOHN GRAY

■

Perfection. Does it exist in an apple pie, a work of art, an electrical appliance, a human being? Are you striving to be perfect?

And if so, what toll is it taking on you, your family, your friends and your coworkers?

Let's face it, everything can be improved upon, if you look at it critically enough.

Let me explain why perfection is the ultimate illusion, says David D. Burns. "There is no such thing. It's the world's greatest con game; it promises riches and delivers misery. The harder you strive for perfection, the worse your disappointment will become because it's only an abstraction, a concept that doesn't fit reality."

Perfectionism is a self-defeating quality that makes everyone around you miserable, including yourself. It has been called "never-enough" thinking. Most people want to do things well, they strive for excellence. But even excellence is not enough for perfectionists. I know writers who never finish anything because each and every word must be exact and all punctuation must be flawless. That's what editors and proofreaders are for—to catch our errors. The writer's job is to spin an idea into words—mistakes, flawed grammar and all that jazz. There's no excuse for sloppiness, so it's important to do the best you can. Then hand it over to a professional—or two. (Thanks, Mom and Nancy, for the great editing jobs!)

Imagine playing golf or tennis and wanting every shot or stroke to be exactly right. I don't think you would be having much fun. When you strive for perfection, all the joy is sucked out of the process. And after awhile you begin to hate what you are doing. Any sense of satisfaction disappears, and your self-image begins to disintegrate. Eventually you give up altogether in disgust. That's what Dr. Burns means when he says: "If you are a perfectionist, you are guaranteed to be a loser in whatever you do."

Here's how one perfectionist described her quest. "It makes me so tight and nervous I can't produce. I become afraid to risk mistakes, which makes me supercritical of myself. I can't enjoy life because I can't admit my successes. Relaxing is impossible, there's always something to fix. I become intolerant of others and end up without friends—because what friends want to be criticized all the time?"

Monica Ramirez Basco, a psychologist and author of *Never Good Enough*, says that many people are plagued by perfectionism, a condition that stems from fear.

"We want to be perfect so people will like us and not reject us," says Basco, a mother of three who lives in Dallas, Texas. "Sometimes it can be a good thing. For example, being imperfect on the job may have serious consequences for an air traffic controller. But when your need to be perfect interferes with your relationships and your quality of life, it's time to take action."

She suggests unlearning perfectionist behavior, which takes time and practice.

Basco tells of one patient who always had flawless hair and makeup before stepping out of the house. Yet she wondered why people at social gatherings avoided her. Then one day she put her hair in a ponytail and went out with no makeup whatsoever. She was astounded by how many people approached her.

The second statements (in italics) on the list that follows, is a sampling of how you can make alterations in your perfectionism.

- I must be perfect or I will be rejected. *I need to do the best job I can.*
- If I make a mistake it will be horrible. *Everyone makes mistakes. Deal with it and move on.*
- If I do it perfectly, I will be accepted. *I want to be accepted for who I am, not what I do. And mistakes happen.*
- I must be perfect so I won't be embarrassed. *A little embarrassment doesn't hurt. It just means you are human.*
- When I achieve perfection I will find inner peace. *This is not the way to inner peace.*
- If I do it perfectly, everything will work out right. *I can do my best, but any number of things that are out of my control can go wrong.*
- I must be perfect or I will fail. *Things might not always turn out my way, but I'm not likely to blow it altogether.*

How can you expect respect from others if your criticism is nonstop? People need appreciation, a pat on the back and a word of encouragement. When you take your perfectionist ideals and project them onto others, you are in a lose-lose situation.

Understanding this deeply ingrained obsession is the first step toward conquering it. The best thing you can do for yourself is to seek professional help, in the form of either a competent therapist or a support group. By exploring the subject—in books, on the Internet, or with a counselor—you will discover the source and learn how to overcome it. Once you are on the road to recovery, life will be more relaxing and more enjoyable and you will respect yourself more. So will others.

> There is no reason not to lighten up even when you're in the thick
> of it. In fact, there's every reason to lighten up.
> —NANCY O'HARA

■

Perfectionism often manifests itself in the form of authority—or as Wayne Dyer calls it, "your authoritarian dominant ego."

The quickest pathway to disrespect by others is to exhibit the following behaviors, outlined by Dyer in *Your Sacred Self*:

- *Bring a conversation back to yourself.* Rather than exploring the ideas, thoughts and feelings of others, you constantly focus their attention on you.
- *Take a hurry-up approach to life.* Behave as if you are in the race of your life: everything needs to be done now—or better, yesterday. Working under a person driven like this can be a nightmare.
- *Give orders and demand perfection.* We have already touched on this negative behavior. It is particularly repellent when done in public places, like stores or restaurants. Remember, nobody is your slave. This goes for children, too. Treat them

fairly when they are young and they will return the favor later in life.

- *Publicly correct others.* You do not endear yourself to anyone when you flaunt a superior attitude, especially in a social setting. Nobody likes to be reprimanded in front of others. If you are in a position of authority, always conduct personal business in private.

- *Withhold intimacy, then place blame.* Do you use the mistakes of your spouse or partner to avoid closeness? Anger and criticism in a relationship always leads to sadness, guilt, and regret.

- *Insist you are right.* During a conversation, do you have to be an authority on every subject? You might get in the last word, but that's all you will get.

- *Build your ego at the expense of others.* Boasting, bragging and self-aggrandizement are not the way to gain the trust and admiration of others.

- *Keep tallies.* Life is a give and take. It is important not only to reciprocate when you are on the receiving end, but to give unconditionally at times, otherwise you will earn the reputation of being a "taker."

- *Hold yourself up as the standard.* You dismiss others who do not speak, dress or behave the way you do. Your judgment of others is based on material possessions, or you hold others up to ridicule.

- *Act in a controlling manner.* You threaten, bully or control by withholding financial support or threatening reprisal. In other words, you are a dictator.

If you recognize yourself in any of the points above, you might want to take a deeper look at your motives and the origin of these negative attitudes. Chances are they stem from childhood. With the help of a competent professional, you can locate the source, address it, and rise above it.

People who have a basically optimistic perspective,
who have the ability to "let go" of a bad event, who can see that it is
impermanent and that their situation will change, tend to be
healthier than their pessimistic counterparts.
                      —Jon Kabat-Zinn

■

How do you talk to others? Do you beg, cajole, whine, threaten, flatter, intimidate?

You only have one chance to make a good first impression. So getting your point across or making yourself understood is of utmost importance. While you might not always select the right word for the situation, you should be mindful of your tone of voice, the urgency you convey, and whether you are speaking through clenched teeth or raising your voice for emphasis or in anger. Some people talk loud and fast; others talk slowly or in a whisper.

We have already dealt with expressing anger; however, communication is a broad topic that requires a closer look. Interrupting, in particular, is done by both men and women alike and is perceived as a conversational bullying—where the one cutting in is the aggressor, the one interrupted is the victim. According to Deborah Tannen, author of *You Just Don't Understand*, these assumptions are founded on the premise that interruption is an intrusion, a trampling on someone else's right to the floor, an attempt to dominate.

Men and women communicate differently. Men tell. Women discuss. Men like to finish their sentences. Women often cut in and talk over each other without incurring resentment or disapproval.

Tannen contends that the key to understanding what is going on is the distinction between "rapport-talk" (the characteristic ways that most women use language) and "report-talk" (the technique many men use as a management technique). "Men feel interrupted by women who overlap with words of agreement and support," she says.

Business communication can seem, at times, to be a contradiction in terms. So many misunderstandings can occur in an office that it's a wonder any work gets done at all. These nine suggestions may be the key to getting your point across effectively.

1. *Cut to the chase.* Forget the preamble. Know what you want done, then say it. Everybody is in a hurry. Put your bottom line up front.

2. *Don't ramble.* It's a nervous habit but it can lead to misunderstandings. Saying more does not mean you've said it better.

3. *Be a problem-solver.* If you want to grab someone's attention, give them the benefit of your wisdom by saying you have an idea that might solve their problem.

4. *Be direct.* Maintain eye contact for effective communication.

5. *Pay attention.* Facial expressions can mean many things: the listener doesn't understand, or there is something else on his or her mind, or an idea is forming. Ask what's happening.

6. *Playback.* Although you think your instructions are crystal-clear, they might instead be muddy or fuzzy. Ask the listener to repeat back what you have said.

7. *Play it again.* Repetition works. Say it and say it again, the way tennis instructors hammer their point home during a lesson.

8. *Follow up.* Mention your earlier conversation and ask how things are progressing. Ask if there are any problems. You might be surprised to find there are setbacks you hadn't anticipated.

9. *Politeness counts.* The words "please" and "thank you" are still in style. Use them liberally, along with "I'm sorry" and "job well done," when appropriate.

A relationship is only as deep as its level of communication.
—ELLEN KREIDMAN

∎

Relationships are based on verbal connections. When people communicate, an exchange takes place that allows a new way of seeing things. The word *communication* itself suggests a flow of energy as well as a bond—although not necessarily one that is in agreement.

Women choose different words than men do to express their emotions. Typically, women use superlatives such as never, everyone, always, nothing. In a conversation it sounds like this: "You *never* listen to me," "*Everyone* wants something from me," "I *always* pick up your socks," "There is *nothing* you can do to make me happy."

Women unwittingly blame men and, with sentiments like these, make them feel guilty. Surely a man picks up his socks now and then. Certainly once in a while he does something to make her happy—if only for a moment. So how does a man respond to those ultimatums? He becomes defensive.

Because most men do not understand that women express their emotions differently, they inappropriately judge or invalidate their partner's feelings. An argument invariably ensues.

"When a woman feels a surge of negative feelings, it is especially difficult for her to speak in a trusting, accepting, and appreciative way," says John Gray, noted author of the *Venus/Mars* books. "She doesn't realize how negative and hurtful her attitude is to her partner."

When you are self-absorbed, or convinced that you are right, a dialogue cannot take place. It becomes a monologue with two people in attendance. If the person you are "conversing" with has strong ideas of his or her own, the battle lines are drawn. It's you against her, or him, or them.

"Even when we are feeling threatened, angry, or frightened, we have the potential to improve our relationships dramatically if we bring mindfulness into the domain of communication itself," says Jon Kabat-Zinn, author of *Full Catastrophe Living* and noted stress-reduction facilitator.

"When both sides expand the domain of their thinking and are willing to consider the other side's point of view, then extraordinary possibilities emerge as the all-too-limiting boundaries in the mind dissolve."

Keeping the lines of communication open are important no matter where you are, or with whom you are conversing. Whether you are at work, at home, with your children, or in a social setting, these tips should help you be more mindful of how you speak to others:

- Don't withdraw during a discussion and stalk off.
- Don't be inflexible.
- Don't evade important issues.
- Don't start an important discussion if you don't have time to finish it.
- Don't have children around if it's a debate among or between adults.
- Don't belittle, accuse, lay blame, name-call or threaten.
- Don't humor the person you are talking to or make wise-cracks at his or her expense.
- Don't adopt a superior, "I'm right" stance.
- Don't judge, criticize or minimize the other person's position.
- Don't pick up the phone if it rings in mid-discussion or mid-disagreement.
- Don't interrupt.
- Do listen actively, and with your complete attention.
- Do accept responsibility if you are wrong.
- Do find a quiet place to talk. At the office, close the door.
- Do put yourself in the other person's shoes.
- Do give the other person the benefit of the doubt.
- Do maintain eye contact.
- Do repeat back what is said.
- Do maintain your sense of humor.
- Do respect the other person's position and ask that he or she respect yours.

It's easier to withdraw than to bring up emotional issues. It is easier to turn a discussion into an argument than to stay calm and rational. However, the best way to make your point and maintain your dignity and respect is to simply say how you feel. Be honest and detached and non-judgmental. Listen without becoming defensive. Do not hold onto bad feelings that will poison your being.

The more you can create an atmosphere of open honesty,
particularly regarding areas of disagreement,
the less likely disagreements will become disagreeable.
—WAYNE DYER
■

AFFIRMATIONS

In terms of respect, what you reap is what you sow. The vibrations you send out to the universe will come back to you. Or, as the Buddhists say, "What goes around, comes around."

If you want to be respected, you must first honor yourself. When you are coming from a place of self-love, and if you act with nobility of manner, you will find that attitude, like a mirror, reflected back to you.

- I will not complain.
- I will not find fault with others.
- I will stop placing blame on others for my own shortcomings.
- I will take responsibility for my own actions.
- I will not react to criticism with defensiveness or anger.
- I will respond to anger with peace.
- I will be polite and helpful at all times.
- I will do my best in any undertaking.
- I understand it is self-defeating to strive for absolute perfection.
- I will be mindful when I speak and will not belittle or criticize.
- I will stand tall and act confident.
- I will respect and honor myself.

> Forgiveness is being fully aware of pain, and feeling resilient
> enough to move on. More important, forgiving others
> is about forgiving ourselves.
> —SCOTT WETZLER

■

RECOMMENDED READING
FOR RESPECT

Anthony, Robert, Ph.D. *How to Make the Impossible Possible.* Berkley Books.

Basco, Monica Ramirez, Ph.D. *Never Good Enough.* The Free Press.

Brothers, Dr. Joyce. *Positive Plus, The Practical Plan for Liking Yourself Better.* G.P. Putnam's Sons.

Emme. *True Beauty.* G.P. Putnam's Sons.

Gray, John, Ph.D. *Men Are from Mars, Women Are from Venus.* HarperCollins.

Johnston, Joni E., Psy.D. *Appearance Obsession, Learning to Love the Way You Look.* Health Communications, Inc.

Sheindlin, Judy. *Beauty Fades, Dumb is Forever.* HarperCollins, Inc.

Tannen, Deborah, Ph.D. *You Just Don't Understand.* Ballantine Books.

Wetzler, Scott, Ph.D. *Is it You or Is it Me?* HarperPerennial.

Nine

IF YOU WANT TO AGE GRACEFULLY

Life is short, and it's up to you to make it sweet.
—SADIE DELANY

■

*T*HE CALENDAR SAYS you are fifty but you don't feel a day over thirty. Or maybe you are thirty and envy the energy of the fifty-year-olds around you. That's because calendar age may not be the best measure of aging. According to Dr. Michael F. Roizen, "real age" is an estimation of how old your body is biologically, rather than chronologically.

Roizen says your genes, the food you eat and the vitamins you take, how you exercise, whether you are prone to accidents and other factors either speed up or slow down your biological clock. For example: Smoking can make you age eight years. By quitting, you can regain seven of those years. Eating breakfast daily (a topic covered in Chapter Seven: If You Want Good Health) adds a year of longevity, and regularly getting a good night's sleep adds another three.

"We have numbers for everything," says Roizen, a Chicago internist and anesthesiologist. "Imagine trying to pay your income tax if there was nothing called money, or judging the circulation of a newspaper if you didn't keep track of how many papers you sold. Yet we ask people to take care of their health without giving them any measuring stick."

Roizen's team analyzed the results of 25,000 studies and found some interesting surprises: flossing regularly can reduce your "real" age by 6.4 years, since gum diseases age the immune and arterial systems.

In a later section you will find some tips for rolling back the hands of time; but first, take a look at one of the world's most glamorous women who, everyone agrees, still looks marvelous.

> If you over-focus on this drooping or that dropping,
> you will not be a happy person. Life after 50 is
> surely for me the best part of my life.
> —JENNIFER O'NEILL

∎

At age sixty-five, Sophia Loren still sizzles with steamy beauty and flawless elegance. The Italian screen legend's face is a gift from God and she swears she has never had a nip or tuck.

Her sultry demeanor, her haughty strut, her well-toned, statuesque figure give hope to aging boomers everywhere. How does she look so good?

"Any woman can look her best if she feels good in her skin," says Loren. "It's not a question of clothes or makeup. It's how she sparkles."

And sparkle she does, the way she did forty years ago when she made *El Cid*. And she continues the tradition. At age fifty-nine, in 1993, she had the moxie to dance a striptease in the movie *Ready to Wear*. And in 1995 she seduced Walter Matthau in *Grumpier Old Men*. She says her secret is lots of rest, good thoughts and exercise.

Loren has been in the public eye most of her life. Before she caught the attention of producer/director Carlo Ponti at a beauty pageant, she was thin, dark and very shy. Her classmates called her *stuzzicadenti*: toothpick.

She was sixteen when Ponti—who was twenty-one years her senior and married at the time—met her. He knew instantly that she was remarkable. After her initial screen test, which did not go well, Loren was urged to have a nose job. She refused and made a few distinctly forgettable films. Then came *Two Women*, a 1961 movie about World War II, in which she played a mother protecting her daughter. The payoff for her gut-wrenching performance was an Academy Award and instant fame.

In 1965 Ponti divorced his wife; he married Loren a year later and their 33-year marriage has endured. Although he is now eighty-five and in poor health, there is a deep and abiding love between them. Instead of focusing on Ponti's illness, Loren concentrates on the family and dotes on their sons, Edoardo, 26, a film director, and Carlo, 30, an orchestra conductor. She looks forward to the day she will become a grandmother.

In a recent interview in *People* magazine, Loren spoke about her life over the past four decades:

"At twenty, I was trying to figure out who I was, what I wanted and how to get it. I was learning about myself.

"In your thirties, you know more about life, what you want, and you think better of yourself. At thirty I wanted to be a mother.

"In my forties, I felt more mature, like I finally had my feet on the ground.

"About fifty, I was like, God, the years go by so fast! What can I do? Yet I had a drive for life that I never had when I was twenty.

"Now, in my sixties, I sometimes think I've found the fountain of youth. Life is serene but exciting. Little things can be good for me."

Those "little things" include taking the very best care of herself. Loren's beauty ritual includes the following:

- She goes to bed early and rises early.
- She uses baby shampoo and colors her hair herself.
- She gives herself manicures.
- She uses a rosewater face lotion and an eye cream made with vitamin A.
- She exercises every day, including 45 minutes of stretching and abdominal crunches, plus a one-hour walk.
- She eats a light breakfast of decaffeinated coffee and an English muffin. A mid-morning snack follows. Lunch is hearty, usually pasta, chicken, salad and fruit. Dinner is small.
- She avoids butter, most red meats and fried foods, and limits her intake of dairy products.

Life has not always been smooth sailing for the international star. She had two miscarriages, two difficult, bedridden pregnancies, plus a seventeen-day stint in jail in Italy for underpaying her taxes. Her beloved mother died in her arms in 1991, and Sophia herself was hospitalized a few years ago when her heart began beating erratically. But her spirit always remains upbeat.

As for aging, the five-foot-nine beauty says: "All seasons of life are beautiful. Aging is a problem only when you stop liking yourself as a person. Fortunately, I still like myself inside and out. I just feel good in my skin."

Being beautiful can never hurt. But you have to have more.
You have to sparkle, you have to be fun, you have to make your
brain work if you have one. I live life day by day and try to
reach new achievements.
—SOPHIA LOREN

■

WHAT'S HOLDING YOU BACK?

Failure is a part of life. We must all go through it.
Regret is a terrible waste of energy.
—PATRICIA HEPBURN

■

At the beginning of the twentieth century, life expectancy for women was just forty-eight years. By now that figure has doubled. Women, as you will see from the stories that follow, are still active in their seventies, eighties and even past the century mark. Statistics from the U.S. Census Bureau indicate there were 37,306 people over the age of 100 in America in 1990. Today that estimate has been revised upward to 70,000—almost double. By the year 2020, the Bureau predicts that figure will rise sharply to 266,000. Remarkably, the over–eighty-five age group, presently numbering over three million, is the fastest-growing segment of the population. *Even more astounding, four out of five U.S. centenarians are women!*

Studies also show that the majority of Americans want to live to be 100, and Roy Walford, a scientist at UCLA, believes that with clean living—no smoking, low-cholesterol diets—we have the ability to reach the 120-year mark.

At age 103, Ella May Stumpe taught herself to use a computer so she could write a book, entitled *My Life at 100*. She says she has lived to such a ripe old age by using moderation with everything and steering clear of pizza and hamburgers.

Never before has there been so much information available on fitness, nutrition and health. Doctors are finally recognizing that women's health issues are just as important as those of men. The Internet is a veritable encyclopedia of advice; and the number of female doctors has risen dramatically. While many large cities now have health centers exclusively for female patients, the sad truth is that too many women simply do not take care of themselves.

This year more than 500,000 women will die from heart-related ailments, 46,000 will succumb to breast cancer, over 10,000 will die of cervical or uterine cancer and more than 13,000 from ovarian cancer. And that's not even counting those who will die from lung cancer, hypertension, diabetes brought on by middle-age obesity, drugs, alcoholism and violent relationships.

The potential for extending your life is now greater than ever, says psychologist David Ryback. "Although many have been brainwashed to believe that much of the physical deterioration associated with growing older is inevitable, this is clearly not so."

The body and the mind are intricately connected. Few things that happen in the body don't start in the mind.

"Feel sadness and your hormonal system goes down one bio-chemical path," he adds. "If something in your life changes that emotion to joy, your hormonal system takes an entirely different path. If you feel that you are old and decaying, your body will respond to that mental message by slowing down and yielding quickly to the aging process."

**Aging is not "lost youth" but a new stage
of opportunity and strength.**
—BETTY FRIEDAN

■

Aging gracefully is not only about not smoking, drinking in moderation, eating right and exercising, it's about lifestyle, outlook and staying in touch with people. Betty Friedan, who wrote the classic feminist tome *The Feminine Mystique,* and *The Fountain of Age*, finds her mature years an "unknown and untested" time of life. Now approaching eighty, she has these tips for remaining vital as the years encroach upon your youth.

- Cherish your choices and maintain control of your own life.
- Commit yourself to your passions in work and love.
- Risk being yourself, who you really are.
- Risk new things, risk new ways, risk failing.

A few years ago, a woman wrote a letter to the editor of our local newspaper, the *Boca Raton News*, saying she thought it was unfair that the senior communities had a minimum age requirement of fifty-five. At the time she was only fifty-one.

"I find myself wishing my life away until the day I can buy a condo at a retirement facility and settle in," she wrote.

Fifty-one and she was wishing her life away! What a waste of precious time—years—living.

Zia Wesley-Hosford, author of *Fifty & Fabulous*, has just the opposite mind-set. "I can't think of anything more exciting than approaching the second half of life with energy, intelligence, glowing health, and all the accumulated knowledge of the past 50 years!" she says. "Once the mind, body or spirit become stagnant or inactive, we begin the decline commonly known as aging or old age."

Are you stagnating? Are you becoming decrepit? Have you given up the spirit of living?

You should not automatically assume that as the years creep ever upward you will fall into such a state of disrepair that you can never recover. Age is as much a state of mind as a state of physical ability. I stopped having birthdays when I hit thirty-three. I figured I'd stick around that age for a while instead of moving on. When my oldest daughter turned twenty, people looked askance. Now that she is twenty-seven, they know I am lying but they haven't a clue how old I really am. That's the way I like it. I firmly believe you are as old—or as young—as you feel.

> Forget about past choices that didn't work out.
> Focus on what you can change.
> —MIMI SOLOMON

∎

Your place of employment may have a mandatory retirement age. Or you may simply look forward to not working any more. However, studies reveal that working at something—focusing your time, energy and devotion—on a satisfying task helps keep you young.

In 1998, Leila Denmark was touted as America's eldest practicing physician. At the time she was a 100-year-old pediatrician dispensing advice from her office in Alpharetta, Georgia. After seventy years on the job, she was still working ten hours a day, six days a week. She graduated from the Medical College of Georgia in 1928 and helped develop a vaccine for whooping cough in the '30s. Her experience is so extensive that she can make a diagnosis just by looking at a child.

Leila says she eats vegetables and protein every day, but most of all, she loves what she is doing. She thought of quitting in 1990, when her husband John died, but she reconsidered.

"When I can't see or think well, I'll quit," she says. "And when I go, I hope it will be right here in this office."

While there is no getting around age discrimination—even Sophia Loren is no stranger to Hollywood's "Pretty Woman" syndrome that idolizes young, beautiful actresses. But you don't have to buy into it. There are numerous skills at which older adults are more proficient than their younger counterparts.

> I see less of certain friends of mine now because they are
> constantly complaining about how they can't do this or
> can't do that. I'm not trying to escape my age,
> but I don't need a constant reminder, either.
> —BARBARA JACOBS

■

Evelyn Irsay of New York was put to Dr. Michael F. Roizen's longevity test. Roizen and a team of physicians determined 126 factors that have been medically proven to affect age. Evelyn's chronological age is eighty-one. Her "real" age is only seventy-seven. To stay mentally and physically challenged, Evelyn still works full-time as assistant director of human resources at a major city newspaper. At age seventy she took up swimming, doing 100 laps a day, five days a week. When a conflict in her schedule put an end to her swimming, she added walking to her daily routine.

Other ways she "reduced" her age were by not smoking, always wearing a seat belt, taking vitamin E and a calcium supplement, eating breakfast, keeping her weight steady and eating 10 percent or less of saturated fat per day.

Additional factors that negatively affect your age include substantial or frequent weight gain or loss, living in or commuting to a large city with polluted air, not getting enough sleep, being a workaholic, smoking, experiencing a major stressful event (death of close relative, divorce, job change), and second-hand exposure to cigarette smoke.

Julia Child, the grande dame of haute cuisine, celebrated birthday number eighty-six in 1999. While she confesses she's "a little creaky" in the knees, she has no intention of giving away her pots and pans.

"If you look at the obits, 80 is nothing!" she exclaims. "If I'm in good health and I've not gone bonkers, I'll just go on living."

How old are you physically, mentally, emotionally? Take this quiz and see where you hold yourself back from fulfilling your maximum potential.

Don't worry about getting older. If you dwell on aging,
you'll feel older. I still look forward to each day,
like something wonderful is going to happen.
—BETTY WALES

■

AGING GRACEFULLY QUIZ

There's no doubt about it, bad habits and negative thinking can put you at risk for aging before your time. How do you fare in the aging quiz?

1. Do you smoke?
   Yes_____No_____
2. Do you drink more than an occasional glass wine or beer?
   Yes_____No_____
3. Do you have a no-can-do attitude?
   Yes_____No_____
4. Do you rely on others for things you can do yourself?
   Yes_____No_____
5. Are you overweight and out of shape?
   Yes_____No_____
6. Do you have high cholesterol?
   Yes_____No_____
7. Are you putting off life-sustaining surgery because you feel it's too late?
   Yes_____No_____
8. Do you feel your best days are over?
   Yes_____No_____
9. Do you worry over things you cannot change?
   Yes_____No_____
10. Do you live in the past, regretting what was?
    Yes_____No_____
11. Do you have friends of all ages?
    Yes_____No_____
12. Do you eat healthy foods?
    Yes_____No_____
13. Do you exercise regularly?
    Yes_____No_____

14. Do you eat a balanced diet?
Yes_____No_____

15. Are you under a doctor's care, or do you get regular check-ups?
Yes_____No_____

16. Do you have supportive relationships?
Yes_____No_____

17. Do you have any interests that make you feel alive and vibrant?
Yes_____No_____

18. Do you go out with friends on a regular basis?
Yes_____No_____

19. Do you have a sense of purpose?
Yes_____No_____

20. Are you close with your children, or with nieces and nephews?
Yes_____No_____

KEY TO QUESTIONS

If you answered "Yes" to more than half of questions 1 to 10, you are not planting the seeds for a healthy old age.

If you answered "No" to more than half of questions 11 to 20, you are doing yourself a disservice by not enjoying your senior years.

FINAL QUESTION:

Would you like to live to be 100, and if so, what are you doing to reach that goal? _____

_____

_____

POSITIVE STEPS FOR GRACEFUL AGING

I climbed Mount Whitney when I was in my late fifties. And there
was a woman in her eighties who climbed Mt. Whitney every year.
—ELINOR GADON

■

In 1900 there were no cars, refrigerators, light bulbs, washing
machines, hormone replacement therapy or heart bypass opera-
tions. Child labor laws were unheard of, and young women
were all but shackled to sewing machines and required to work
for ten- or twelve-hour days. In rural areas, farming was a back-
breaking way of life. Vaccines had not been invented, and doctors were few and far between. Childbirth was an invitation to
infection and early death.

Today we have luxuries beyond the wildest dreams of our
grandparents. The woman of the millennium microwaves her
breakfast, tosses a load of laundry into the washer and sets the
dials, then hops into her car or onto the train and is transported
to her job, where she has the latest technology at her fingertips.

Then why can't we live to be any age we want?

Noted writer and septuagenarian Doris Lessing says she
wants to make one thing perfectly clear: "People decide to get
old. I've seen them do it. Why they do this, I don't know. But I
do think it's terribly important that people not make that inner
decision. Because then they sit around and they're old. In fact,
it's not about *staying* young but about *not* getting old."

As Karin Bivens approached the big five-oh, she wanted a
challenge—one that would make her feel a whole lot younger.
She decided on a marathon as a test of her endurance and vitality. The 26.2-mile trek through the redwood forest of California
was her goal. But she was no runner. Prior to her decision, she
had alternated running with walking in the few small races she

had entered. Then she came across an organization called 50 Plus Fitness Association (www.50plus.org). Her role model became a woman in her sixties who was still running marathons.

Says Bivens: "I started looking forward to my long runs. They became a stress release for me and they really cleared my head."

As a wife and mother of two, she carved time from her hectic home and work schedules. Her husband didn't think she could go the distance. But at age fifty, Karin ran her first marathon in 3 hours and 52 minutes, which qualified her for the famous Boston Marathon. Now, five years later, she predicts she'll be running for another 20 years. "It made me feel that if I can do this, I can do just about anything," she says.

> It's never too late to start exercising. Even 90-year-old people are exercising and receiving benefits... it's just never too late.
>
> —KARIN BIVENS

■

Rose Edwards, a feisty septuagenarian, is a real-estate agent by day. But at night, she comes out of her corporate cocoon and morphs into a butterfly—one that dances in the altogether. A few years ago, Rose discovered something truly amazing about herself—that she had a killer body and that she didn't mind flaunting it. This New York senior hired a teacher and soon made her debut as a stripper for private parties. She says she was less nervous about performing without clothes than without her bifocals. And the audience loved it—and her.

"My dancing came from a desire to express myself in a way that tapped into my own sexual energy," says Rose, who resembles an older Cher. Everything is hers except the breasts, which are man-made. Rose not only shakes her ample assets, but also really enjoys what she does. She says: "One night I lost my bikini top, but I also lost my hearing aid."

If stripping isn't your thing, get into the computer age—like Marge Minz of Toronto, Canada. After buying a computer at the age of seventy-nine, she learned how to surf the Web and now teaches other seniors how to have fun in the age of high-tech communication.

"It opens up a whole new world," she says.

And if neither of these pastimes suit you, try exercising, like Anne Clark—who was born ninety years ago in a tent along an Oklahoma roadside. She didn't start exercising until she was sixty-four. Now she has more than 136 medals for running and has set 40 national running records. She even teaches fitness classes at retirement homes.

"It just goes to show you anyone can start exercising at any age," says Anne, a widow who lives in Carol Stream, Illinois. "Before that I was an extremely sedentary person, never interested in exercise. Then one morning my car wouldn't start and I had no choice but to walk to work."

On her seventy-fifth birthday, Anne ran her first marathon— in Paris. Her husband and two sons thought it was absolutely incredible. She says her goal was simply to finish, but the former second-grade teacher found herself winning in her age group, and after one race her picture was on the front page of the *Chicago Tribune*.

Amazingly, Anne says that her inspiration is a student in her stretching class: a woman who walked two miles a day, every day, until the age of 104!

"I've met a lot of wonderful people," adds Anne. "Running has made my life much happier."

And while many of us would give up gardening at the age of eighty or ninety, Beth Davidson still uses her green thumb at the ripe age of ninety-two. The Toronto native keeps the balcony of her downtown high-rise blooming with purple pansies, geraniums, begonias and impatiens. She also has dwarf evergreens, an orange tree and a variety of house plants.

"It's so good for us to get our hands in the soil," says Beth, who suffers from arthritis. "It relaxes me," she adds, "but it's also hard work. Planting my window boxes nearly killed me."

The great grandmother of gardening says, "I'm full of arthritis and osteoporosis. But you have to learn to live with these things when you get old and not bore people. I don't allow myself to get down."

I'm a positive person. I don't pay much attention to time. I like life.
—BETH DAVIDSON

∎

Whether you want to take up belly dancing, yoga, aerobics, marathon racing, computerizing, gardening, or returning to school for a degree, these tips can help you roll back the hands of time.

- Take vitamins C, D, E and calcium.
- Floss and brush daily to avoid periodontal disease, which causes aging.
- Use a seat belt, don't use your cell phone while you're driving, and do buy a car with an air bag.
- Consider hormone replacement therapy. It is the most powerful anti-aging agent for women—a good hedge against crippling osteoporosis.
- Have monogamous (and safe) sex.
- Laugh often. It strengthens your immune system.
- Eat a diet that's low in calories and high in nutrition, including plenty of fruit, vegetables and grains and a limited amount of red meat.
- Sleep seven hours a night.
- Turn off the TV and stimulate your mind with reading, crossword puzzles and anything else that makes you think—including adult education classes.
- Wear plenty of sunblock when you are exposed to the sun.
- Don't smoke, and do avoid secondhand smoke.
- Exercise on a regular basis and build muscle tone with strength training (weight lifting).

Of course it goes without saying that common sense will help you stay alive and kicking well into your later years. This means wearing protective gear when participating in sports, not exceeding your limit of endurance, keeping up on your immunizations (flu, measles, mumps, hepatitis B and pneumonia vaccines), drinking alcohol only in moderation—or not at all if there is a family history of alcohol abuse or addiction—drinking at least six to eight glasses of water daily, seeking competent medical care for health problems, taking medicines as directed and avoiding needless drugs and vitamin supplements.

> I used to think that 60 was old and that old people don't do it.
> And if you told me I'd be doing it, I wouldn't have believed it.
> Now I am now one of those old people who have sex.
> —CAROLE CASTAGNOLI

■

Two of America's most famous octogenarians are Ann Landers and Abigail Van Buren, who turned eighty-one on July 4, 1999. Esther Pauline Friedman was born seventeen minutes before her twin sister, Pauline Esther. Esther was nicknamed Eppie and became *Chicago Tribune* advice columnist Ann Landers in 1955.

Pauline Esther was nicknamed Popo and auditioned for the *San Francisco Chronicle* only eighty five days after her sister landed her job. She was hired on the spot and picked the name Abigail from the Old Testament and Van Buren from the eighth president.

The twins both played the violin and attended Morningside College in Sioux City, where they lived with their two older sisters and parents. They dressed alike until they were married; both majored in journalism and both dropped out of school two days before their twenty-first birthday. They married in 1939 in a double wedding and went on a double honeymoon. Ann and Abby became Mrs. Jules Lederer and Mrs. Morton Phillips, respectively.

Ann and Jules divorced in 1975, after thirty-six years of marriage. They have a daughter, Margo. Abby has been married sixty-one years and has three children, Edward, Jay and Jeanne. Ann had a nose job, Abby didn't. Both stand five feet tall.

These American icons still work daily, sorting through thousands of letters and grinding their columns out on IBM typewriters. Their advice is read by more than 90 million people in 1,200 newspapers nationwide.

Says Abby, "I don't know what I'd do with my time if I wasn't working. My job isn't a burden to me. It really is a pleasure. I can't wait to get to work in the morning." Neither can her sister, Ann.

> **Aging sucks. Put more elegantly, it's lousy.**
> **Nobody wants to get older. Nobody wants to lift her arm**
> **and see crepe paper, but there it is.**
> **—JOAN RIVERS**

■

If anyone tells it like it is, it's the wisecracking Joan Rivers, who is using every trick in the book to dance around Father Time. She says: "Anyone who tells you that age is wonderful is lying." And she plans to fight the wrinkles every inch of the way.

"It's better to take stock of where you are chronologically, to realize all the baggage that comes with aging, and then not to accept it," she advises in her book *Don't Count the Candles*. "Fight age constructively and intelligently. Be the best that you can possibly be."

By changing your diet, your wardrobe and your attitude, you can reshape and recharge your life.

The tart-tongued comedienne—who looks fabulous at age sixty-five—has these tips for looking, feeling and living younger.

- *Keep up with high-tech advances.* Get a computer and learn to use it. Get a fax machine and a cell phone. Modern life is a challenge; accept it.
- *Keep current by reading the newspaper and magazines.* Read a

best-selling book, see the latest movie. Be hip, not square.

- *Ditch the dowdy look.* There's no reason to look frumpy when you can look fabulous. But dress appropriately for your age—no micro-miniskirts or eye-popping cleavage exposure.
- *Recognize your physical faults and assets.* If you have great legs, show them off. But if your arms flap in the breeze, forget the tank top.
- *Fight gravity with control-top pantyhose or body-shapers.*
- *Wear your hair at an appropriate length for your age.* Long hair, she says, is for kids and dogs.
- *Update your home.* Don't live in a museum stuffed with old things. Keep it light and cheerful, burn scented candles, get flowers and plants and update your framed photos.
- *Get a pet:* If you live alone, it will provide company—even a parakeet can be a bosom buddy .
- *Surround yourself with younger friends so you don't find yourself all alone one day.*
- *Get out more, and not just to the doctor's office.* If you like people or need some spare cash, get a part-time job. Or volunteer at a shelter or thrift shop.
- *Don't diet.* Just stop eating so damn much. Too many ladies are sloppy fat because they have given up. They feel they are old so why bother? No matter what age you are, keep fit so you can be proud of the way you look.
- *Walk whenever possible and use the stairs to build muscle and strong bones.* Exercise also guards against obesity and helps your heart, circulation and respiration.
- *Travel.* There are plenty of affordable group tours, senior excursions, or tours for women traveling alone. Life is a glorious journey.

Have cosmetic surgery. Beg for or borrow the money, she says. Charity begins with you—your face, your body and any other part that needs repair.

The older you are, the more makeup you should use, but keep it current. So ditch the blue eye shadow and take a look at these tips.

Neutral tones are best for everyone—grays, browns and smoky shades. As for eye shadow, the lighter the eye, the darker the tone.

Follow the lip line with liner. Do not use liner that is darker than your lipstick.

To minimize flaws, play up another asset. Go easy on the rouge; it makes you look older. Instead, contour with soft blush.

Aging is a disease. I don't have it and I don't intend to get it.
—KELLY NELSON

∎

Kelly Nelson of East Wenatchee, Washington, remembers the day her husband John walked into the house lugging a set of weights. She was fifty-two and out of shape. Although petite, Kelly had never been sports-minded. She struggled as she began swinging the 10-pound dumbbell; she had no technique whatsoever.

"Then I heard about a local coach who had set up a makeshift gym in his basement," she recalls. "I called and within weeks I saw my muscles growing."

Encouraged by the change in her physique, she learned about toning, pumping and conditioning. A year later she entered her first bodybuilding competition. Now, at age seventy-two, she is still going strong. At the time of this writing, she has entered 32 competitions. Her daughter, Colleen Fisher, who is in her mid-forties, joins her mom—sometimes onstage for the awards ceremonies. Both women are buff in their bikinis.

"In the Oregon State Bodybuilding Championship Colleen won her class and I won my class," crows Kelly, who worked for 55 years, most recently as manager for a car-rental company. "We had the privilege of posing together for the overall photo up there on the stage. It was a thrill."

Their training schedule includes a 100-mile bike ride each week during warm weather, and cross-country skiing in winter.

She says that to age gracefully each of us should think about our dreams of long ago: and when we no longer have to work every day, we should pursue those desires. Kelly and Colleen are making an exercise video to show there is no age difference when it comes to working your muscles.

"I think in each of us is a athlete trying to get out," Kelly says. "When people say 'I can't,' they mean 'I won't.' I'd get up at 4:30 in the morning so I could work out before going to the office. Consistency is the answer. You can do it if you choose exercise as a lifestyle."

> Get up and help others. Go out and talk to your politicians. There's no sense in being old and grumpy. There's no sense in resting. You got eternity to rest. No sense in starting now.
> —ENOLA MAXWELL

■

The easiest and best way to age well is to eat healthy foods in moderate servings. Diets create frustration and engender poor self-esteem when the pounds stay on. Eating is something we do at least three times a day, every day of our lives. Making a lifestyle change to include wholesome low-fat foods and to exclude foods that are poor in nutritional quality, high in fat and sugar and filled with chemical preservatives will help you to live longer and enjoy your later years.

David Ryback, author of *Look Ten Years Younger, Live Ten Years Longer—A Woman's Guide,* has ten rules on his fit-for-life anti-aging plan. He claims that if you stick to these rules faithfully, you will be treating your body with the respect it deserves.

1. *Set reasonable goals.* When determining your ideal weight, keep in mind the ratio of muscle to fat. A woman who is out of shape may be in the right box on the weight charts but out of whack when it comes to

muscle-to-fat ratio. Consult a nutritionist or dietitian if you want a personal evaluation.

2. *Don't lose sight of reality.* Slow, gradual weight loss works best—ideally, one to two pounds a week. With dramatic weight losses the pounds tend to come right back on, making you feel you are a failure.

3. *Convert poor eating habits to good ones.* Keep a journal of everything you eat, when you eat and how you feel at the time. Note whether you are upset, lonely, angry or frustrated. Once you understand why you eat, you can begin a program to alter your eating habits.

4. *Follow a balanced low-fat food plan.* Choose from the basic food groups and include lots of fruits, vegetables and grains.

5. *Avoid high-fat foods.* Forget hot dogs, luncheon meats, processed foods, baked goods (like cookies, cakes and especially doughnuts), fried foods, gravy and cream sauce, crackers, chips, whole milk and cheese, ice cream and too many nuts.

6. *Find the eating pattern that is comfortable for you.* When you feel satisfied with your healthy food choices, you will begin to lose weight. Otherwise, you will continue to cheat or binge.

7. *Steer clear of sodas.* They are loaded with sugar and caffeine. Instead, substitute water with a twist of lemon.

8. *Learn to limit libations.* No more than one or two alcoholic drinks a day.

9. *Exercise.* The best defense against regaining any weight you have lost is to get the body moving. Use it or lose it.

10. *Create meaningful milestones and celebrate your success.* Set a goal of five, ten or twenty pounds. When you reach it, reward yourself with something tangible—a piece of jewelry, tickets to a show, dinner out with someone special.

Women begin losing bone density from the age of thirty at the rate of .05 to one percent every year. That increases with breast feeding to three percent; and postmenopausal women experience another three percent of bone loss *every year*. Most women consider osteoporosis just a nuisance, but according to the National Information Network, it is one of the *top three most life-threatening diseases* in the United States. It affects over 28 million Americans and is the most common disease of the bones.

Essentially new bone cells form all the time. However, as we age, the number of new cells fails to keep up with the number of dying old cells. When this happens the older osteoclastic cells (large cells closely associated with areas of bone resorption) cause the formation of pores, fissures, holes or "spaces" in the bone. Over time, as these spaces expand, the bones become fragile and the risk of fracture increases. The result is low bone density and osteoporosis.

A major problem nowadays is that young women are ingesting sugar, salt, caffeine and alcohol, and they are smoking and having babies early—all of which interfere with building healthy bones during the formative years. They are setting themselves up for osteoporosis when they get older, but have no idea how drastically their quality of life will be affected.

> Growing old is a rich experience.
> Maybe we should just relax and enjoy the ride.
> —JEAN WEISS

■

It is inevitable that the years will creep up on us. When we hit forty, our bodies begin to undergo significant changes that affect all aspects of our lives: how we look, feel, think, and act. The aging process may begin with a mid-life slump which is heralded by a decline in the amount of energy you have. Perhaps that's where the expression "I'm running out of steam" originated.

Julian Whitaker, M.D., founder of the Whitaker Wellness Institute in Newport Beach, California, says every human activity requires energy. To satisfy this demand, our bodies function as energy-producing factories.

"It begins with the food we eat," he explains, "which is digested or broken down into smaller components in the gastrointestinal tract. After food is digested it must be metabolized, or broken down even further into a form that can be utilized by the cells of the body for fuel. This fuel is converted into energy by tiny structures called mitochondria, which are 'power plants' inside our cells. As we age, the mitochondria begin to run down and lose their ability to produce energy as efficiently."

This energy shortage affects the entire body. Everything slows down. Cells lose their ability to repair themselves. Our immune system functions less efficiently. Our skin dries out. Our endocrine system stops producing hormones the way it used to. Most important, our metabolism slacks off, making it difficult to burn calories. As a result, we store fat, put on weight, and lose muscle tone.

That is one important reason to eat right. Teenagers can get away with pizza, burgers, fries and junk food and not gain a pound, even though they are doing their bodies a disservice. As a responsible adult, it is imperative that you treat your body with respect. Local bookstores and libraries are well-stocked with cookbooks filled with healthy recipes. However, it is important to know that the ten food choices listed here are highly recommended by nationally-known nutritionist Jean Carper, author of *Miracle Cures*. These foods have been selected for their contribution to your longevity.

- *Tomatoes.* Because they are rich in lycopene—an antioxidant and cancer fighter—tomatoes help decrease the risk of prostate, lung and stomach cancer. "Tomato eaters function better mentally in old age and suffer half as much heart disease," says Carper.
- *Olive oil.* Research shows this was a major ingredient in Mediterranean diets, which were considered the most healthy type of eating. Olive oil is high in antioxidant activity and helps reduce the risk of heart attacks.

- *Red grapes.* Drinking red wine in moderation increases longevity because of the antioxidant power of red grapes. Grape juice is a good nonalcoholic substitute.
- *Nuts.* Almonds and walnuts lower blood cholesterol. And while nuts are high in fat , it is mostly monounsaturated— or good fat. Nuts, in moderation, are a valuable source of protein and studies now show they can help reduce the risk of heart-attack deaths in women.
- *Whole grains.* "The more whole grains you eat, the lower your odds of death," says Carper, according to a study at the University of Minnesota. That means more dark breads, old-fashioned oatmeal, and bran cereals.
- *Salmon.* Certain cold-water fish, such as salmon, sardines, mackerel, herring and tuna, are rich in omega-3 fatty acids which fight myriad chronic diseases. Omega-3 fatty acids also help your heart beat properly and prevent your arteries from clogging.
- *Blueberries.* Carper says, "They are so powerful in retarding aging in animals that they can block brain changes leading to decline and even reverse failing memory."
- *Garlic.* Used since Biblical times, garlic helps fend off cancer, heart disease and aging. It's loaded with antioxidants and may prolong your life by years.
- *Spinach.* Rich in folic acid, spinach protects aging brains from degeneration and may help prevent Alzheimer's disease, according to studies at Tufts University in Boston and New University of Kentucky. It's a terrific health promoter and is loaded with iron and vitamins.
- *Tea.* Green tea and black tea both help decrease the risk of heart disease by fifty percent.

Aging slowly allows us to enjoy life to the hilt, rather than expend our energies resisting Father Time.

—BRUCE GOLDBERG

Marianna Prieto came to America from Cuba as a child and became a writer. During her heyday she wrote dozens of books in English and Spanish and thousands of articles, published in numerous magazines.

Now a widow living in Miami, Florida, Marianna spent the first six months of 1999 in and out of the hospital. She broke her hip, which required surgery and a metal pin to hold her together. Then she fell again when her walker slipped and was hospitalized a second time, bruised from head to toe.

She's back home now and can't wait to get back to her typewriter. Still sharp as a tack at age eighty-seven, Marianna called me to ask if I could give her an assignment. She says: "At the end of each day I write something positive that happened. Perhaps it was a pleasant phone call or a visit from a friend. That way I can look back and see that life is getting better day by day. As long as you have a hobby or an interest, your mind will be occupied."

And there is feisty Florence Foster of Johnson, Michigan, who began her own business at the age of ninety-three!

During a hiking trip in Arizona with her daughter, she realized she needed a cane to help her walk. Horrified at the thought that people would think she was old if she used an ugly metal one, she bought a clear plastic tube, filled it with small silk roses and put a rubber tip on one end and a Lucite handle on the other. The first Foster Designer cane was born.

People went wild for her creative canes. "She's no granny in a rocking chair," says Tom Wilson, a marketing expert who helped Florence get her company started.

She met with five high-powered executives from an autodetailing manufacturer to arrange for mass production of her unique product and knocked their socks off with her enthusiasm and youthful spirit.

"I'm ninety-three years old and I'm not buying any green bananas," says Florence. "But if my experiences have inspired any other older people to follow their dreams as I did, it will be reward enough for me."

People don't wear out through years of activity. They rust away as
soon as they put their feet up and begin to take life easy.
                    —NORMAN FORD

■

THE FAMILY CIRCUS.   By Bil Keane

"Grandma doesn't have any REAL
kids. Hers turned into grownups."

AFFIRMATIONS

Now that you know it is within your power to live life to the fullest, it is time to make these affirmations part of your daily routine of eating right, exercising and positive thinking.

- I will treat my body with respect.
- I will not dwell on the inevitable.
- I will appreciate every moment of every day.
- I will not worry about the future.
- I will give myself a complete makeover.
- I will eat healthy foods and do some form of exercise every day.
- I will stop any habits that will prevent me from aging gracefully.
- If I want cosmetic surgery, I will treat myself to it. I am worth it.
- I will set old grievances aside and make peace.
- I know that every day is precious and I will not waste time feeling sorry for myself.
- I will stay busy and give to others.
- I will live in the moment, not the past or the future.
- Life is a blessing and I am blessed.

Life is a banquet, and I still have a place at the table.
—CINDY JUDD HILL

■

RECOMMENDED READING
ON AGING GRACEFULLY

Barnard, Dr. Neal. *Eat Right, Live Longer*. Harmony Books.

Chopra, Deepak. *Ageless Body, Timeless Mind*. Harmony Books.

Ford, Norman. *18 Natural Ways to Look and Feel Half Your Age*. Keats Publishing.

Kotulak, Ronald, and Peter Gorner. *Aging on Hold: Secrets of Living Younger Longer*. Tribune Publishing.

Lamm, Steven, M.D. *Younger at Last: The New World of Vitality Medicine*. Simon & Schuster.

Love, Susan M., M.D. *Dr. Susan Love's Hormone Book*. Random House.

Monte, Tom, and the editors of *Prevention* magazine. *Staying Young: How to Prevent, Slow, or Reverse More than 60 Signs of Aging*. Rodale Press.

Powell, Douglas H. *Nine Myths of Aging*. W. H. Freeman & Co.

Rivers, Joan. *Don't Count the Candles*. HarperCollins.

Roizen, Michael F., M.D. *Real Age*. HarperCollins.

Rountree, Cathleen. *On Women Turning 70*. Jossey-Bass Publishers.

Ryback, David, Ph.D. *Look Ten Years Younger, Live Ten Years Longer—A Woman's Guide*. Prentice-Hall.

Warga, Claire, Ph.D. *Menopause and the Mind*. The Free Press.

Wesley-Hosford, Zia. *Fifty and Fabulous*. Prima Publishing.

Whitaker, Julian, M.D., and Carol Colman. *Shed 10 Years in 10 Weeks*. Simon & Schuster.

Willix, Robert Jr., M.D. *Healthy at 100*. Shot Tower Books, Inc.

CONCLUSION

■

MARJORIE HERTZ, OF Naples, Florida, started taking dancing lessons at the age of three. She still cuts a rug twice a week, although she turned 100 on May 2, 2000. On days that she doesn't dance, she walks a mile to stay limber. "Without that I'd be stiff as a board," she quips.

Ruth Livingston is the state of Washington's oldest licensed driver. At age 104, she still drives her Buick wherever she wants to go. Each morning before getting up, she stretches in bed. Ruth eats judiciously, practices reflexology, thinks positively and delights in the world. "I love good music. I love nature. I love gardens. But I'm not so crazy about animals," she says.

And at age seventy-three, Cindy "Gams" Judd Hill has great legs and can still kick them high over her head. In one of her routines, she bounds onstage in a skimpy red outfit and four-inch spike heels. The nursing-home residents in Pittsburgh, Pennsylvania, where she lives, love every minute.

"We've come a long way, but we've got a long way to go," says Hill, who holds the titles of Ms. National Senior Citizen 1993-'94 and Ms. Pennsylvania Senior America 1992. "The world is definitely better, but I wouldn't say it's easier."

Then there's Minnie Van Duren of Boca Raton, Florida, who has been helping people most of her life—and she's not about to stop, even though she is ninety years old and wheelchair-bound. For more than fifty years she taught Bible studies. Now that hip and heart problems have slowed her down, she has found a new way of giving—by crocheting baby blankets, which she gives to migrant workers. Minnie crochets every day except Sundays, and turns out about eighteen blankets a year.

"You should see the look on the children's faces when they get them," she says beaming. "It is something you can never forget."

These are just a few American women who are hooked on life with enthusiasm, good grace and an optimistic outlook, and who have retained their spunky spirit well into their golden years.

Being happy, having peace of mind or financial security and finding someone to love who will love and respect you in return can be yours for the taking, if you believe in yourself.

Learn to take criticism with a grain of salt and learn from your mistakes, like Janet Fitch, forty-three, author of *White Oleander*. Fitch had submitted a short story by that name to the *Ontario Review*, where it was rejected by noted writer Joyce Carol Oates. Accompanying the manuscript was an encouraging note from Oates, saying it looked like the beginning of a novel. Instead of being discouraged, Fitch took the suggestion to heart and turned the short story into a book. At the present time it is number two on the best-seller lists and has been optioned as a movie.

You may have to work at being empowered and successful. Respect yourself and others will respect you. Good health and living well into your later years are within your grasp.

294 L . A . J U S T I C E

Remember, *you* are your own best friend, or your own worst enemy. Only *you* can make your dreams come true. You have the power. Your inner self has the answers, if you listen. And nobody can take your happiness away, unless you let them.

May you live long and prosper.

To thine own self be true.

—WILLIAM SHAKESPEARE

■

INDEX

D

E

F

G